▼ ▼ ▼ ▼

T H E
PARADOXICAL
VISION

▼ ▼ ▼ ▼

T H E
PARADOXICAL
VISION

A Public Theology for the
Twenty-first Century

ROBERT BENNE

Fortress Press, Minneapolis

BT
738
.B 397
1995

THE PARADOXICAL VISION
A Public Theology for the Twenty-first Century

Interior design: Peregrine Graphics Services
Cover design: Spangler Design Team

Library of Congress Cataloging-in-Publication Data
Benne, Robert.
    The paradoxical vision : a public theology for the twenty-first
century / Robert Benne.
        p.   cm.
    Includes bibliographical references and index.
    ISBN 0-8006-2794-6 (alk. paper)
    1. Sociology, Christian (Lutheran)   2. Christian ethics—Lutheran
authors.   3. Two kingdoms (Lutheran theology).   4. Church and state—
United States—Lutheran Church.   5. United States—Religion—1960–
6. Lutheran Church—United States—History.   I. Title.
BT738.B397   1994
261'.08'8241—dc20   95-18251
                                                                                          CIP

The paper used in this publication meets the minimum requirements of American National Standard for Information Sciences—Permanence of Paper for Printed Library Materials, ANSI Z329.48-1984.   ∞™

Manufactured in the U.S.A.   AF 1-2794

99   98   97   96   95   1   2   3   4   5   6   7   8   9   10

CONTENTS

▼ ▼ ▼ ▼

PREFACE

▼ ▼ ▼ ▼

The homogenous culture of eastern Nebraska seems an unlikely place to nurture a compelling interest in religion and
society. But such an interest, like the call to a religious vocation, does occur in mysterious ways. Both happened to me
and there has been no turning back.

The surprising call to some sort of religious vocation came
first. But then my intense interest in the Christian faith was
drawn toward religion and societal concerns by my introduction at Midland Lutheran College to the early writings of
Reinhold Niebuhr and to the biting social commentary of
Søren Kierkegaard. The powerful prophetic critiques of their
respective societies resonated in my idealistic soul. The comfortable fifties of my growing up years seemed to need a
vigorous shake-up. Niebuhr and Kierkegaard certainly provided that.

As a Fulbright student at Erlangen University in Germany
in 1959–60, I continued my interest in religion and society
by concentrating on courses in Christian ethics given by Walter Künneth, a Lutheran who, with a number of other generally unnoticed conservative Lutherans, had honorably resisted Nazi claims to the extent that he spent most of the war
under house arrest. Though certainly not as bold intellectually
or politically as Dietrich Bonhoeffer, Künneth had resisted
on the basis of his understanding of a Lutheran social ethic.
For him, as for Helmut Thielicke, the two-kingdoms doctrine
had led to a sharp rejection of Nazi ideology. Künneth's teaching was at that time somewhat controversial, since the Germany of the late 1950s was still caught up in serious debate
about the connection of the Christian, but particularly of the
Lutheran, posture to Germany's political struggles during the
Nazi time and before. It was a bracing time to consider my
religious tradition's relation to political, economic, and cultural life.

Things got even more interesting when I entered the University of Chicago Divinity School in 1960. The Divinity School was pioneering in what were called "dialogical fields," one of which was entitled Ethics and Society. Gibson Winter and Alvin Pitcher, both sharply critical of the American church and its relation to what they thought was a pervasively unjust society, were my teachers. They pressed us toward the critical edges of the social ethics of Richard and Reinhold Niebuhr as well as Paul Tillich. The emergence in the early sixties of the civil rights and community organization movements, both particularly intense in Chicago, were vivid occasions for Christian social-ethical reflection and action.

But such occasions now seem mild compared to the conflagration that engulfed us in the late sixties and early seventies when I was a young professor at the Lutheran School of Theology at Chicago. The Black Power and antiwar movements and the beginnings of the ecological, feminist, and gay rights movements presented powerful challenges to American society. Traumatic assassinations and riots gave a generally apocalyptic hue to American religious and social life. By this time I was teaching Christian ethics to seminarians caught up in the dynamism of that hectic time.

My reflections on that era (1965–75, the years we think of as the 60s) were offered in two books dealing with religion and society. My first, entitled *Wandering in the Wilderness: Christians and the New Culture* (1972), attempted to relate the Christian vision to the emerging currents of the 60s. As I look back, it represents an unduly optimistic assessment of those currents, but at least it maintained a critical distance between the central Christian religious and moral claims and the spirit of the times.

A second book, which came out right before the American bicentennial and was coauthored with colleague Philip Hefner, probed Christianity's relation to America at a seriously theological level. *Defining America: A Christian Critique of the American Dream* (1974) wrestled with the question "How can a person be Christian and American at the same time?" We tried to avoid both easy denunciations and affirmations in our dialectical approach.

From 1975 onward I gradually shifted to what many have called a neoconservative perspective. Such a move was at least in part my response to an increasingly negative attitude toward capitalism by most American Christian intellectuals. After engaging in extensive self-education in the field of economics, I came to the conclusion that the combination of political democracy and market economic systems was not only morally defensible, but was perhaps the best arrangement for developed and developing countries alike. My book entitled *The Ethic of Democratic Capitalism: A Moral Reassessment* (1981) did not lack a critical posture in relation to democratic capitalism, nor did it move toward any sort of "Christian economics," as if the transcendent truth of the Christian vision could be domesticated in any kind of human system. But the book did lead to a heightened sense of tension for me as I taught in a seminary increasingly influenced by feminist and liberation theologies, perspectives on the world that are not characterized by their friendliness toward market economic arrangements.

For a number of reasons, I moved to a Lutheran-related liberal arts college, Roanoke College, in 1982, where teaching undergraduates pressed upon me the crucial importance of teaching the basics of Christian faith and life to young people who have an ever-diminishing connection to a living religious tradition. Such teaching aims led me to write a book entitled *Ordinary Saints: An Introduction to the Christian Life* (1988), which was an attempt to make contemporary the generally Protestant, but specifically Lutheran, notion of vocation. Its goal was to sketch a vision of Christian personal life for those persons intrigued by Christianity.

I am now interested in collecting my thoughts on Christian social ethics, Lutheranly conceived. I am interested not so much in applying those Lutheran insights to specific social issues, as I have in the past, but rather in elaborating the basic theological-ethical framework for engaging the Christian vision with its surrounding public environment—political, economic, cultural, and intellectual. Such a task of engagement currently goes under the name of *public theology*, though there are nuances in the usage of that term that differ from the earlier term, *social ethics*. I shall have more to say about the definition of public theology in chapter 1.

The willingness to present my settled convictions for public scrutiny and conversation comes primarily from the belief that such convictions are crucial to any adequate elaboration of Christian public theology. Operating as a public theologian over the past quarter century has convinced me not so much that I am right on the particular issues I have taken up, but rather that the basic framework within which I have implicitly operated needs to be made explicit so that vital Lutheran insights might be added to the ongoing conversation about the public relevance of Christianity. I do not in any fashion claim that Lutheranism or its social-ethical framework has all the answers. Indeed, our tradition seems to have as many possibilities for perverse distortion as other traditions. It has been healthily challenged and changed by its immersion in world and American Christianity. Without that larger conversation Lutheranism would be much less interesting and persuasive than it is now. My intent is simply to give Christian public theology a nudge in a Lutheran direction by contributing something authentically Lutheran to the discussion, no more than that but certainly no less.

I have divided the book into three parts. The first deals with the nature and challenge of Christian public theology at the dawn of the twenty-first century. The second part deals with the paradoxical vision itself. It outlines the contours of the Lutheran perspective, its distinctiveness in relation to other Christian traditions, and its public legacy in America. The third part discusses practical ways in which religious traditions in fact do engage the public environment that surrounds them. It focuses on the *how* of public theology.

I am grateful to many individuals and institutions for the opportunity to pursue this project. The persons who have told me over the years that my writings are important to them have given an important boost to my confidence. James Lewis and the Louisville Institute for the Study of Protestantism and American Culture, not only encouraged this Lutheran venture into public theology, but also provided the financial assistance to help make possible a full year's sabbatical. Roanoke College's sabbatical program contributed the other necessary assistance.

Mark Noll, American religious historian at Wheaton College, articulated in two recent articles ("The Lutheran Difference," in *First Things,* and his review of Martin Marty's *The Noise of Conflict* in *The Christian Century*) just the right set of notions to set me off in the proper direction. In both articles he called for a Lutheran perspective on American religious history and American public theology to challenge the overwhelmingly Calvinist character of most Protestant outlooks. While I cannot address the former, I can make a credible attempt at the latter, a Lutheran version of public theology.

—Robert Benne

P A R T I
▼ ▼ ▼ ▼
AMERICAN PUBLIC THEOLOGY AT THE DAWN OF THE TWENTY-FIRST CENTURY

Academic theology seems to have lost its voice, its ability to command attention as a distinctive contributor to public discourse in our culture. Can theology speak persuasively to an educated public without sacrificing its own integrity as a recognizable mode of utterance? . . . To gain a hearing in our culture, theology has often assumed a voice not its own and found itself merely repeating the bromides of secular intellectuals in transparently figurative speech. . . . Can a theologian speak faithfully for a religious tradition, articulating its ethical and political implications, without withdrawing to the margins of public discourse, essentially unheard?

Serious conversation with theology will be greatly limited if the voice of theology is not recognizably theological. . . . Conversation partners must remain distinctive enough to be identified, to be needed.

Jeffrey Stout, *Ethics after Babel*

▼ ▼ ▼ ▼

THE CHALLENGE
OF PUBLIC THEOLOGY

THE MEANING OF PUBLIC THEOLOGY

This chapter aims to explore the difficulties that any living religious tradition has in making a signficant impact on the world in which we live. But before we get to that task, we need to sketch out what we mean by public theology. Any new and stirring concept is apt to have a somewhat fuzzy meaning. As a "buzz word" in current theological discussion, public theology has more elasticity of meaning than most theological expressions. It can refer to a very specific intellectual task, as in David Tracy's efforts in *The Analogical Imagination* and *Plurality and Ambiguity*, to identify the common criteria of truth that theology might share with other disciplines, common criteria that then would give theology's truth claims credibility in the search for public truth.[1] Or it can mean something broader, as in Ronald Thiemann's definition: "Public theology is faith seeking to understand the relation between Christian convictions and the broader social

1. David Tracy, *The Analogical Imagination* (New York: Crossroad, 1981), *Plurality and Ambiguity* (San Francisco: Harper and Row, 1987), and "Defending the Public Character of Theology," *Christian Century* 98 (1 April 1981): 350-56.

and cultural context in which the Christian community lives."[2]

Max Stackhouse gives a similar, broad definition of public theology. He says that theology can be called public for two reasons:

> First, because that which we as Christians believe is not esoteric, privileged, irrational, or inaccessible. It is something that we believe to be both comprehensible and indispensable for all, something that we can reasonably discuss with Hindus and Buddhists, Jews and Muslims, Humanists and Marxists. Second, such a theology will give guidance to the structures and policies of public life. It is ethical in nature.[3]

Some thinkers give public theology more of a social-critical thrust. For example, Linell Cady emphasizes this function when she writes that a public theologian seeks to "sustain, interpret, critique, and reform a particular religious worldview and its concomitant way of life . . . [and to] contribute to the upbuilding and the critical transformation of our public life."[4]

With these definitions in mind, I will attempt my own definition, which is perhaps yet broader than even the more expansive definitions above. Public theology, I think, refers to the *engagement* of a living religious tradition with its public environment—the economic, political, and cultural spheres of our common life. This definition, like those above, affirms an integrity, a *sui generis* quality, for a religious tradition. It assumes that a particular religious worldview is an authentic

2. Ronald F. Thiemann, *Constructing a Public Theology: The Church in a Pluralistic Culture* (Louisville: Westminster/John Knox Press, 1991), p. 21.

3. Max Stackhouse, *Public Theology and Political Economy* (Grand Rapids: Eerdmans, 1987), p. xi.

4. Linell E. Cady, "The Task of Public Theology," in *The Legacy of H. Richard Niebuhr,* ed. Ronald F. Thiemann (Minneapolis: Fortress, 1991), p. 119.

quest for ultimate truth and that people of that tradition actually shape their lives according to their religious vision.
Religion is not simply a function of something else—a reflection of class interest, an irrational expression of unconscious psychological need, or an arbitrary but illusory im-
position of meaning on a meaningless reality. Religion is not
merely epiphenomenal, nor is it purely private or irrational.
I certainly do not mean to say that all religious claims are
true, for if all religious claims were true, then none would
be true.

The demand to recognize the integrity of the religious
enterprise means that we must hold open the possibility that
religion is an intellectually credible path to the nature of ultimate reality, the character of nature and history, the nature
and destiny of the human being, the character of human
fulfillment, and a model for moral life. A living tradition is
an argument about the deepest meaning of our world and
our place in it, an argument to whose truth people often
commit their whole lives. At its most profound, a religious
tradition does not point to itself, but rather to the final reality
that it believes is disclosed in its tradition, and it enlists millions in its vision over the stretch of hundreds, if not
thousands, of years.

In the modern world, of course, religion does not exist in
a vacuum. It interacts with other spheres of life that have
grown independent from the religio-cultural wholes that
made up archaic human societies. Modernity has meant that
economics, politics, and culture have their own existence.
They are differentiated from religion and each other; they are
characterized by specialization and often bureaucratic organization. In short, they have a significant degree of autonomy.
They operate according to their own principles, rules, and
goals. But even so they are not completely autonomous.
Politics and economics depend on the meanings and values
supplied at a deep level by the culture of the society. Politics
and economics obviously affect each other profoundly. The
cultural system, by which I mean the guidance system of the

society—its coherent pattern of meanings and values (often supplied at least in part by its religious inheritance), is heavily dependent on a modicum of economic and political stability and success. Moreover, the culture is affected by the practices adopted in economic and political spheres. They, too, produce and sustain values. The culture also embraces the intellectual and aesthetic resources of a society, its educational institutions, thinkers, writers, and artists. Further, the political, economic, and broadly cultural spheres also have an impact on the religious traditions of the society. Thus, the various spheres of society are overlapping and interdependent, though an argument continues about which are the most powerful independent variables in the mix.

But, be that as it may, all these sectors of society are radically dependent on thinking, valuing, and acting human beings. These human beings may be ensconced in various roles shaped by the institutional systems in which they live and work, but they still remain moral agents within those systems. As such, they are influenced by their religious and moral convictions. Human agency is an indispensable factor in all the workings of society, no matter how much they seem at times to be determined by fateful necessity.

So we have for our purposes roughly two poles—religion and society—that are distinguishable but certainly not separable. *Religion*, for the purposes of this book, is not religion in general, but religion in the form of particular traditions. These traditions are describable and recognizable and are almost always embodied in institutional form. They are borne and transmitted by organized patterns of knowledge and action through which their vision is sustained and the practices indispensable to their existence are maintained. Naturally individual adherents are not the carbon copies of their traditions that officials in the organization would like. Particularly in the modern world, individuals are free to, and often do, choose their own combination of religious and moral values. The modern pluralistic world, and even more so the postmodern fragmented world, condemn us to choose, to be heretics, as Peter Berger has argued in *The Heretical Imperative*.[5] Many persons fall into their own idiosyncratic concoction, called "Sheilaism" by Robert Bellah, after an archetypical practitioner of individualized religion interviewed in his *Habits of the Heart*.[6] But others remain true to the basic affirmations of their tradition or choose another coherent tradition. In either case they are identifiable adherents of a particular tradition.

The other pole is the public context in which a tradition exists—*society*—which consists of economic, political, and cultural spheres. Religious institutions and their adherents live within this public context. They are part of what I am calling the cultural sphere. While some religious traditions attempt to separate themselves from the larger public spheres of economics, politics, and culture, the vast majority of religious traditions not only intend to exist within and interact with them, but also aim to affect those public spheres.

Thus the public environment is *engaged* by most religious traditions. It is engaged by individual adherents of a tradition who have been formed by that tradition, as well as by the formal religious organizations themselves. When a religious tradition becomes practically engaged with its public environment, either intentionally or unintentionally, religion becomes publically relevant. I will call this practical engagement "public theology" from here on, although in many ways I am referring to publically engaged religion. But I will use public theology in this broader sense, meaning by it the public engagement of a religious tradition.

A tradition's practical engagement with its public environment entails both knowledge and action. A religious tradition has an intellectual component—it claims truth for its vision of the world. Its vision is made up of stories and symbols, concepts and ideas. Sometimes great systematic theologies

---

5. Peter Berger, *The Heretical Imperative* (New York: Doubleday, 1971).
6. Robert Bellah et al., *Habits of the Heart: Individualism and Commitment in American Life* (Berkeley: University of California Press, 1985).

are constructed by religious traditions such as the Roman Catholic or Lutheran. Other traditions purport to get along on much less propositional baggage, but even they have to stipulate doctrinally the boundaries of their tradition.

A religious or theological intellectual tradition engages the public world in at least two important ways. First, that intellectual tradition moves outward from the tradition toward the world. It *interprets* the public world in the light of the religious tradition. It tells the world how it looks through the prism of its vision. This can run from prophetic denunciation to cool analysis to sycophantic affirmation.

Moreover, the intellectual tradition may be used to *persuade* the world of the cogency of its vision of how things ought to be in the public spheres of life. That is, there may be an apologetic thrust in the tradition. It may aim at convincing the world to follow its interpretation of the divine will for all of life. A related task in this intellectual movement outward is to interpret the religious tradition to the world. Historians of religious communities are particularly called to this task among others.

There is a second way that the tradition's intellectual tradition engages the world. The world is interpreted and assessed by its teachers and scholars for the use of the tradition itself. The community needs a constant interpretation of the world it is facing if it is to survive, let alone flourish. Its own members are affected by the world, sometimes unconsciously so. The tradition needs to clarify the character of the world so that it might resist where it needs to and adapt where it can. An interpretation of the world must be brought back to the tradition for the sake of its own integrity. At times this interpretation of the world may mean a critique and revision of the tradition itself. Certainly the scientific revolution has meant important reinterpretations of the intellectual traditions of many religious communities. Even those who have resisted it vehemently, such as the fundamentalists, have been conditioned by its spirit and methods. But there are very important issues here. On what bases are the revisions made?

How far can we go in our revisions before we sell our birth-right for a mess of zeitgeist pottage? What is essential to the tradition and what is negotiable? Who is to decide? So this internal critique on the bases of worldly challenges is no simple matter. The survival of the tradition is at stake as the answers to these questions are given.

To suggest that the forming capacities of a tradition are exclusively, or even primarily, in its intellectual practices would be a mistake. Formal teaching of the tradition, while essential, is not the only way that minds are formed in the tradition. Minds are persuaded and formed by other important practices of a tradition: hymns, liturgy, prayer, pastoral care, fellowship, and governance, as well as other informal activities. Even more importantly perhaps, hearts are formed, nurtured, and sustained by the practices of a specific religious tradition. A living tradition grasps the affections and will of persons, forming them according to its exemplars. Both hearts and minds are formed within living traditions.

I argued above that the practical engagement of a religious tradition with its public world entails both knowledge and action. And I have offered some reflections on the intellectual component of a religious tradition becoming public. Another dimension of public theology goes beyond knowledge to action. Action into the public world of economics, politics, and culture is taken by both institutions and individuals. The institutional engagement is easy to see. Churches make social pronouncements, they divest their money from corporations or countries that obstruct human rights, and they advocate certain kinds of legislation, to list a few examples.

Perhaps an even more powerful engagement with the public world is an indirect one. Individuals who have been deeply formed in a tradition may become active agents for the values of that tradition in their worldly roles in economics, politics, and culture. They are in the public places that matter. They can bring their religious understanding to bear on their world-ly roles and act according to the religious vision they have. They are not completely free to do whatever they decide to do in these worldly roles, since most of the time they are limited by the demands of their roles, but there are always interstices of freedom where their vision can become relevant in a significant way. This "witness" may or may not be recognizably "religious" as it is publically expressed, but in either case it flows from the hearts and minds of persons deeply formed in a religious tradition. I argue later that this is the most important way that public theology is expressed in the contemporary world.

For a religious tradition to engage effectively, it must make an intelligible case for its vision, it must have access to the public spheres of life, and it must have credibility—that is, it must possess the religious, moral, and intellectual virtues necessary for it to be taken seriously. The public world must *receive* the insights and actions of the religious tradition in some way that affects it (sometimes even unwillingly) if it is to be a genuinely public theology. I say much more about these requirements in Part III, where I examine the practical ways in which religious traditions do in fact engage the public world.

Finally, as I move into my argument, it is important to recognize that I will be limiting my treatment of religious traditions to Christian religious traditions, though I would hope that much of what I say is applicable to other traditions. Indeed, the primary religious tradition I will be dealing with will be the Lutheran, though insofar as Lutheranism is a reforming movement in the Western church, much that is said from its perspective is essentially biblical and Christian. Further, the public context I will be dealing with is American, though in this increasingly interdependent world our public worlds share so much with those of other Western nations that there should be little problem with a more general applicability.

THE ENLIGHTENMENT PROJECT AND THE MARGINALIZATION OF RELIGION

As we examine the challenge of doing public theology at this time in history, we might ask, What is behind all this concern for public theology? If religious traditions are indeed alive and if institutions and individuals are free to express their convictions in the public world, then we automatically have many instances of religion becoming public. Indeed, it might be argued persuasively that we do have a lot of public theology, perhaps too much for religion's own good. By that I mean that religious traditions are all too likely to make a public case for an issue before they have done their homework. This leads to contempt for such careless public posturing.

A closer look, however, reveals that the call for public theology is responding to a genuine set of historical realities. There are powerful currents driven by both intentional and unintentional forces to move religious notions and spokespersons to the margins of public discourse. Later I will discuss why this is the case. For the moment, however, I will focus on my contention that these currents are real.

I begin with a seemingly mild illustration. Glenn Tinder, a political philosopher of some note, has written an important book in which he argues the importance of Christian values for political life. Writing particularly to the secular academy to which he belongs, Tinder finds it necessary to conclude the preface of his book with a somewhat plaintive plea:

> I write, therefore, with the hope of finding non-Christian, as well as Christian, readers. Is this not reasonable? It is taken for granted that non-Marxists should read and learn from Marxist writings; people who reject the atheism and materialism of Freud readily consult the writings of Freud and his followers. It seems arbitrary and hazardous to be less open-minded toward Christianity.[7]

An excerpt of Tinder's book *The Political Meaning of Christianity* appeared in the December 1989 issue of *The Atlantic Monthly*, under the provocative title "Can We Be Good Without God?" It precipitated the largest outpouring of mail the

7. Glenn Tinder, *The Political Meaning of Christianity* (Baton Rouge: Louisiana State University Press, 1989), p. 5.

Atlantic had ever had, most of it negative. Some of the mail was filled with contempt for the suggestion that biblical notions about the sacrality of the individual were necessary for the sustenance of any humanly decent polity.[8] Religious ideas were neither necessary nor, for that matter, welcome in the discussion of fundamental political values. It was assumed by these cultural despisers of religion that religious values are either harmful or irrelevant to the public enterprise.

Tinder's brush with secularism is seconded by a Catholic Christian teaching at a distinguished law school. In a recent book entitled *Love and Power,* Michael Perry calls for an "ecumenical political dialogue" in which serious religious beliefs about the human good are welcomed. He obviously believes that in our current intellectual culture such an invitation is withheld. He approvingly quotes David Tracy at length on the subject:

> As David Tracy has written, in our society religion is "the single subject about which many intellectuals can feel free to be ignorant. Often abetted by the churches, they need not study religion, for everybody already knows what religion is: It is a private consumer product that some people seem to need. Its former role was poisonous. Its present privatization is harmless enough to wish it well from a civilized distance. Religion seems to be the sort of thing one likes "if that's the sort of thing one likes."[9]

That American intellectuals for the most part would like to banish religious ideas and values from public deliberation is not a new observation. Richard Neuhaus strongly pointed to it in his book *The Naked Public Square* in 1984.[10] But that was only the systematic account of a process that has been

8. This is an anecdotal account given to the author by Tinder.

9. Michael J. Perry, *Love and Power* (New York: Oxford University Press, 1991), p. 67.

10. Richard John Neuhaus, *The Naked Public Square (Grand Rapids: Eerdmans, 1984).*

noticed for years by many astute persons, both religious and nonreligious alike. As long ago as the early 1920s, Carl Becker starkly pronounced as irrelevant and unintelligible any theological claims to truth or morality.[11] They simply did not mesh with the modern worldview and were on their way to the dustbin of history.

This intellectual contempt for the contributions of theology and religiously based morality can be traced in many areas of human learning. Scores of books on business ethics rely solely on a secular basis for ethics when in fact a large majority of businesspersons are practicing Christians or Jews who take their religious values seriously in their work. Most texts on medical ethics bracket out religious insights into tough issues such as abortion, euthanasia, heroic medical efforts, and so on, when in fact overwhelming numbers of Americans take seriously those insights when making up their minds about the quandaries of medical ethics. Books on suicide often do not even mention the long-standing religious aversion to taking one's life, which is perhaps the single most important factor holding back our culture's push toward a radical doctrine of suicide. Educators banish the Judeo-Christian religious and moral heritage from their accounts of American history and social life, as well as in their attempts at moral education. In the field of international relations, the religious factor is generally neglected as an important ingredient in media or university-based analyses of world events. Thus, many great political events of the post–World War II era have been misunderstood by those blind to the religious factor.

Economists derisively call their opponents "theologians" when they want to add insult to injury. A typical secular attitude to traditional Christian moral reflection was displayed by an editorialist in *The London Times* as he commented negatively on the use of the term *subsidiarity* in recent debates on the development of the European Community. The term nis taken from Catholic social thought, in which it is argued

11. Carl Becker, *The Heavenly City of the Eighteenth Century Philosophers* (New Haven: Yale University Press, 1921), p. 17.

that problems should be dealt with at the most immediate level consistent with their solution. This pundit simply could not accept that helpful principles could come from theological ethics. He ended his diatribe with this: "The wilder shores of theology are better left to the theologians, who get centuries of pleasure out of such gobbledegook."[12]

Such overt hostility is not as common as simply ignoring religion and religious-based morality. For example, Gary Becker, the Nobel Prize-winning economist from the University of Chicago, argues that self-interested economic rationality is at the heart of decisions governing marriage and family life.[13] Such an approach, if claimed to be an exhaustive accounting of guiding values, eliminates *all* other-regarding motives for marriage and family life, not only religious ones.

The dominant intellectual attitudes of the elite of our universities certainly do affect the practical life of institutions and individuals over the long run. One of the most dramatic examples of this effect is the secularization of hundreds of Protestant and Catholic colleges and universities over the course of the past fifty years. A careful study of one of them, Vanderbilt, which was to have been a premier Methodist graduate school, has been made by James Burtchaell.[14] The story he tells is so familiar that the same description could be used for a great many colleges and universities. One would only need to substitute their names for Vanderbilt. The upshot of this process is that the sponsoring religious tradition of the school makes less and less difference to the intellectual, social, and moral life of the school. Religious sources of intellectual insight, moral guidance, and institutional identity have plainly been totally eliminated or dramatically marginalized in the life of so many of these schools.

12. Philip Howard, "Defining the S-word Is Driving Some People Bananas," *The London Times,* 15 October 1992, p. 16.
13. Gary Becker, *The Economic Approach to Human Behavior* (Chicago: University of Chicago Press, 1976).
14. James Tunstead Burtchaell, "The Decline and Fall of the Christian College," part 1, *First Things* 12 (1991): 16-29; part 2, *First Things* 13 (1991): 30-38.

In the case of one school that was undergoing a lively debate about whether the president of the school ought to be a member of the sponsoring religious community, an influential member of the board of trustees put his viewpoint this way: "The Board of Trustees should not care what the President does with his weekends."[15]

Practical economic life has been so conditioned by reliance on a pragmatic utilitarian morality that other moral visions have trouble making any impact whatever. Law has gradually been detached from its moral and religious moorings by a strong positivist attitude. Perhaps politics is the most open to the insights of Christian theology and ethics, as it has turned more and more to "values issues." Politics has become a struggle on issues like abortion, family life, affirmative action, homosexual rights, patriotism, euthanasia, and so on. While economic policy is still the most important focus of political debate, contention over foreign policy has been diminished by the cultural wars that have erupted in our political life. Politics is less dominated by elite opinion than either the academy or the media, so it becomes the arena for the people's concerns over values issues. And since ordinary Americans are overwhelmingly connected with Christian religious traditions, politics becomes the most likely public channel for the expression of their convictions. Indeed, recent elections have been contests about who can capture populist streams of opinion.[16]

Too much of the political debate on values issues, unfortunately, is marred by sloganeering and sensationalistic rhetoric. Careful arguments from a serious religious point of view are few and far between. Degeneration of political debate in

15. As a combatant in this struggle to maintain the requirement that the president of Roanoke College be a Lutheran, which had been a stipulation of the school's charter for almost 150 years, I had the privilege of seeing the correspondence generated by the board about this issue.

16. See the book by Jeffrey Bell, *Populism and Elitism* (Washington, D.C.: Regnery Gateway, 1992), for an insightful analysis of the political attempt to appeal to populist sentiments.

general does further harm to the prospects of public theology in the eyes of the cultural elite.

So when we reflect on these strong tendencies to expunge theology and theological ethics from the public sphere, one can readily see why there is a call for a credible public theology. Articulate members of living religious traditions have watched in anguish as our public life has become increasingly impervious to the contributions that these traditions can make to our deliberations. They long for a public relevance and influence commensurate with the numbers and weight of their communities.

This drift toward a naked public square has taken centuries to exert its full impact. The great religious and moral capital of Christendom has not been easily or quickly sentenced to the periphery. Indeed, the Anglo-American Enlightenment itself began, not as a rejection of Christianity, but as an affirmation of its fundamental values through other means. Carl Becker argues that the Enlightenment shared more with the preceding Christian centuries than we moderns would like to admit. In fact, he asserts that the key values of the Enlightenment were rational distillations and translations of Christian values. The Enlightenment approached the Heavenly Throne not through revelation, as the Christian church had claimed, but through reason. The early intellectuals of the Enlightenment thought they were doing "natural theology"—discerning God's eternal law by rational means. Reason and science, rather than revelation and theology, were to become the guiding instruments of a new chapter in human history, a chapter that would lead to progress toward a heavenly city built here on earth.[17]

The ethos of American life at its earliest inception was a combination of Protestant—mostly Calvinistic Puritanism—and Enlightenment themes. The moderate English Enlightenment blended well in the hearts and minds of American leaders with the biblical motifs deeply ingrained in them by

17. Becker, *Heavenly City,* pp. 28-31.

Puritanism. This combination became the persisting guidance system for American public life. It provided the civil religion that glued together the far-flung elements of American reality. Its Protestant ethic offered moral restraint and direction for ordinary citizens and the framework of reference for American public discourse. This "righteous empire" was nurtured by the great mainstream Protestant traditions—the Puritans, who became the Congregationalists; the Presbyterians; the Episcopalians; and later the Methodists and Baptists.

That earlier, relatively coherent world is fast declining, as I shall argue in the next section. Its passing has been facilitated by a complex of causes. Earlier on, the religious wars among Christians themselves did much to sentence religious themes to the periphery of public life. Enlightened persons, many Christians among them, dealt with the explosiveness of religious differences by keeping those differences distant from public life. There is still a modicum of sense in such a posture—but only a modicum.

Another reason for an increasingly naked public sphere is the loss of confidence by the leadership of the religious traditions themselves in the efficacy of their own vision's capacity to contribute to public discourse. They often capitulate before the forces of secularization by supplanting their own vision's insights with those from sources more acceptable to the secular despisers of religion. Psychology, sociology, philosophy, and particularly politics provide more "relevant" substitutes for the tired offerings of theology. So when they try to speak they merely wrap secular ideology in sacred clothing. This general waning of confidence among mainstream Protestant religious groups also makes it less likely that persons of great strength and capacity will rise among them. No one of the stature of the Niebuhr brothers has appeared from these traditions in recent decades.

However, the naked public square is not simply the result of the foibles of religion. It is the result of many historical factors over which religious communities had little control. The rise of science-based knowledge has rendered all "softer" approaches to truth less credible. Even the human sciences are tempted to claim a natural science model for their fields of learning. The modernization of society brought forth by the ascendance of science has made religious claims suspect, especially among the elite. Secularism as an ideology has strengthened among that very elite. A fragmentation of society has made it difficult for *any* authoritative voices to be heard. Misinterpretations of the First Amendment have led to legal decisions that seem intent on making all public life religion-free. Backed by these rulings, government regulations deracinate many institutions that receive government support. Militantly secular organizations such as the American Civil Liberties Union attempt to press these rulings to their logical conclusion, a completely naked public square.

So it is clear why there are renewed calls for public theology. In a country where religious communities are strong and where a vast majority of the people claim allegiance to some religious tradition, it is incredible that the public impact of religion is diminishing. This fact takes on particular poignance when we look at the condition of our public life in general, a task to which we now turn.

THE DECONSTRUCTING WORLD

"A world in fragments" seems to be the dominant image projected by our most influential thinkers. It is the key image in Alasdair MacIntyre's seminal book *After Virtue*.[18] Andrew Sullivan, editor of *The New Republic*, asserts, "There is, these days, only subculture. . . . There is no longer any sustaining broader culture to take its place."[19] Jeffrey Stout entitled his book *Ethics after Babel* to indicate the plurality of cultures and

18. Alasdair MacIntyre, *After Virtue,* 2d ed. (Notre Dame, Ind.: Notre Dame University Press, 1984).
19. Andrew Sullivan, "Disappointed," *The New Republic,* 28 September 1992, p. 45.

their varied moral perspectives.[20] There is an important distinction between a healthy and a chaotic pluralism, and many scholars fear we are tending as a society toward the latter. Contrary to Sullivan, who celebrates the loss of a sustaining broader culture, many influential thinkers envision a society breaking into warring parties, each with its own version of the truth.[21]

Others, like Robert Bellah, worry that the fragmentation of our deconstructing world is taking the form of a radical individualism instead of warring groups.[22] He argues that older sources of virtue—republican and biblical—are being replaced by hyperindividualism. Individualism is stimulated by both our current political and economic cultures. Our contemporary political culture emphasizes individual liberty and rights at the expense of commitment to the common good. Our economic culture encourages the quest for short-term pleasure for the individual.

Two new lifestyles have emerged from these powerful currents to challenge biblical and republican ideals of the human good. One of these is called "utilitarian individualism." It is the model of economic man. Individuals assumed in classical and neoclassical economics are utility maximizers. They know what their interests are, and they use reason to

20. Jeffrey Stout, *Ethics after Babel* (Boston: Beacon Press, 1988). While Stout admits the plurality of moral perspectives, he believes that a neopragmatic approach (his, among others) can restore the needed common ground for moral discourse in the public realm. He also invites the perspectives of religious ethics into this discourse, though he believes that religious ethics have fallen on bad days for many of the reasons we catalogued earlier.

21. Many thinkers voice these fears. Among them are some I have already mentioned: MacIntyre, Neuhaus, and Thiemann. But there is a general sense among social commentators that "interest group liberalism" has exaggerated the contextual element in truth claims so strongly that we have fallen into a radical perspectivalism, i.e., that truth is relative to the social group to which one belongs. We are left then with a kind of "epistemological tribalism" that denies any common ground for truth claims.

22. Bellah, *Habits*.

maximize those interests. Reason in this case is not the elevated reason of classical Greek or Roman philosophy, the exercise of which can lead the rational person toward the good, the true, and the beautiful. Rather, reason is the practical capacity that enables individuals to find effective means toward whatever ends they choose. Bellah believes that such an orientation leads toward self-interested individualism. Indeed, even commitments to others are viewed as useful means to the end of individual satisfactions.

However, the second kind of individualism, which Bellah calls "expressive individualism," is perhaps even more subversive of human community. Expressive individualism assumes that it is both liberating and fulfilling to express whatever internal states the individual has within. With obvious connections to romantic movements past and present, this expressivism ranges from the ridiculous to the sublime. Petty emotions as well as soaring creative capacities are encouraged to be expressed. One is invited, perhaps even obligated, to make one's life an artistic expression, the more intense and colorful the better. All repressive internal and external restraints are the enemy. One must overcome them to reach the liberated life. Rock stars living short and intense lives become the inheritors of the mantle of earlier Romantic poets.

In either kind of individualism, commitments to other persons, communities, and institutions are qualified by one's own wishes, be they utilitarian or expressive. Perhaps persons and communities are useful to the interests or needs of the utilitarian or expressive self; perhaps they are not. It all depends on the individual's gauging of his or her interest or need.

At root this individualism posits an innocent and harmless self. The exertion of utilitarian interest or expressive need will not harm others by either intent or neglect. Indeed, the exertions and expressions of individual selves will lead to a miraculous harmony among self-interested and self-expressing parties. The liberation of the self means at the same time the liberation of others. So the illusion avers.

However, any cursory look at the social scene in America bears quite a different message. Our society has soaring rates of early and promiscuous sex, sexually transmitted diseases, AIDS, cohabitation of loosely committed pairs, marital discord and divorce, children born out of wedlock, the feminization of poverty, abortion, single parenthood, crime, murder, and high rates of incarceration. Stimulated by various forms of egoistic individualism—either utilitarian or expressive—persons gradually lose their sense of commitment and moral responsibility. No longer shored up by communal consent, external restraints in law and culture are weakened and allow the individual free reign without any concomitant increase in self-discipline. Liberty becomes chaotic and disordered. The imperial self is not harmless and innocent; it is a self-obsessed and self-centered agent.

The effects of the liberation of the imperial self on the primary units of social life are devastating. Society becomes a gigantic hospital for treating the persons harmed in the breakdown of healthy communal and associational life. Even at the middle-class level we detect signs of malaise. People indulge their selfish impulses by refusing to enter into commitments beyond themselves.

A selected page of the *Sunday Times* of London leaves an indelible impression of the movement of at least a part of modern culture.[23] An article entitled "Going Solo by Choice" gives a rationale for the rapid rise of single-person households in Britain. It is a paean to unencumbered utilitarian and expressive individualism. It begins with an attack on the family: "The more we know about the history of the family, the more we become aware that people living in the family were not mad keen on it and were waiting to escape." The article goes on to catalog those who have escaped both marriage and family. One young woman observes: "Because of my independence and income, I have become more aware of what I might lose in marriage. My own private space and income

23. *The Sunday Times,* London, 20 September 1992, sec. 5.

are all put at risk when I enter a relationship, and I am no longer prepared to make those sacrifices." A twice-divorced man puts it this way: "Living alone is a luxury because you can be as selfish as you like. I spent fifty years of my life terrified of being on my own, but now I can smoke in bed, make a mess and not feel guilty about it in the slightest. I got over being lonely about seven years ago. One morning I woke up and thought, 'My God, I'm free.'"

It is difficult to know whether to feel worse about these individuals' condition or their illusory satisfaction with their condition. At any rate, there is something deeply disturbing about people who retreat from deeply shared commitments with others. The very structure of human life itself—its covenantal structure—seems to be blithely rejected. On the same page of the newspaper cited above are two further articles, one on the explosion of paranormal practices among people in their early twenties in Britain. The other is on the ever-increasing use of sex to establish successful magazines. It seems that the unencumbered indeed look to something beyond themselves for meaning, no matter how kooky it is, and they look for the quenching of their thirsty spirits through more and more sex, either real or imagined.

Before this depletion of the moral capital of Western culture, the Enlightenment project of rational, scientific progress seems helpless. The vaunted possibilities of science serve to magnify and intensify human capacities but have little to contribute to the task of guiding those capacities in proper paths to ennobling ends. Science certainly improves the external conditions of life—no mean achievement—but contributes little to the internal aspirations of the spirit.

The Enlightenment confidence in reason's capacity to discern substantive goals has waned dramatically. Reason is mostly viewed as the practical instrument to achieve whatever ends we choose. In the moral sphere reason still recognizes the ethical demand for persons to consent to actions upon them. What is right and good amounts to whatever adults consent to.

The current inheritors of the Enlightenment project, the philosophical liberals and pragmatists, have difficulty both discerning the human good and stipulating the means—including rules—to move toward it. Motivational concerns seem not even to enter their outlook; rather, procedural concerns dominate their purview. Lacking more substantive notions of the human good, they seem incapable of stemming the powerful downward tug of contemporary mass culture.

As Phillip Rieff has argued in *The Feeling Intellect*, philosophical liberalism has no way to prevent us from sinking into the "abyss of our own possibilities."[24] Reiff believes that the minimalistic ethic of mutual consent is powerless before the tendency to say "Why not?" when confronted by harmful or even degrading human practices, as long as those practices are engaged in by consent.

The current worldwide impact of pop star Madonna illustrates well what we have been saying. The substance of what she is publicly offering is sheer expressive individualism. Admitting to the suggestion that she sees herself as a sexual revolutionary, she elaborates:

> In all my work, my thing has always been not to be ashamed. . . . People are afraid of their own feelings and I am saying: don't be afraid. It's OK to have whatever feeling you have, . . . If people were comfortable with the way they felt—they didn't feel like they had to play all these different roles for society and other people, if they just could be honest about who they were this world would be a better place.[25]

When asked later in the interview whether sadomasochistic sexual feelings are included in what people should feel OK about, Madonna fervently argues that they should be. She could hardly say otherwise, since a portion of her best-selling

---

24. Phillip Rieff, *The Feeling Intellect: Selected Writings* (Chicago: University of Chicago Press, 1990), p. 31.

25. "Laid Bare," an interview with Madonna by Andrew Neil in *The Sunday Times Magazine,* 18 October 1992, p. 20.

book, *Sex*, has a considerable number of sadomasochistic scenes. But pressed as to whether such activities should be engaged in involuntarily, she of course demurs. Further, she adds, all this should not be taken seriously since her book is simply a flight of imagination; reality should be something different. In spite of all, she isn't against "family values."[26]

Why then, all this lustful weirdness? Besides Madonna's confused notions of liberation, she is admired in show business as the epitome of projecting and selling her "image." Perhaps she really doesn't believe in what she is selling, but the utilitarian individualism that drives her leads her to do whatever she needs to do to maintain her fame and sell books, videos, and records. She is willing to pander to the lowest desires and impulses in order to become successful. This no doubt is combined with a rationalized desire to be part of the cause of liberation. This cause is replete with both direct and indirect attacks on Christian symbols, traditions, and moral principles. It is a willful flirtation with evil. She senses that her Christian background is precisely the enemy in her struggle to liberate the expressive self. Christian notions of service to others, the Christian ethic of sex, and certainly the Christian value of modesty are her explicit targets.

Some radical feminists have seen Madonna's efforts as important supports for the attack on conventional sexual identities and roles. She is a dangerous goddess enlisted in the task of deconstruction. Tremendous amounts of talent, expertise, technology, and effort have gone into promoting Madonna and her image. These differ only in scale from what is devoted to other entertainment stars. And even the vast promotional efforts made for entertainers are dwarfed by those made for advertising products of all sorts.

These products in profusion are viewed as elements essential for the good life. Human ingenuity is harnessed in the process of selling the good life. All this reminds one of Augustine's famous depiction of late antiquity as a society of

26. Ibid., p. 21.

splendid vices. Great human talent and ingenuity are focused on promoting more and more ignoble practices. Sensate values are pursued with all imaginable means.

This downward tug is not the whole story. Many subcultures are devoted to humane values and practices, but a struggle is on. The older cultural coherence is gone. New interest groups practice their hermeneutic of suspicion on whatever is left of it. Individuals are free to find their own way in this confusing maelstrom of possibilities. In this context, religious traditions are called to find their public voice. Their public theologies must articulate their vision of the human good, not only for the sake of their own communicants, but also for the sake of an unraveling public world, a world that could well be moving toward dissolution. Perhaps that world retains enough health to know of the danger it is in and to listen to a voice that has provided the moral capital of the West for aeons. This possibility depends at least partially on the capacity of Christian communities to speak with a credible public voice. We will turn next to an examination of those capacities.

2

▼ ▼ ▼ ▼

CURRENT OPTIONS
IN AMERICAN
PUBLIC THEOLOGY

THE DECLINE OF PROTESTANT MAINLINE
PUBLIC THEOLOGY

The Kingdom of God in America

It has been argued conclusively, I believe, that the spirit of American religion and of America itself, insofar as it has been penetrated by religious themes, has been thoroughly Calvinistic, rather than Catholic, sectarian, or Lutheran. One of the essential themes of that Calvinistic spirit holds that the kingdom of God will come in history. At its best, the kingdom is purely God's work and will come with judgment as well as affirmation of the American project. In its more domesticated form, American Christians themselves will be able to discern God's will clearly and bring it to fruition, aided by the Holy Spirit, who confirms and legitimates all their best efforts.

H. Richard Niebuhr, in his classic, *The Kingdom of God in America*, believed he had grasped the guiding motif of American religion when he wrote in his preface:

> It appeared possible, then, that the expectation of the kingdom of God on earth was the great common element in our faith and that by reference to it one might be able to understand

not only the unity beneath the diversity of American religion but also the effect of Christianity on [American] culture.[1]

Commenting on Niebuhr's contributions to understanding American religious history, Harry S. Stout writes, "Niebuhr extracted a common core of meaning and ethos that centered around the impulse to transform the raw American environment into the kingdom of God."[2]

Stout goes on to argue that Niebuhr had indeed identified the Christian transformist theology and movement that "provided America with a radical, even democratic, social and political ideology."[3] Other major historians of American religion confirm this broad analysis. Martin Marty extended it with a book entitled *Righteous Empire*.[4] Sydney Ahlstrom, in his monumental *A Religious History of the American People*, points to the Puritan theme of America's providential destiny as central to American religion and life. America is the redeemer nation called to realize a new order for the ages. America, like Israel, is in a covenantal relationship with God. If America lives up to its calling as a covenanted people, it will receive God's blessing. The millennium will appear in America, and the Christian "errand into the wilderness" will be brought to fruition. These powerful Old Testament notions, taken up first by the Puritans and broadened and deepened in the First and Second Great Awakenings, gave decisive direction to the American project.[5]

1. H. Richard Niebuhr, *The Kingdom of God in America* (New York: Harper and Brothers, 1959), p. xi.

2. Harry S. Stout, "The Historical Legacy of H. Richard Niebuhr," in *The Legacy of H. Richard Niebuhr,* ed. Ronald F. Thiemann (Minneapolis: Fortress, 1991), p. 88.

3. Ibid., p. 95.

4. Martin E. Marty, *Righteous Empire: The Protestant Experience in America* (Fort Worth: Dial, 1970)

5. Sydney E. Ahlstrom, *A Religious History of the American People* (New York: Doubleday, 1975), and "American Religious Values and the Future of America," in *American Religious Values and the Future of America,* ed. Rodger Van Allen (Philadelphia: Fortress, 1978), pp. 5-23.

Others besides Americans have come to the same conclusions about the underlying soul of America. André Siegfried, following in the footsteps of Alexis de Tocqueville, argued that America had developed as an "essentially Calvinistic" country where a Reformed perspective nurtured "the feeling of social obligation that is so typically Anglo-Saxon." This feeling was responsible for "the missionary spirit which animates the crusades against cigarettes, alcohol, and the slums, and such movements as feminism, pacifism, anti-vivisection, Americanization of immigrants, and even the gospel of eugenics and birth control."[6]

Mark Noll, whose use of Siegfried I have just cited, agrees with this overall analysis that the spirit of America has been decisively shaped by a particular kind of Calvinism. Its essence, he believes, lies in a strong doctrine of sanctification whereby the Christian soul is brought to purity by the Holy Spirit. The sinner's soul is transformed by the Spirit so that he or she can clearly discern God's will and actually do it. But the process does not stop there. This transformation of the soul brings about the urge to transform society in like manner. Indeed, Noll holds that Calvinist Protestantism of the American sort intends to "transform society as an analogy to the transformation of the soul."[7] Thereby God's kingdom in the individual soul will be translated into God's kingdom in society.

One should not underestimate the positive effects of this active, robust form of "constructive Protestantism," as H. Richard Niebuhr termed it.[8] As Noll puts it:

Such Reformed attitudes toward life in the world have had an immeasurably great effect on American history. Calvinistic

6. André Siegfried, *America Comes of Age: A French Analysis* (New York: Knopf, 1927), as quoted and interpreted by Mark Noll in his review of Martin Marty's *The Noise of Conflict, 1919–1941*, Vol. 2 of *Modern American Religion* in *The Christian Century*, 15 May 1991, p. 556.

7. Noll, p. 557.

8. Niebuhr, *Kingdom of God*, p. 43.

convictions about living all of life to the glory of God led to the remarkable experiment of seventeenth century New England where Puritans created the freest, most stable, most democratic society then existing in the entire world. In the eighteenth century a more diffuse Puritan passion for public justice provided, if not the specific ideology, at least much of the energy for the American Revolution and the creation of a new nation. During the nineteenth century a more general evangelical Protestantism fueled immense labors of Christianization and civilization—subduing a continent, democratizing a people, evangelizing at home through revival and abroad through missions, reforming institutions, attitudes, habits, and social practices, and surviving a civil war that ended with the prohibition of slavery.[9]

Noll goes on to argue that in recent days secularism has changed the substance but not the form of public activity. Instead of God and Scripture being the agents of change, science and progress have taken their place. But the reform of all of life has remained the goal. The crusading mentality has been constant. "Thus, though modern Americans may differ in nearly every particular from their Puritan and evangelical ancestors, they still are deeply committed to working out their salvation, and the salvation of everyone else, through the restructuring of public life."[10]

Certainly it was mainstream Protestant Christianity that presided over this Calvinist project. Congregationalists, Presbyterians, Methodists, Baptists, and to some extent Episcopalians bore not only the key religious motifs but also the capacity to translate those motifs effectively into public life. They were the carriers of "constructive Protestantism." They shaped *the* culture of American life. And they produced the public theologians who were able to articulate the meaning of these religious themes into an effective public rhetoric.

9. Mark A. Noll, "The Lutheran Difference," *First Things* 20, February 1992, p. 38.
10. Ibid.

From the early Puritan divines through Jonathan Edwards to Richard Niebuhr and Paul Ramsey, Calvinist Christianity held sway over the public face of American religion.

The confidence by mainstream Protestantism that America was the fit vehicle for God's kingdom lasted right up until the 1950s. When the National Council of Churches succeeded the old Federal Council in 1950, Henry Knox Sherrill, its first president, said that the council's formation marked "a new and great determination that the American way will be increasingly the Christian way, for such is our heritage. Together the churches can move forward to the goal—a Christian America in a Christian world."[11] The transformist intentions are still present, as is the confidence that America is a hospitable location for the fruition of God's kingdom. Furthermore, confidence remains that we can discern the clear marks of God's will for American public life and translate them into public policy.

The Great Reversal

A great distance exists, not in terms of time but of posture, from that mainstream hope for the kingdom of God in America to the current mainstream despair for America. Instead of America being a fit vehicle of God's transforming actions through his people, America is a tragic perversion of God's intentions, fit only to be deplored. The same National Council of Churches, the creature of the Protestant mainstream, proposes a two-hour "learning journey" through the study of its quicentenary study document, *Columbus Explored: Retracing Our Roots*. The Puritans, as well as other later European Christians, came at the expense of America's first peoples. The colonial process should not be celebrated, for it brought devastation to indigenous peoples. Indeed, Christianity contributed to the "exploitative worldview" that brought, and continues to bring, that devastation. Jim Wallace of *Sojourners*

---

11. As quoted in Mark A. Noll, "The Public Church in the Years of Conflict" *The Christian Century*, 15 May 1991, p. 553.

drives home that point: "There is, in fact, no new world order; we are still being governed by an old one whose economic, political, philosophical, environmental, and especially spiritual roots can be traced back to the conquest and colonization of the Americas." In light of this, we are called to "repentance and renewal" so that the dark past might be transformed.[12]

There could scarcely be anything more different than the two contrasting attitudes we have just examined. Since the mid-sixties, mainstream Protestant Christianity has turned its back on the American experiment it has had so much part in shaping. Its public theologians, perhaps epitomized by Robert McAfee Brown, claimant to Reinhold Niebuhr's mantle, illustrate this disaffiliation. Brown has identified strongly with liberation theology, replete with its Marxist analysis of the relations of rich and poor, north and south, in the emerging modern world. At the World Council of Churches meeting in Africa in the mid-seventies, Brown refused to speak in English, the language of the capitalist oppressors of the Third World. He asserted that "the structures of our democratic society that benefit me here at home (the vote, the capitalist system, the police) often destroy others both at home and abroad." This systemic evil must be rejected and radically transformed toward socialism. The clues toward the direction we must move are in the liberation movements around the world, such as those in Central and South America.[13]

Perhaps one could argue that the transformist urge is still there, and that would be correct. But what is dramatically different is the assessment of the possibilities of America for the context in which God's kingdom will draw near. America has lost it. She has broken the covenant and no longer holds

12. National Council of Churches, *Columbus Explored: Retracing Our Roots* (New York: NCC, 1992).

13. Robert McAfee Brown, *Theology in a New Key: Responding to Liberation Themes* (Louisville: Westminster, 1978), pp. 15, 69.

promise. There can only be judgment before wiping the tarnished slate clean. And the signals for renewal will not come from our own history even though it has been dramatically conditioned by mainstream Protestant Christianity. Nor will it come from a direct reading of biblical injunctions. No, the signals of renewal will come from the nations and liberation movements struggling against us. They will come from China, Cuba, Nicaragua, and the many African countries involved in creating African socialism. Even the Soviet Union and its satellites can contribute to building a new society here, for they have emphasized social and economic rights rather than political rights. They can complement our one-sided emphasis on liberal, procedural rights. They have much to teach us. So went the argument of the Protestant mainstream through much of the last two decades.

This disaffiliation from America and the West went so far during the Cold War that most mainstream Protestant groups claimed that America was the main source of the arms race. The thinking was that if we would freeze our weapons development, the Soviet Union would feel less threatened and diminish its capacity for making war. We were the major aggressor, or so it seemed to the mainstream.

The redeemer nation had become the destroyer nation. James Reichley, in his massive *Religion in American Public Life*, chronicles this gradual turn from hoping for the kingdom of God in America to hoping for it from almost anywhere else but America. The mainstream denominations increasingly identified with the left wing of domestic politics and the liberation movements of the Third World, neither of which had much appreciation for the American experiment. The ecumenical organizations sponsored by the mainstream denominations identified even more strongly with those adversarial parties. The World and National Councils of Churches were less restrained by grassroots sentiments than the denominations themselves. Meanwhile, the laity that supported these denominations and their ecumenical agencies were much more moderate or conservative in their orientation, as was the American populace in general.[14]

Thus, in a curious way, the mainstream denominations, their intellectual spokespersons, and their headquarters and ecumenical agencies became disengaged from the American experiment they had had so much influence in constructing, as well as from the people they had formed in their own churches. They were too estranged from them to have a genuinely constructive conversation. All they could do was denounce. And those laypersons responsible for society turned away from such denunciations. The mainstream no longer had much of a public to address. Its public theology, as it were, had no public to receive it.

The political and economic centers of power ignored mainstream pronouncements for several reasons. After some time it was clear that the intellectuals and the headquarters spoke only for a very small portion of the members of the Protestant mainstream. Businesspersons and politicians are smart enough to read the polling data about the real political, economic, and social opinions of mainstream Protestant Americans.

Besides, the elite of the Protestant mainstream had distanced themselves so sharply from American economic and political practice that they could say little relevant or helpful to those involved in the real processes of American life. While the mainstream voice claimed itself to be prophetic, it was merely alienated and distant from the society it had so deeply affected. It had little to say of practical importance.

Political and Cultural Pilgrims

Beginning in about 1970, the Protestant mainstream leadership, especially its intellectuals, searched for God's kingdom everywhere but in America. The period from 1970 to about 1985 saw a search for a *political* manifestation of the kingdom.

14. A. James Reichley, *Religion in American Public Life* (Washington: The Brookings Institution, 1985), pp. 243-81.

Some saw China as a place where Mao's cultural revolution was doing Christ's work without mentioning his name. Many others saw African socialism—particularly that of Julius Nyrere in Tanzania—as the drawing near of God's kingdom of justice and peace. When those began to go sour, the Sandinistas in Nicaragua became the carriers of the banner. Other insurgent groups in Central and Latin America, South Africa, Namibia, and the Philippines were also of great interest and hope. Revolutionary praxis was where God was active in bringing forth his kingdom, a kingdom for the poor and against the rich. God was bringing forth his kingdom, and his prophet was Karl Marx.

Since America seemed to be against these insurgencies and the Soviet Union for them, there was also sympathy for the revolutionary intentions of the granddaddy of revolutionaries. Indeed, the Protestant mainstream, the World and National Councils of Churches, and the religious intellectuals who spoke for them could find little difference in the kinds of imperialism represented by the Soviets and the Americans. The suspicion was that America's was worse since it was more subtle and sophisticated. Only infrequently had American imperialism broken into its murderously open manifestation, but Vietnam was certainly one of those instances. And once again America was on the wrong side of history, impeding God's revolutionary action. At best there was a moral equivalence between East and West; at worst, there was more suspicion that the West, with America as its leader, was guiltier than the East. Consequently "political theologians" like Dorothee Soelle heaped scornful judgment upon Western "militarism" and excused the arms buildup of the East as a defensive response to the aggressive West.

As "real, existing socialism" collapsed in Central and Eastern Europe, and Marxist-Leninism evaporated as a formative political ideology, most liberation movements have either sought negotiated compromises or changed their ideological justifications.

The Protestant church and society bureaucracies have shifted their political hopes to base communities in Latin and Central America, which now seem far less enamored of Marxist-Leninism, and, moreover, are in danger of being swamped by the growth of charismatic and fundamentalist Christianity. Even Cuba, the last outpost of "real, existing socialism" in the Western hemisphere, is losing its allure as an alternative to Western democratic capitalism for those liberationists in the Protestant mainstream who looked on Castro with affection and sympathy.

The Marxist project now seems over. Except for backwater places like North Korea and the minds of a surprising number of Western intellectuals, the seventy-year revolutionary project has come to an abrupt end. (Certainly the direction China is taking is more akin to authoritarian capitalism than classic Marxist-Leninism.) But the search for the revolutionary project has not stopped. The political pilgrims who searched for a political manifestation of God's kingdom anywhere but in America now look for it in cultural disclosures within America's adversarial movements. Salvation will come from the revolutionary cultural praxis of gender feminism, homosexualism, multiculturalism, or militant ecological movements.[15]

Gender feminism—in distinction from equalitarian feminism, which seeks nondiscriminatory treatment of women in public life—posits a radically different feminine essence in

---

15. It is fascinating how basic Marxist analysis still underlies many of these adversarial movements. The Marxist notion that dominant groups have arranged society and culture for their own exploitative purposes remains a key to their perspective. Power relations between the oppressed and oppressor (relations of groups are never seen as more complex) provide the dominant model of analysis. Following from this, it is assumed that those who are oppressed by the dominant group (male, straight, European, capitalist) have a particularly relevant grasp of true reality. Since they are not blinded by the ideological screens that surround the oppressor, they are able to see clearly and move decisively toward justice. Their revolutionary praxis will bring wholeness to the oppressed and, in the longer run, to the whole society. The dream of a sinless and unerring proletariat has not been given up. It has simply been translated into new categories.

the female of the species. This essence is intuitive, cooperative, nonhierarchical, empowering, nurturing, and compassionate. Women, as the possessors of these virtues, have been
suppressed by males with their malevolent (to make an intentional pun) values. Indeed, the deepest and most fundamental oppression is sexual oppression. As women throw off
the patriarchal structures of oppression, the long-suppressed
virtues of women will finally be released to free and reform
all structures of life. Feminist practice will reveal the liberating
energies of the divine, now "imaged" as Goddess the Mother
rather than God the Father.

Gay and lesbian liberation groups identify the oppressor as
the straight white male who has established heterosexism as
the dominant ideology of the West. The attendant homo-
phobia has sentenced gays and lesbians to the closet, or, in
cases of public exposure, to violent and cruel oppression.
Because of domination by the heterosexist establishment, human sexuality has been badly distorted. The only path for
renewal is to discern the signs of undistorted sexuality among
the oppressed—gays, but especially lesbians. Indeed, the president of the Society of Christian Ethics suggested to the as-
sembled crowd at a recent annual conference that we must
look to lesbian sexual relations to gain clues about what
healthy, unoppressed sexual relations are like—never mind
the millions of Christian couples who have lived out their
Christian vows of marriage throughout the ages.

Multiculturalists take aim at the European-Americans and
their heritage that allegedly oppress minority cultures within
church and society. African Americans, Hispanics, Native
Americans, and other groups whose native language is other
than English, raise the charge of hegemony of both power
and culture. (Interestingly enough, while even the deaf—or
hearing impaired—are often included in the list of oppressed
groups, European groups, no matter how poor or oppressed,
are not included.) On a superficial level, the multiculturalists
are right. The normative culture of America has been shaped
by those of European heritage. Likewise, since they have been

in the country the longest, Americans of European heritage have accumulated power and status. The multiculturalists in church and society seem to want to delegitimate any normative culture, even the broadly American one into which the "Europeans" have melded. Without any sense of danger about what the balkanization of American society might be like, they assume that the interplay of self-consciously ethnic and racial groups (whose identity has been sharpened by resentful accusations toward the majority "Europeans") will be harmonious and creative. For them the road to peace and justice is through an affirmation of radical pluralism.

Ecological militants look for a renewal of the earth by adopting themes from archaic cultures, especially Native American. These cultures, suppressed by the industrial cultures of the white, straight, capitalist "European" male, have the resources to reconnect humans and their societies with the natural environment from which they sprang. Moreover, other cultures and religions, particularly those that emphasize goddess worship, provide other sources for correction and renewal.

These four adversarial sources for reversing the putative destructive trajectory of American culture are often in cooperation with each other. They have a common enemy. And key thinkers from any of these four movements frequently articulate themes drawn from all four. Witness the writing of a leading feminist theologian, Rosemary Radford Reuther:

> A healed relation to each other and to the earth calls for a new consciousness, a new symbolic culture and spirituality. We need to transform our inner psyches and the way we symbolize the interrelations of men and women, humans and earth, humans and the divine, the divine and the earth. Ecological healing is a theological psychic-spiritual process. . . . We must see the work of ecojustice and the work of spirituality interrelated, the inner and outer aspects of one process of conversion and transformation.[16]

16. Rosemary Radford Reuther, *Gaia and God: An Ecofeminist Theology of Earth Healing* (San Francisco: HarperCollins, 1992), as quoted in *First Things,* November 1992, pp. 73-74.

Certainly the Calvinist concern for transformation toward earthly fulfillment is vigorously present in these movements. But they assuredly do not look to the American tradition of historic "constructive Protestantism" for guidance. Nor do they look for clues in the ongoing practices of American life that mainline Protestantism so powerfully shaped. Normative principles must come from outside those traditions because they are so hopelessly distorted. But even more seriously in these latter days of cultural pilgrimage, the very biblical vision that brought those Protestant traditions forth is suspect, as is orthodox Christian tradition through the ages. For those vehicles—the Bible and tradition—are themselves the source of patriarchy, heterosexism, ethnocentrism, and the exploitation of nature. They must either be rejected or thoroughly purged of their perversions according to the principles revealed by contemporary liberating praxis.

Thus the self-destructive course of mainstream Protestantism has now intentionally taken aim at its own foundations. It hopes for transformation guided by sources from the cultural adversaries of traditional Christian life. The inheritors of "constructive Protestantism" do not look for the kingdom to come in the America they helped build, nor do they look for America to be guided by the constructive Protestantism from which they have descended. Discouraged by their failed efforts to be gods in history, they look for new gods (or goddesses) from among those most clearly opposed to the culture they have had so much a part in constructing.

To charge the whole of mainstream Protestantism with such machinations would be inaccurate and unfair. Certainly the local parishes of Presbyterian or Methodist or United Church of Christ or Episcopal persuasion are not all moving headlong in this direction. The preceding analysis, however, points accurately to strong trends among the church and society bureaucracies, the intellectual leadership, and the seminaries of many mainstream Protestant denominations. A day at a typical mainstream or interdenominational seminary could not go by without these tendencies being strongly articulated by representative figures.

Why the Reversal?

It is difficult to account for this dramatic shift, but let us propose several explanations. First, religious traditions of all kinds have had powerful challenges to the truth and efficaciousness of their core visions by the Enlightenment. Revelation and theology have been replaced by reason and science as the way to truth for the educated elite of modern societies. Religious doctrines have been consigned to the margins of private life, as I argued in chapter 1. In the face of such a challenge, religious traditions, particularly those of a liberal posture, have been tempted either to dilute or displace their core religious vision with more promising and "relevant" insights derived from secular sources. As its confidence in religious themes waned, liberal Protestantism looked to ethics, politics, and psychology for guidance. Indeed, the liberal Protestantism of the late sixties and the seventies looked for the world to set the agenda for the church. What better way to diminish the role of one's own religious vision than to give "the world" religious authority? If you can't beat them, join them.

This secularization process accounts for the worldliness of liberal Christianity, its search for transcendence in worldly sources rather than through its own religious vision, but it does not explain the negative turn toward the American experiment, which it had so deeply conditioned. Certainly the trauma of the sixties (1965–75) provides part of the explanation. Prior to the sixties, mainstream Protestantism was still hopeful that its own project could be carried out—the coming of the kingdom of God in America. True enough, as H. Richard Niebuhr had shown, the grand, classic Calvinist themes of the sovereignty of God and the reign of Christ had been reduced to a more domesticated set of tunes that Protestant Christians themselves were to invent and realize without great pain or judgment. What more biting words have ever been written about the loss of Christian transcendence than these: "A God without wrath brought men without sin into a kingdom without judgment through the ministrations of a Christ without a cross"?[17] The optimistic myth of American (Protestant) innocent progress was still deeply ingrained in the Protestant mainstream self-definition. Of course such an optimistic assessment was never an accurate account of American history itself, as Reinhold Niebuhr argued strongly throughout his career, perhaps most persuasively in *The Irony of American History*.[18] But fond illusions persist, and it took the trauma of the sixties to blow them away, and then with extreme and unhealthy effects.

The sixties were a time in which America was seriously put to the test. Its smoldering problems broke into flames. The enduring problem of racism, degradation of the cities, careless treatment of the environment, limitations on women, and intolerance toward homosexuals were all challenged by organized protest movements. The tensions created by all these were immeasurably exacerbated by an unsuccessful war in Southeast Asia. A huge population of baby boomers was caught up in the spirit of protest. The assassinations of two Kennedys and Martin Luther King Jr. added a frightful edge to already serious traumas. Apocalyptic analyses abounded. Many thought America as we knew it was coming to an end.

And indeed it was. Many of the young were convinced that our heritage and tradition were corrupt. The myth of American guilt replaced the myth of American innocence. Instead of America being the exaggerated font of every good thing in the world, it became the source of every bad thing. We were the most guilty of all the world's peoples. Our democracy was a sham, our capitalism exploitative, our Eurocentric culture repressed and murderous, our institutions untrustworthy, our leadership corrupt, and our prospects for constructive contributions in the world close to nil.

17. Niebuhr, *Kingdom of God*, p. 193.
18. Reinhold Niebuhr, *The Irony of American History* (New York: Scribners, 1952).

This excessively dark definition of contemporary America was the flip side of the excessively bright definition of an earlier time. The coin was violently turned by the dramatic exposure of the dark side of the American dream, a dark side that had been long suppressed by the innocence and optimism of the dream itself.[19] This traumatic turn convinced many people, but especially the young, that America was certainly not the place where the kingdom of God could come. Rather, it was the antithesis of the kingdom.

We must look elsewhere, anywhere else, for signs of peace and justice. The most credible signs were found in places and movements that were in opposition to America and its tradition.

This radical redefinition was not held by the majority of the American populace. Instead of "power to the people," the radicals got Richard Nixon. But the myth of American guilt was lodged in many important sectors of American culture and society. The educational, religious, and media elite were most affected. The "knowledge class," as some have termed it, were more likely to accept the new definition of America than were the older middle classes. In economic and political life, however, where one has either to sell one's product or to win an election, such radical interpretations of America were soon moderated, though they lived on in the left wing of the Democratic Party. But in the more protected spheres of cultural life—education, religion, entertainment, and the media—the myth of American guilt carried considerable force. Likewise, the adversarial politics and culture that fed off the myth of American guilt flourished in these sectors. Perhaps among these "soft" institutions, religion was the most vulnerable. Many convinced by the myth of American guilt slowly moved into the bureaucracies and seminaries of mainstream Protestantism. From those locations they could translate the myth of American guilt into "prophetic messages"

19. Robert Benne and Philip Hefner, *Defining America: A Christian Critique of the American Dream* (Philadelphia: Fortress, 1974).

to the people, and they could provide a platform for the adversarial politics and culture that keyed off that guilt.

Thus it came to be that the Protestant mainstream turned against its own legacy. And it turned against it with such force that it seriously damaged the channels of communication it once had, not only to its own grassroots constituents, but also to the broader society. Its estrangement severely damaged its public voice.

At the root of the Protestant mainstream's problems, however, was not simply an inaccurate assessment of American possibility, but rather a theological flaw. From the beginning of American Protestant constructive Christianity, expectations for human history were too expansive. The Calvinist strain in American religion led to anticipation of the saving acts of God in public national life. The kingdom of God was to come on earth as it is in heaven, ushered in by committed Christians. Transcendent fulfillment was expected in history. This great worldly hope then became the occasion for worldly despair when those expectations were disappointed. Where too much is expected, too much blame is laid when the longed-for does not appear. Then judicious relative judgments cannot be made. The careful judgments of the relatively good and bad, which are so crucially important in any adequate exercise of historical responsibility, are foresworn. The nerve of prudential wisdom is cut.

This problem flows not simply from placing too much hope in a particular nation; it is rather a case of assigning salvific significance to any collective achievement in human history. It is, to use Noll's phrase, to expect a transformation of society analogous to the transformation of the individual soul. Indeed, we could press the critique further. Calvinist doctrines of sanctification anticipate too complete a transformation of the soul. Following from that, perfection of society becomes too much of a possibility.

It should be mentioned after this long critique of mainstream Protestantism that the same theological errors crop

up in the expectations of fundamentalist or extremely conservative churches. For them, however, America is still the
locus of God's coming kingdom or Christ's return. But it is
the America of another time and place that is idealized into
a fit vehicle for God's redemption of the world. The Christian
America of yore will be regained under the leadership of these
churches; their sanctified churches will sanctify society back
to the future.

Lutheran views are very different. The soul is never fully
transformed. We remain sinful even as we are justified before
God. Our righteousness is an "alien" one that we can never
fully possess. Further, society is definitely not the instrument
of God's saving acts. Politics, economics, and culture cannot
be vehicles of God's justifying grace. There can be no pro-
jection of what happens in the life of an individual's soul onto
the life of society. We cannot be gods in history.

Certainly not all mainline Protestant public theology has
suffered from such self-destructive patterns. Figures such as
Paul Ramsey and James Gustafson have had an effective public
voice. Historians of religion such as Martin Marty have played
an important role in interpreting American religion to the
public world. Robert Bellah, at times close to the kind of
estrangement described above, nevertheless engaged sym-
pathetically enough with the American tradition to be heard
by large sectors of the American public. Many other lesser-
known figures have focused on issues in medical and business
ethics. Others have examined just war theory and delved into
social philosophy. But in the larger debate on American politics and economics, few mainstream authors are heard beyond churchly or religious academic circles.

In the last several years, however, writers such as Max
Stackhouse have attempted to draw mainstream Protestant
public theology back into the center of American reflection
on political and economic affairs. In his *Public Theology and
Political Economy* and especially in his (with Dennis McCann)
"A Postcommunist Manifesto," Stackhouse tries to call Protestant public theology to a mutually critical and constructive

conversation with American democratic capitalism.[20] Instead of the rejectionist stance so typical of Protestant mainstream public theology, Stackhouse and McCann call for a respectful dialogue with American businesspersons, especially the leaders of American corporations.

THE RISE OF CATHOLIC AND NEOCONSERVATIVE PUBLIC THEOLOGY

Before embarking on our examination of new players in the game of public theology, it will be helpful to reflect a moment on a rather curious phenomenon, the impact of Stanley Hauerwas on American public theology. Hauerwas, a son of the Methodist mainstream educated at Yale Divinity School, has played a significant role in summoning his brothers and sisters in the Protestant mainstream to take more seriously their own sources of religious identity and behavior. During his teaching stay at Notre Dame, Hauerwas was deeply influenced by John Howard Yoder, a Mennonite whose *The Politics of Jesus* argued the classic sectarian notion that the teachings of Jesus were to be applied directly to Christian life in politics and economics. Such a position leads to a thoroughgoing pacifism, albeit not a withdrawing type. Hauerwas took up much of the substance of Yoder's vision, so much so that he has called himself a "high-church Mennonite."

More than the Mennonite substance of Hauerwas's work, however, his formal emphases have had an amazing impact on the Protestant mainstream. His emphases on the church as a community of character, on a virtue ethic, and particularly on the story of Jesus as the key source of Christian formation have served to recall Protestants to the Bible and the church as the guiding beacons for Christian existence in the world. He has rejected secular politics and psychology as important

20. Max L. Stackhouse, *Public Theology and Political Economy* (Grand Rapids: Eerdmans, 1987) and with Dennis P. McCann, "A Postcommunist Manifesto," in *The Christian Century,* 16 January 1991, pp. 1, 44-47.

sources for Christian reflection. He has been particularly contemptuous of American liberalism and denies that it has any
helpful contributions to make to Christian theology and
ethics. This "odd" perspective, coming from a Methodist
Texan, has caused many to sit up and take notice. His work
has been a healthy prod to critical self-examination among
all Christian groups, compromised as so many are by their
comfortable accommodation to modern secular nostrums.
This "Christ against culture" perspective, to use the termi-
nology of H. Richard Niebuhr, has served as an important
reminder to many Christians to think seriously about whose
drumbeat they are really marching to. So, while on one level
Hauerwas seems to eschew the task of public theology, on
another he has helped the Protestant mainstream regain an
authentically Christian—rather than a political or psychological—voice by which to address the public world.[21]

Catholic Public Theology

With the election of John F. Kennedy in 1960, the Roman
Catholic (hereafter designated simply "Catholic") community gained public legitimacy. At roughly the same time the
work of the Jesuit theologian John Courtney Murray proposed strong arguments for religious liberty and a legitimate
role for a Catholic voice in the pluralist American political
scene. Up until that time Catholics entered the public sphere
mainly to fend off policies inimical to their communal cause
and to further their own communal self-interest. With public
legitimacy Catholics have been able to turn their attention in
more positive directions. In the last three decades they have
found a public voice commensurate with their large numbers.
Indeed, they have increasingly taken over the leading role in
making the Christian vision relevant to the public world of

21. Many books and articles express his themes, but Hauerwas early
on articulated them clearly in *A Community of Character* (Notre Dame,
Ind.: University of Notre Dame Press, 1981), and in *The Peaceable Kingdom*
(Notre Dame, Ind.: University of Notre Dame Press, 1983).

politics, economics, and culture. As the Protestant mainline has weakened, the Catholic public voice has taken its place. It has become the closest thing we have to a public church in this age of religious realignments.

Individual Catholic intellectuals, both clergy and lay, have exerted an important influence in the public discourse of our day. In academic circles, David Tracy's massive and erudite writings have made credible a role for theological claims in learned discourse. Lay Catholics, cohering around *The New Oxford Review*, have argued that their religious convictions, far from disbarring them from fruitful discussion of the political, social, and aesthetic issues of our day, have in fact contributed to new and fresh insights to the discussion. Robert Coles, Christopher Lasch, and the late Walker Percy, among others, are certainly no intellectual slouches. Their expertise in their "secular" fields have provided them with an audience that takes seriously their religious insights as well. Indeed, their religious insights are thoroughly integrated into their "secular" expertise.

The National Conference of Catholic Bishops provides the official church with a powerful public voice. Two pastoral letters in particular have entered the national discussion of two key issues, the quest for peace and the direction of the American economy. *The Challenge of Peace: God's Promise and Our Response* (1983) and *Economic Justice for All: Catholic Social Teaching and the United States Economy* (1986) have demanded the attention of a wide range of secular commentators. During the several drafts that each letter went through and upon the presentation of the final draft by the bishops, almost every newspaper op-ed page and editorial column carried comments on their arguments. The bishops genuinely entered into the national debate.

In part 3 I will give closer attention to the reasons why the Catholic pastoral letters have been so much more publicly relevant than the Protestant social statements. (One wag has suggested that the Catholic bishops are like the tolling of a huge bell—boom, boom, boom—and the Protestants are like the tinkling of a tiny handbell—tinkle, tinkle, tinkle.) Suffice it to say here that the bishops carry more weight because they argue from genuinely Catholic religious and moral premises, they speak with more authority than their Protestant compatriots, they argue more carefully and thoroughly, they remain more open to a diversity of perspectives in their formulation process, they handle guiding principles by making very useful distinctions between different levels of authority with regard to those principles and judgments, and, above all, they do not engage in wholesale denunciations of American political and economic practice. In other words, they are not so badly infected by the myth of American guilt as are their Protestant counterparts.

Pope John Paul II has also furnished the Catholic tradition with a powerful voice. Again, his letters inevitably call forth responses from important actors on the American scene. Two recent ones, *Sollicitudo Rei Socialis* (1988) and *Centesimus Annus* (1991) have effectively joined the recent debates on political economy. The most recent letter, *Veritatis Splendor* (1993), on the objectivity of moral truth, has also drawn serious consideration in secular circles as well as religious.

Far more than their Protestant contemporaries, Catholic leaders have spoken more authentically from their religious and moral traditions. While generally tipping toward the left in political and economic matters, and to the right on social issues, they appear to operate with more fidelity to their own defining principles, not the secular ideologies of the day. Nor do they intentionally attack their own defining principles, as is the case in so many Protestant attempts at public theology. Operating from their own core religious vision gives them a more unpredictable record on a host of issues, at least as viewed from a secular perspective. Viewed from their tradition, however, little is unpredictable about their positions.

Neoconservative Public Theology

Second only to Catholic preeminence in public theology has been the band of theologians of many denominations bound together under the general rubric of the neoconservative movement. The vast majority of these neoconservatives were liberals, if not radicals, up to the cataclysm of the sixties. Some, like Richard Neuhaus and Michael Novak, did in fact identify with the more radical elements of the various protest movements of the sixties. But all of them turned away in disgust and anger amid what we earlier called "the great reversal." As the various protest movements turned more dramatically toward the myth of American guilt, a significant number of liberals and radicals departed. Sometimes their departures were gradual, sometimes swift, but in the end all were decisive. The neoconservatives assessed the American tradition—its economy, political arrangements, and culture—more positively than their left-liberal counterparts. The religious conservatives among them also affirmed the role of religion in this more hopeful American project.

As neoconservative theologians departed from the liberal consensus, they were shocked to find how sharply negative the response of their former friends and colleagues toward them could be. They and their organizations were anathematized by the Protestant mainstream. The vigorous denunciations and aggressive investigations of the Institute for Religion and Democracy by the Protestant mainstream illustrate this point.[22] Such negative reactions led the neoconservatives to believe that liberal Christianity had indeed been too closely conflated with left-wing political, economic, and cultural causes. Upon their disaffiliation from that fusion, the neoconservatives believed that in hindsight they could see the

22. Reichley tells the story of the IRD in his *Religion in American Life,* pp. 334ff. I add an anecdote with regard to mainstream reactions to the rise of neoconservative institutions such as the IRD. I became sympathetic with the aims of IRD after years of chafing under the denunciations of American democratic capitalism by American mainstream Protestantism. After joining its board of advisors and appearing on its masthead, a high official of the Lutheran Church in America told me that I must cut all relations to the IRD if I ever wanted to be included in the LCA's official public theology. He warned that such associations would tarnish my reputation indefinitely.

substitution of radical ideology for classic Christian theology only too clearly in the groups from which they were departing. This led them to emphasize the transcendence of Christian truth over all penultimate concerns, even as they turned toward more conservative organizations and causes.

Their "conversions" coincided with the ascendance of conservative political fortunes, especially that of Ronald Reagan, and a number of neoconservatives found ready access to political figures and positions in that era. A number held office in the Reagan administration. But their influence was not confined to political circles. Prolific writers and discussants, they wrote books, launched journals, wrote editorial columns, and appeared on talk shows all over the land. They reappropriated theological giants such as Reinhold Niebuhr, Jacques Maritain, and John Courtney Murray as their theological beacons. Indeed, excepting the Catholic bishops, the neoconservatives were the most effective public theologians in the years from 1975 to 1990. Their religious convictions were related creatively to the public discussions of the day, and they were listened to and read by a large public. Religious ideas were taken seriously again in the public square, thanks in large part to this group.

By and large the contributions of the neoconservatives were ignored or dismissed by the Protestant mainstream and partly so also by the Catholic bishops. They were charged with being merely religious legitimations of conservative politics, a charge the neoconservatives themselves vehemently denied. Indeed, one can read through many tomes of mainstream Protestant public theology without coming across any of the names of the neoconservative theologians, though the neoconservatives have certainly been more influential in public discourse than their detractors.

Who are these neoconservative public theologians? Certainly one could not account for the neoconservative movement without giving due attention to those Jewish intellectuals, who, though not being theologians per se, were knowledgeable about and committed to their religious heritage. Irving Kristol, Norman Podhoretz, Midge Decter, Nathan Glazer, Seymour Martin Lipset, and Gertrude Himmelfarb are names that come immediately to mind. The magazine *Commentary* is a primary instrument for getting their message out.

These Jewish intellectuals have supported and cooperated with their Christian brothers and sisters in the movement. Among very active Catholics are the lay theologians Michael Novak and George Weigel as well as the legal philosopher Mary Ann Glendon. Weigel's Ethics and Public Policy Center is a Washington hub for publications and conferences. Novak, holding an endowed professorship in the American Enterprise Institute, is an indefatigable writer and lecturer who has carried his arguments effectively and often into the public sphere. Mary Ann Glendon, a Harvard Law School professor, writes in a wide variety of scholarly journals, often taking on radical feminists on the subject of family policy.

The Institute for Religion and Democracy (IRD), led until recently by Kent Hill, an energetic and gifted evangelical scholar, has been a feisty and controversial vehicle of neoconservative public theology from its inception in 1981. The IRD has spun off a number of publications and action groups that have focused on bringing the institute's views into mainstream denominational debates.

Peter Berger, the eminent sociologist, and Richard John Neuhaus have added Lutheran voices to the movement, although Neuhaus recently left Lutheranism for Roman Catholicism. Together the two have written a number of influential books, none more effective as a public theological document than *To Empower People: The Role of Mediating Structures in Public Policy*.[23] They have cooperated in founding high-quality journals, first *This World*, and then later, *First*

23. Peter Berger and Richard John Neuhaus, *To Empower People: The Role of Mediating Structures in Public Policy* (Washington, D.C.: American Enterprise Institute for Public Policy Research, 1977).

Things: A Monthly Journal of Religion and Public Life. Neuhaus has been editor of both. (*This World* no longer has any connection with Berger and Neuhaus.) Neuhaus, of all the neoconservative public theologians, has been the most prolific and energetic on a number of fronts. He has written copiously, has appeared as an editorialist in national newspapers and journals, has lectured widely, and has held many significant conferences under the auspices of his Institute on Religion and Public Life in New York. Most of the symposia sponsored by that institute have resulted in a series of books edited by Neuhaus. *First Things* and the Institute on Religion and Public Life have provided an important sounding board for many voices in the overall movement. Indeed, it is hard to imagine any Christian theologian in America who has had more exposure in ongoing public debate than Neuhaus. In a later chapter I shall argue that he is one of the most persuasive representatives of the paradoxical vision in our national discourse.

A number of evangelical figures have recently begun to shine as public theologians. Two historians of American religion, Mark Noll and George Marsden, have been very important in interpreting evangelicalism to a broader American public. James Davison Hunter has projected an evangelical voice in the world of sociology. Charles Colson has entered the popular discussion of many issues with his robust evangelical perspective. James Skillen, with his Center for Public Justice in Washington, has provided an alternative to the mainstream advocacy groups there. Many more such voices will likely arise in the future as the evangelical communities produce more leaders in American life, especially in American religious life.

THE FUTURE

The future of public theology in America will certainly not unfold without mainstream Protestant voices. A number have not fallen fully into the mythology of American guilt and will have much to say in the future. Mainstream Protestantism itself may experience a renewal in which the classic sources of Christian identity will come to the fore in place of liberationist themes. The political climate may change and become more hospitable to left-liberal public theologies. Even now, public theologians such as Martin Marty possess enormous authority in the broader world. Robert Bellah's sociology and social philosophy express his deeply held Christian convictions and are widely read in American society. James Gustafson, who never did imbibe the adversarial spirit, is widely read among natural scientists and medical ethicists.

Catholic public theology will continue to bear significant fruit if the bishops carry on their carefully crafted statements and Catholic theologians maintain their grounding in the Catholic tradition. However, there will likely be increasing tension between Catholic conservatives and liberals, a problem I address in more detail below.

Will the change in political climate spell the end of neoconservative public theology? Was that movement a function of the insurgency of political conservatism that was itself a response to the alienation of political liberalism from mainstream America? Will it wane with Reaganism? That seems unlikely for several reasons. One is that conservatism as a political phenomenon will not disappear and in fact may become better defined. There will continue to be a ready political ear for neoconservative public theology. Moreover, what these public theologians have been saying is not only relevant to conservative ears; many of their arguments are persuasive to a much larger segment of the political spectrum. In a fragmenting society the confident and substantive voice of conservative public theology may perhaps have even more currency. People are simply not content with chaotic pluralism or purely procedural liberalism.

But neoconservative public theology will not go away for another reason, though the movement may no longer be a movement nor have the tag "neoconservative." Neoconservative public theology claims to be grounded in the classical tradition of Christian faith. It makes important distinctions between its fundamental religious commitments and the specific mission of the church on the one hand and its political judgments on the other.[24] Insofar as it is true to its commitments, it will have credibility among Christians and the American public alike. Its operation out of unabashedly Christian commitments will wear well, as will its reluctance to equate its political conservatism with those fundamental commitments. Its attractiveness will increase if mainstream Protestants continue their rush into finding salvation in feminism, multiculturalism and ecotheology.

What will happen, it seems to me, is suggested by James Davison Hunter's analysis in *Culture Wars: The Struggle to Define America*. Hunter argues that the great divide in America's culture wars is between the "orthodox" and the "progressives."[25] This war, which Hunter believes is essentially religious in nature, pits those who are committed to "an external, definable and transcendent authority" (the orthodox) against those who share "the tendency to resymbolize historic faiths according to the prevailing assumptions of contemporary life."[26] I argued above that the Protestant mainline denominations have tipped strongly toward the progressive side, accommodating strongly to current secular ideologies of liberation—Marxist, feminist, gay, and ecological. These

24. See, for example, the founding document of the Institute on Religion and Democracy written by Richard Neuhaus: "The first political task of the Church is to be the Church . . . a sustaining community of faith and under the discipline of Christ." Its primary responsibility is to "proclaim and demonstrate the Gospel," though it should not "withdraw from participation in other communities" (*Christianity and Democracy* [Washington, D.C.: Institute on Religion and Democracy, 1981], pp. 1-4). The document goes on to forge a close link between the working out of the Christian mission in history and the democratic project, though it stops short of making a fusion of the two. This link was then used to criticize sharply the mainstream Christian bodies that were unduly friendly toward Marxist-Leninist countries and movements.

25. James Davison Hunter, *Culture Wars: The Struggle to Define America* (New York: Basic Books, 1991), p. 48.

26. Ibid., pp. 44-45.

ideologies, which have made strong inroads into the nerve centers of Protestant mainstream theologies, are not only adversarial to the general American Protestant heritage, but are corrosive, at least in their more militant form, of the classical biblical and Christian tradition as well.

Those who move in this progressive direction will find their allegiances among the like-minded across denominational lines. Strong progressives can be found in all the major Protestant denominations as well as in Catholicism. As a general judgment, it could be argued that the progressives are dominant in the official leadership centers of mainstream Protestant churches and their ecumenical agencies. On the Catholic scene the situation is reversed. The hierarchy is increasingly orthodox, being shaped by Pope John Paul II in that direction. But many Catholic intellectuals and laity tend toward the progressive side.

In contrast, a great affinity is being increasingly realized among the orthodox of all religious traditions. Catholics, Lutherans, evangelicals, and Protestants of the mainstream tradition who hold orthodox convictions often feel closer to each other than they do to progressives in their own denomination. The same holds true with regard to the vast majority of African-American Christians—the grass roots hold firmly to their orthodox heritage while their well-known theologians (well known among the elite of the Protestant mainstream, at least) bend in the progressive direction. These black Christians find that they are compatible with their orthodox compatriots of other Protestant traditions.

Fundamentalists, who vehemently claim the orthodox label, are attracted to this orthodox axis, even as the orthodox are immensurably more hospitable to the fundamentalists than either the progressives or the surrounding secular culture, both of which camps derisively single them out as the most benighted and dangerous of American subcultures. Fundamentalists seem to be the only American subculture unprotected by political correctness. As a segment of fundamentalism moderates its claims, it will join the orthodox camp.

Certainly this coalition of the orthodox will not be in a majority either in the society (far from it!) or even in the major American denominations. Nor will the various orthodox factions pull away from their own indigenous religious communities into some sort of realigned superchurch. Rather, they will gather around independent journals such as *The New Oxford Review*, *First Things*, and *Pro Ecclesia*, as they are already beginning to do. Their theological commitments will be unabashedly orthodox, but their public theologies may well be very different from each other. They, as well as other organized groups within the churches, will galvanize a large minority of laity for the cause of orthodox Christianity.

It will be likely that these orthodox groups will proceed in a manner that is, in Martin Marty's words, both "committed and civil." But their agitation within their larger denominations will certainly not bring serenity to any of them. Because of their felt tension with the more progressive environment of their denominations and the surrounding society, their identities will be sharpened. Their public theologies will be distinct, interesting, and self-consciously connected to classic Christian sources.

The larger progressive majorities will be enriched by this active minority and may be restrained from accommodating unduly to the secular ideologies of the day. Perhaps a synergism of the two camps may emerge in which the churches experience a renewal of their lives. At the very least it will be an interesting time.

As the broader public society increasingly fragments and particular identities are celebrated over any larger encompassing identity, the orthodox perspective will gather more attention in both church and society. It will have a clear and firm base from which to argue, and its public theologies may become far more persuasive than they are now. Fragmentation will mean a new openness to confident and wholesome particularities. The Christian vision may again become a persuasive voice in the public sphere. Theology may again become public.

PART II
▼ ▼ ▼ ▼
THE
PARADOXICAL
VISION

"America has enjoyed a surfeit of Reformed tendencies and a very occasional nudge in the Lutheran direction. A better balance is possible."

Mark Noll, "The Lutheran Difference," *First Things*, February 1992, p. 38

3

A
CONTEMPORARY
INTERPRETATION

IN SEARCH OF THE VISION

In his review of Martin Marty's book, *The Noise of Conflict,* Mark Noll criticizes Lutheran Marty for not taking seriously enough his own tradition's perspective on American life and history. Among other things, Noll lifts up Lutheranism's posture toward public life as a neglected item in Marty's investigation. He suggests that this "Lutheran attitude" is an important alternative to the generally Calvinist outlook of American religion.[1]

Noll again probes this issue in another article, "The Lutheran Difference." There he suggests that American Christianity sorely needs a Lutheran approach to public life. He writes approvingly of the two-kingdoms doctrine, rightly applied. He laments that such an approach has not been articulated forcefully in American religious and public life.[2]

I certainly agree with Noll's first contention—that American public theology needs more nudges in the Lutheran direction. In this chapter I articulate what I think the paradoxical

1. Mark A. Noll, "The Public Church in the Years of Conflict," *The Christian Century,* 15 May 1991, pp. 556-59.
2. Mark A. Noll, "The Lutheran Difference," *First Things,* February 1992, p. 38.

vision (the Lutheran attitude) is and how it differs from the dominant Reformed tendencies of American religious tradition. However, I disagree with Noll's second contention—that the "Lutheran attitude" has not been articulated forcefully in American religious and public life. It has been articulated in a body of Lutheran public theology produced by the Lutheran churches of America, particularly the Lutheran Church in America. More decisively, the "Lutheran attitude" has been articulated with great impact by important thinkers who have had little or no connection with official Lutheranism. Both official and unofficial examples of Lutheran public theology will be dealt with in some detail in chapters 4 and 5.

Noll can certainly be pardoned for not recognizing these individual, "unofficial" articulations of the Lutheran posture. Two out of the three public theologians I will construe as "Lutheran"—Reinhold Niebuhr and Glenn Tinder—did not or have not identified themselves as such. The third—Richard Neuhaus—has identified himself as such but has left the Lutheran church for the Roman Catholic. Noll, however, is correct in his judgment about the small impact of official Lutheran public theology, especially considering the size of the Lutheran churches in America. Lutherans are one of the largest Protestant groups in America, making up more than seven million adherents.

Lutheranism's lack of public voice is not for want of trying. The last forty years have been characterized by the production of an excellent body of Lutheran social thought, which I shall examine in chapter 4. Its quality deserves more attention than it has been given. If it were taken more seriously in American religious and public life, the additional nudge that Noll calls for would have already occurred.

But certain factors account for at least some of the inattention shown Lutheran social thought. Like Catholics, Lutherans have been a church of fairly recent immigrants. For much of their early history, they devoted a great amount of time and energy to evangelizing and nurturing their own.

Also, given the far-flung and diverse nature of Lutheran immigration, a high priority was given to reaching consensus on basic theological matters. Public stances on the controversial issues of the day would have added too many divisive elements to churches already struggling to find accord on basic items of faith and practice. As they found common ground and merged into larger churches, Lutherans did begin to be concerned about issues of broader public concern.

Still, the Lutheran churches did not and do not speak on social issues as often as their mainstream brothers and sisters. There is an authentic Lutheran note in this reticence to "go public," as I later argue in more detail. Lutheran theology has been reluctant to assert the church's competence on "worldly matters." The state, not the church, under the law of God has the primary responsibility to make just policy. Likewise, the laity in their several callings, not the theologians, are better placed to make discerning judgments about these matters. The theologians of the church, conversely, are primarily called to articulate the meaning of the faith to each new generation. Lutheran theologians have typically been church theologians, above all else.

This reticence has brought forth charges of political quietism. Indeed, a number of American scholars have attempted to connect this traditional Lutheran reticence with the rise of Nazism in Germany.[3] Faced with this allegedly tarnished heritage in political ethics, Lutherans have made a strong effort to defend Luther and Lutheranism from such attacks.

Closely related to the preceding point, the negative verdict pronounced by Ernst Troeltsch on Lutheranism's social teaching did not enhance the reputation of Lutheran public theology. Troeltsch argued that Lutheranism docilely adapted to any political system. Its tendency to bow abjectly to any political establishment gave it little chance to contribute constructively to social change.[4] Reinhold Niebuhr, as well as

---

3. William McGovern, *From Luther to Hitler* (Boston, 1941), and Peter Wiener, *Martin Luther, Hitler's Spiritual Ancestor* (London, 1945).

4. Ernst Troeltsch, *The Social Teachings of the Christian Churches* (London, 1941), pp. 501ff.

other more recent theologians such as Jürgen Moltmann, have continued this general verdict. While any fair examination of American Lutheran social thought would sharply qualify these charges, they do account for some of the lack of attention given to Lutheran public theology.

In response to the situation described above, the argument of this book is twofold. First, I contend that the Lutheran paradoxical vision provides a valuable, if not indispensable framework for any adequate Christian public theology. This framework protects the radicality and universality of the gospel itself as well as the integrity of the church. The paradoxical vision itself does not provide a substantive public theology, i.e., one that leads to specific policy positions. But, in addition to protecting the gospel, the paradoxical vision provides a framework that ought to condition Christian public theology's assessment of human nature, of God's governance of the world, and of the historical process itself.

Within this framework provided by the paradoxical vision, Christian public theology can move in liberal or conservative directions. The framework itself does not move necessarily toward specific public-political ideologies, though it sets a general direction for such ideologies. Later, when I give examples of influential recent practitioners of the "Lutheran attitude," I use public theologians who have moved in rather different political directions: Reinhold Niebuhr (activist reformer), Glenn Tinder (hesitant liberal), and Richard Neuhaus (neoconservative).

The second part of my argument concerns the presence of the "Lutheran attitude" in American public theology. In chapter 4 I argue that official Lutheran public theology has deserved more public attention than it has received. In chapter 5 I contend that the "Lutheran attitude" has been publicly effective in the work of the three thinkers mentioned above who have operated outside the boundaries of official Lutheranism.

THE PARADOXICAL VISION[5]

The concept of "paradox" has long been used to describe the Lutheran construal of the Christian faith. Perhaps the best known of these assignations in recent times is H. Richard Niebuhr's characterization of the Pauline-Lutheran vision as "Christ and Culture in Paradox."[6] Dictionary definitions of

5. In the following I will draw upon many classic and modern sources of the Lutheran vision. Much comes from Luther himself, who powerfully articulated the radical biblical message of God's grace. Other sources include the writings of modern interpreters of Luther and the Lutheran tradition. The literature on Luther and the Lutheran tradition is massive. From this vast scholarly heritage, I have relied on a number of relatively recent works. Among them are Gustaf Wingren, *Luther on Vocation* (Philadelphia: Muhlenberg, 1957), which I consider to be the best single book on Luther's doctrine of the calling of all Christians; Gustaf Wingren, *Creation and Law* (London: Oliver and Boyd, 1961); Einar Billing, *Our Calling* (Rock Island, Ill.: Augustana Book Concern, 1951); Gustaf Aulen, *Church, Law and Society* (New York: Scribners, 1948); Anders Nygren, "Luther's Doctrine of the Two Kingdoms," in *Ecumenical Review,* vol. 1, no. 2 (Summer 1949); George Forell, *Faith Active in Love* (Minneapolis: Augsburg, 1954), perhaps the best introduction to Luther's ethics; William Lazareth, *Luther on the Christian Home: An Application of the Social Ethics of the Reformation* (Philadelphia: Muhlenberg, 1960); *God and Caesar: A Christian Approach to Social Ethics,* ed. Warren Quanbeck (Minneapolis: Augsburg, 1959); and *Luther and Culture* in *Martin Luther Lectures,* vol. 4 (Decorah, Iowa: Luther College Press, 1960). More recent sources include Ulrich Duchrow, *Two Kingdoms: The Use and Misuse of a Lutheran Theological Concept* (Geneva: Lutheran World Federation, 1977); Eric Gritsch and Robert Jenson, *Lutheranism* (Philadelphia: Fortress, 1976); and Carl Braaten, "God in Public Life: Rehabilitating the Orders of Creation," in *First Things* 8, December 1990. I will draw on general concepts from this Lutheran corpus without citing the sources. When I quote directly, I will cite the specific source.

6. H. Richard Niebuhr, *Christ and Culture* (New York: Harper and Brothers, 1956), pp. 149ff. This is an accurate and sympathetic portrayal of the paradoxical vision. Strangely enough, Niebuhr does not include Augustine in this category even though most historians of Christian thought see Augustine in strong continuity with Paul on the one side and Luther on the other. Niebuhr rather puts Augustine in the "conversionist" type of Christ-culture relations, along with the gospel of John and Calvin. It seems to me a bit of a strain to do that. Augustine is perhaps more

paradox emphasize its meaning as "mystery, enigma, contradiction, or a seemingly absurd statement," but go on to clarify its more nuanced character.[7] A paradox refers to two statements that apparently contradict each other but are ultimately true. That is the essence of paradox.

The central paradox of the Christian faith is that God's salvation of the rebellious world is wrought through the life, death, and resurrection of an obscure Jewish figure, Jesus of Nazareth. That central affirmation of Christian faith is built upon other paradoxes: the election of the Jews, a little-known people of the Near East, to be the vessel for bringing forth a Savior; the enfleshment in a Jewish boy of the all-powerful Creator God himself; and the ministry of this Jewish "Messiah" aimed at neither the powerful of the world nor at establishing any sort of visible earthly kingdom. What odd ways for the love of God to overcome the sin of humankind!

These background paradoxes, however, blanch before the one already mentioned: that in the unique and specific event of Jesus as the Christ—his ministry, death, and resurrection—the lost world in its entirety and for all time has been retrieved by a loving God. Such an assertion indeed is "foolishness to the Greeks and scandalous to the Jews." And, except that its paradoxical edge has been taken off by thousands of years of common usage, such an assertion is as incredible now as it was then, for it asserts that apparent ignominious defeat is in fact glorious victory and that a very specific event in time and space has universal and eternal significance. Throughout the ages countless attempts have been made to analyze and extract meaning from this stunning affirmation, which would have been quickly dropped had it not been for its surprising confirmation in the resurrection. Though it has been described in many different ways, I will convey its essential meaning in the following way.

---

pessimistic than Luther about the possibilities for constructive change in human history. The two cities comingle, but there is little hope for the City of God to transform the Earthly City.

7. *The New Universal Dictionary* (Cheshire, 1958), p. 531.

God chose to reconcile the world to himself through Christ by bearing on the cross the consequences of our sin. God in Christ became vulnerable to all the death-dealing efforts of the forces of darkness. Such an act means that God suffered out of love for us. Indeed, the cross led to the death of the Crucified One. But that seeming defeat turned to victory with the resurrection of Jesus on the third day. The forces of sin, death, and the devil—our ancient foes—gave it their best shot but were defeated. Christ's sacrifice and victory are objective facts. They have been done for us, and they are an anticipation of the final victory that will be realized at the end of time. We live now between that anticipatory revelation of God's victory and its fulfillment in the eschaton.

For us who receive the benefits of this divine action, several things become clear. First, as we in faith cling to Christ, we too shall be brought through the terrors of sin and death to reconciliation with God, both here and in eternity. We participate through the Spirit in his victory. We are enabled to join in that great caravan of Christ's people that proceeds to the right hand of God himself, there to enjoy the blessed community of God and all the saints.

Moreover, when we are "in Christ" through faith, we also participate in what Luther called the "happy exchange." Christ takes our sin and gives us his righteousness. God's extravagant love makes us righteous before him, not by our works but by our faith in Christ. We are justified by God's grace through faith on account of Christ. Through faith in God's mercy toward us we may grasp the invitation to participate in the life of God, in his kingdom, both here in this life and in the life to come.

Justification by grace through faith on account of Christ is the glowing core of the Lutheran interpretation of the Christian gospel. Obviously such an interpretation is explicitly present in the New Testament and in the whole of the Christian tradition. It is not a Lutheran idiosyncracy, but it is a Lutheran emphasis, thus holding up the radicality of God's grace.

This emphasis was vigorously and concisely professed by Luther in his *Treatise on Christian Liberty*. There he says that "the soul needs only the Word of God for its life and righteousness, so it is justified by faith alone and not any works; for if it could be justified by anything else, it would not need the Word, and consequently it would not need faith."[8] Einar Billing tells us:

> Whoever knows Luther, knows that his various thoughts do not lie alongside each other, like pearls on a string, held together only by common authority or perchance by a line of logical argument, but that they all, as tightly as the petals of a rosebud, adhere to a common center, and radiate out like the rays of the sun from one glowing core, namely, the gospel of the forgiveness of sins.[9]

Even our acceptance of God's grace in Christ is not an occasion for boasting. The Holy Spirit leads us to repentance and the grateful acceptance of God's grace. Finally, when all is said and done with regard to our salvation, the glory belongs to God—Father, Son, and Holy Spirit.

Regarding our salvation, then, the human posture is one of pure receptivity. We *receive* the grace of God in Christ; we do nothing to earn our salvation. We need only, in Paul Tillich's inimitable words, "accept the fact that [we] are accepted." Further, as we become aware of God's gracious activity on our behalf, we have a growing awareness of our unworthiness. The law of God, which exerts God's demand on us as creatures, brings us to bad conscience and repentance. This sense of the terrified conscience before the Holy God is heightened when we compare the pure love of God for us with our own self-obsession and pride. Before God, then, as Luther said, "We are all beggars." And in a strange way, there

8. Martin Luther, *Treatise on Christian Liberty* (Philadelphia: Fortress, 1985), p. 9.

9. Einar Billing, *Our Calling*, trans. Conrad Bergendoff (Rock Island: Augustana Book Concern, 1951), p. 7.

is solace in this radical affirmation of the pervasiveness of sin in all of us. We all stand equally in need of grace. "It is comforting," Søren Kierkegaard observed, "to know that before God we are always wrong."

Starting from this moment of contrition, our souls are lifted by God's extravagant love. In Christ, God stoops to gather us up for communion with him, in spite of our sin. We are made "free lords of all, subject to none," by God's mercy. The human response to this is one of grateful joy and renewed faith in the promises of God. With regard to our relation to God, we are truly liberated from all that binds our souls. We are freed by his grace for reconciliation with him. Nothing or no one can take this from us.

At the same time that we are free lords of all, subject to none, we are, paradoxically, "dutiful servants of all, subject to all." The love that we have received from God in Christ moves through us toward our neighbor. Our incurved wills are warmed by the Spirit so that they spontaneously move outward toward others. "Love grasps the hand that need holds out."[10] This love, however, does not just float freely into an amorphous world. It flows from individual Christians through their various callings to the world. God gives each of us locations to exercise our Christian discipleship. We are family members, workers, citizens, and members of religious communities. Love of neighbor motivates us to perform and transform our responsibilities in the world into authentic Christian callings. Christian love, both corporate and individual, becomes a leavening influence in a fallen world. It stretches mundane responsibilities toward a more inclusive love and justice. Such efforts are not without cost, however. As we stretch our roles we risk a backlash from the world. If we take love and justice seriously in our callings, Luther says, we will not need to seek the cross; it will find us.[11]

10. Joseph Sittler, *The Structure of Christian Ethics* (Baton Rouge, La.: Louisiana State University Press, 1958).

11. I have explicated these elements of Christian vocation in my book *Ordinary Saints: An Introduction to the Christian Life* (Philadelphia: Fortress, 1988). This book is an attempt to put the Lutheran view of the calling of the Christian into fresh and contemporary language.

We must enter two qualifications of this brief portrait of the Christian life as response to the grace of God. One is that Christian love is rarely expressed directly into the institutional world, though it may more frequently be communicated in personal relations. Christians must take their roles as workers, citizens, and parents seriously. Each of these has built-in expectations that take into account the finitude and falleness of the world. Each role often demands "hard" actions that on the surface do not accord with Christian love. Without ignoring these demands, Christians nevertheless respond to the special summons of love. In this way, worldly reponsibilities are tempered, but not negated or ignored, by love. Christian love does not leave the world unchanged.

A second qualification is this. Christians always remain sinners both before God and in their worldly callings. They are *simul justus et peccator*—at the same time righteous and sinful. Insofar as the Spirit infuses the love of Christ in their hearts, Christians are righteous. Insofar as the old Adam remains active in their lives, they remain sinners. Unfortunately, the old Adam can only be fully conquered in the last times, not in this worldly life. So Christian life on earth will be a struggle in which the Spirit of Christ and the old Adam are in unending conflict. This does not mean there is no forward movement in the Christian life, but it does mean that the victory of the Spirit will never be complete in this life. The paradoxical vision allows no total victories within the confines of human existence.

A Framework for Public Theology

Given the religious vision I have elaborated above, we are now ready to explore the various themes constituting "the Lutheran attitude." These themes provide a framework for doing Christian public theology. Moreover, these themes are crucially present in the biblical and Christian tradition generally, and they are neglected at the peril of authentic Christian teaching and practice. It is also important to note again that these themes do not necessarily press toward any particular set of political policies—that is, they do not themselves constitute a political ideology. But they do provide a framework that ought to condition everything that Christians say or do with regard to the public world. The following four themes or principles comprise our framework for public theology.

1. THE QUALITATIVE DISTINCTION BETWEEN GOD'S SALVATION AND ALL HUMAN EFFORTS

If the foregoing explication of the paradoxical vision is at all clear, it ought to be evident that the saving work of God in Christ is totally the work of God. Before God with regard to their salvation, humans are purely receptive. God's redemption is a gift, pure and simple. However, humans simply will not allow God to save them. Individually they want to earn their salvation or at least cooperate with God in it. Hence there is always the human temptation to add something to the gospel to assure that our efforts are taken seriously by God and our fellow human beings. We want to maintain our pride in the process. But such cannot be the case, Christianly speaking. Before God none can stand, and God's gift of unmerited grace recognizes that fact. We must recognize it too.

If pride is evident in individual desire to subvert the gospel, it is even more rampant in corporate attempts to usurp the saving power of God. Groups are incapable of repentance and the reception of grace. But humans nevertheless have longings for salvation that groups claim to fulfill. Unable to repent and receive the grace of God, however, they substitute their own efforts for those of God and then claim salvific significance for their efforts. All sorts of groups make such claims, from self-help groups to revolutionary movements to powerful nations. When, as Glen Tinder argues, the God-man (Jesus as the Christ) is rejected, the man-god rushes in to take his place. Enlightenment claims to bring the heavenly city to earth through reason and science, Marxist-Leninist promises to bring paradise to earth through revolution, Nazi attempts to establish a thousand-year reich, the Freudian promise of health through psychoanalysis, and the thousands of variations on these themes demonstrate the human propensity to claim salvific significance for their schemes.[12]

Perhaps the most pernicious of human claims to bring forth salvation are those legitimated by overtly religious symbols. Great nations backed by exalted religious traditions often claim to be the salvation, not only of their own people, but also of the world. The avowals made by and for Holy Mother Russia come immediately to mind. The Nazi movement, legitimated by pagan religious themes, is another example. Militant Afrikaners, fueled by a degenerate Calvinism, claimed to be the vehicle of salvation for whites in South Africa.

Nobler, but every bit as damaging to Christian faith, are the salvific claims put forth by some types of liberation theology. The revolutionary praxis of the poor and oppressed (inevitably led and ideologized by intellectuals) is the vehicle of salvation in these scenarios. Faith in political, social, and cultural transformation is sacralized by Christian theology in many of the varieties of liberation thought, including some feminist and gay versions of it.

One would think that the world has had enough experience of revolutionary change to obviate any claims that political and social "transformation" lead to anything remotely resembling human fulfillment. Such a judgment comes from ordinary human observation and experience. But for religious people to make such claims is even more baffling.

Such sacralizing claims are ruled out by the paradoxical vision. We obviously are not capable of our own salvation. The paradoxical vision, however, aims at cutting off such claims for even more profound reasons than their lack of empirical validity. It does so for the sake of the gospel, for its radicality and universality. The radicality of the gospel insists that salvation is pure gift; we do not earn it. If we do

12. Glenn Tinder, "Can We Be Good without God?" *The Atlantic Monthly*, December 1989, pp. 78ff.

not recognize that, we dishonor God who gave his Son in this unique and decisive saving act. When we claim a part in the drama of salvation, we at the same time insist that God's action in Christ is not good enough. Something else, presumably our virtuous action, must be added.

Furthermore, the universality of the gospel is compromised if we fail to make a sharp distinction between God's saving act in Christ and all human efforts at improving the world. In any overt or covert claim for human effort as a constituitive part in our own salvation there are always those who are on the right side of the struggle and those who are on the wrong side. Some are saved and some are damned, not because of their faith or lack of faith in God's work in Christ, but because they either are or are not participants in the group or process that claims to be bringing redemption.

In this loss of universality, the proletariat and their sympathizers are saved, the bourgeoisie are not. The Germans are saved; the non-Germans are not. The enlightened and educated are saved; the lesser ranks are left out. Those under psychoanalysis are blessed; others are objects of pity. Those with the right opinions are in; the wrong-headed are out. Democrats are in; Republicans are out.

The picture is clear; the claims of the man-god always exclude. The gospel simply does not exclude. All humans, regardless of what group they belong to, are equidistant and equally near the grace of God in Christ.

The New Testament gospel of the suffering God who abjured all worldly power and all worldly group identifications simply rules out those schemes that compromise the radicality and universality of the gospel. The cross of Christ freed the gospel from enmeshment in all human efforts to save the world. No one was with Christ on the cross to die for our sins. Or viewed differently, *everyone* was with Christ on the cross, but only as passive inhabitants of his righteous and suffering person.

No boasting is permitted. Therefore, the paradoxical vision rules out salvific politics. All human efforts are relativized before the gospel. They belong in the penultimate sphere. But precisely here is a real danger. Lutheranism, because of its profound grasp of the misery of the human predicament and glory of God's grace in Christ, has been tempted to show contempt for, or at least little interest in, the important relative distinctions between the better or worse among efforts at human improvement. In comparison with the grandeur of the highest peaks of a mountain range, the surrounding foot-hills all look the same pitiable height. Lutheranism has been tempted to combine a deep religious mysticism with political cynicism. But that is a perversion of the Lutheran view. Rather, when we are free from the need to look for salvation in human schemes, our eyes should be clearer to make the very important distinctions among the relatively good and the relatively bad in the realm of human action. Liberated from worry about our salvation, we can turn unobsessively to the human task of building a better world, not by prideful claims of transformation, but by determined yet humble attempts to take small steps for the better.

Certainly this relativization of human efforts does not make them unimportant for Christians. The Christian response to God's grace is faith toward God and love toward one's neighbor. Faith and love go together. In this sense, faith without works is indeed dead. So obedience follows faith; it is not the route to salvation, but rather its result.

Thus the essential mission of the church is made clear: its reason for being is to proclaim the gospel, for no other agency will do that. It must attend to its core vision, not only proclaiming it, but attempting to be faithful to it in all its practices and endeavors. The church cannot insure that its gospel vision will prevail in the hearts of human beings; only the Holy Spirit can capture those hearts for the gospel. But the church is called to proclaim. In so doing it must also guard the gospel, protecting it from human distortions.

What is contained in this core vision? At the very center is the event of Jesus as the Christ. Surrounding it is the biblical and early church's witness to the events of Jesus' life, death, and resurrection. This apostolic witness is both a record and interpretation of that revelatory event. It incorporates not only the "glowing core" of God's forgiveness of sins on account of Christ, but also the key teachings without which the gospel makes little or no sense. The Old Testament background, the doctrine of the Trinity, the eschatological tension between the Christ event and the coming kingdom, and the calling of the church and individual Christians to their mission in the world are all essential elements in this core vision. These are well summarized in the ecumenical creeds.

This core vision ought to be held with clarity and confidence by the church. Its main elements do not change with time, though they must be interpreted afresh for each new generation. This core makes up the great tradition that can be traced from the time of the apostles to the present day. Its main tenets are not negotiable if the Christian faith is to remain the Christian faith.

Closely related to this central religious core is the central moral vision of the Christian faith. The Ten Commandments, the calling of all Christians to faith active in love and justice, the preciousness of all created life redeemed by Christ, and the covenantal structure of God's creation (which includes the special covenant of man and woman in marriage) constitute the moral core of the Christian vision. They too are constant through time, though they must be applied creatively to each new historical situation. It is difficult to imagine authentic Christian identity without them, though they are often under attack from the world and sometimes are subverted even by religious communities themselves, as I argued in chapter 2.

The next concentric circle away from these two inner orbs are the more speculative theological reflections of the church, including its social teachings. This band represents the efforts of the church to apply its religious and moral vision to the dynamic world around it. These efforts entail significant steps in moving from the core vision to its application to specific problems. Each step means an increasing chance for disagreement among Christians who hold their core vision in common. Theological reflection on society, the arts, science, and so on, and social teaching on economics, politics, and society are examples of this extension of Christian meaning. Ventures in this direction are important in the life of the church, but unanimity on them is highly unlikely. The church needs to allow a good deal of latitude for disagreement and plurality of opinions. Its clearest litmus test should be that these extensions do not conflict with the core vision itself.

Finally, there is a concentric circle that represents the church's posture on specific public policy issues. Such specific commitments on the part of the church ought generally to be quite infrequent, as I argue later in the book. But in special times with regard to special issues, the church may have to stand for or against them. In normal times, however, it is important for the church not to commit to particular policies since there are many other agencies through which Christians can exert their influence. Further, there will be much difference of opinion among intelligent Christians of goodwill on such specific policies.

It is essential that the church be able to distinguish these different circles and to hold their contents with differing degrees of commitment and passion. The central religious and moral visions ought to be held with clarity, confidence, and steadfastness. They have the highest degree of authority and consensus in the church. The outer circles are much more susceptible to genuine and permissible disagreement. Moreover, as one moves toward the outer circles, the church has less and less warrant and knowledge for pronouncing or acting upon its judgments. (Again, there are exceptions here. If a social practice is glaringly in opposition to the Christian religious and moral core, the church must speak and act. I will deal with these issues in more detail in part 3.)

One of the great problems with portions of the liberal mainstream churches is that they often are confused about the core but dogmatic about the periphery. Denial of the decisiveness and uniqueness of Jesus as the Christ creates little alarm while disagreement over the strategy of divestment in

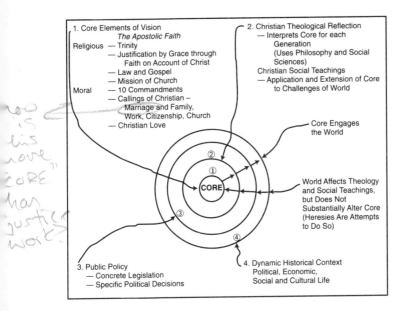

1. Core Elements of Vision
    The Apostolic Faith
Religious — Trinity
    — Justification by Grace through
      Faith on Account of Christ
    — Law and Gospel
    — Mission of Church
Moral   — 10 Commandments
    — Callings of Christian –
      Marriage and Family,
      Work, Citizenship, Church
    — Christian Love

2. Christian Theological Reflection
    — Interprets Core for each
      Generation
      (Uses Philosophy and Social
      Sciences)
Christian Social Teachings
    — Application and Extension of Core
      to Challenges of World

Core Engages
the World

World Affects Theology
and Social Teachings,
but Does Not
Substantially Alter Core
(Heresies Are Attempts
to Do So)

3. Public Policy
    — Concrete Legislation
    — Specific Political Decisions

4. Dynamic Historical Context
Political, Economic,
Social and Cultural Life

South Africa warrants near excommunication. Serious confusion over the church's sexual ethics is combined with utter clarity on policy in Central America. This, it seems to me, is a confusion in priorities and a symptom of decaying religious traditions. It is a desperate substitution of political ideology for the religious and moral core. No longer clear or confident about their central reason for being, such religious groups turn to secular sources for their identity.

If the church does recognize the qualitative distinction between what God has done in Christ and all human actions for improving the world, and also prizes its unique mission to proclaim the gospel, one of its public policy propensities ought to be to support religious freedom everywhere. It must insist that the world leave room for the proclamation of the Word of God. At the same time it must identify and criticize all claims by humans to offer redemption to individuals or society. Above all, it must guard its own core vision so that it does not fall into false promises of salvation through human means. Any adequate public theology must hold to these provisos.

2. THE PARADOX OF HUMAN NATURE

"Whatever your heart fastens to, that is your god," said Luther. And from the perspective of the paradoxical vision, humans are irretrievably committed to finding something other than God to which to fasten their hearts. This analysis of inescapable sin, however, is not simple. We do not fasten to the unalluring and worthless things of the world. On the contrary, we fasten to those things that really tempt. Highest among our temptations is devotion to ourselves. We are obsessed with ourselves and make ourselves the center of the universe. Our attention to ourselves crowds out everything else, except those things we want in order to feed the image of ourselves that we have concocted. This obsession may be one of willful assertion or self-pitying negation, but in either case it makes a mockery of the divine command "to love the Lord your God with all your heart, mind and soul." We love ourselves and the things that lend us some semblance of importance and immortality.

Before God, then, the Lutheran perspective holds that we are without hope. Our self-obsession leads to sins against others, but the primary religious condition to which our self-obsession leads is separation from God. We follow in Adam's footsteps and can find no way of properly relating to God out of our own capacities. It is with regard to this "vertical" relation to God that Luther is so contemptuous of human capacities. Human efforts to rise up in worthiness to God are the height of sin and are in many ways the most dangerous, because some persons in their sin and pride actually think they are righteous. This makes them even more dangerous to their fellow human beings than those who know they are sinners or who are cynical about human capacities in general.

So the most precious thing in human existence—our desire for a fulfilling relationship with God—is the most vulnerable to corruption.

This Augustinian view of human nature extends to human action in society. Luther thought that without the external restaints of positive law, humans would act like beasts. They would particularly do so in groups, which lack conscience and prudence. Human sin is particularly expressed in collective situations.

The indelible character of sin persists even in the faithful Christian, as I noted in the preceding section. The Christian remains *simul justus et peccator*, simultaneously justified and sinner, even after faithful response to God's Word. Transformation of the self is never complete. Indeed, claims of perfection are the most telling sign of ongoing sin and self-deception. The righteous know they are not righteous. This does not mean that there is no growth in the Christian life, but rather that growth always proceeds out of a continuing repentance and openness to the Spirit, which alone can move our self-obsessed souls to care for our neighbors.

There is little sentimental optimism about human nature, if any, in the Lutheran tradition. Yet humans are not dirt. Even in their fallen state they possess qualities of their creation in the image of God. They long for wholeness and completion but cannot heal or complete themselves. Our longings for something beyond ourselves—God and the companionship of others—do not disappear, but rather are misdirected to the gods we cling to. Indeed, our rationality, though fallen, can help us to discern what is right and just behavior with regard to our fellow human beings. We are capable of "civil righteousness." By "we" I mean all human beings, whether Christian or not. Luther believed that non-Christians were as capable as Christians in the areas of life that demanded human rationality and prudence. He famously pronounced that he would rather be ruled any day by a wise Turkish prince than by a silly Christian.

On the "horizontal level"—that is, in relations with our fellow human beings and the world, we can do the right thing. We can act civilly and justly. Before others we can appear quite upright and healthy. (One of the paradoxes of human life is that outwardly we can be the most successful and "happy" of persons, while inwardly we are desperately empty.) Moreover, human virtues on this plane can be learned and practiced. Luther had no qualms about Aristotle's approach to this kind of human training in virtue as long as it did not extend to our "vertical" relation to God. Reason is a whore only when it tries to rise up in wisdom and righteousness to God. Further, this "civil righteousness" is not to be confused with authentic Christian love, which flows from the Spirit-grasped person in response to God's justifying grace.

Humans are also exalted by the fact that all are the recipients of God's objective saving act in Christ. All are given an "alien" dignity on account of Christ. This does not mean that humans necessarily respond to the reconciling activity of God, but it does mean that they never lose their relation to God, who wills to draw them back to himself.

Thus we humans find ourselves in a paradoxical predicament. Created and redeemed by God, we are exalted individuals. We have a capacity for love and justice, yet we use our freedom to fasten to lesser things, creating a hell for ourselves, our fellow human beings, and the world around us. We are a paradox of good and evil, manufacturing idols of the good things we are given. We cannot solve this predicament on our own, nor can any efforts from other human beings release us. Only God can save, and he does.

3. GOD'S PARADOXICAL RULE

Perhaps the most difficult element, yet the most important, in the Lutheran attitude is its doctrine of the twofold rule of God, sometimes called the "two-kingdoms" doctrine. As the most difficult it has also been the most vulnerable to distortion. Karl Barth was the first actually to call this Lutheran teaching "the two-kingdoms doctrine," and he was not paying a compliment to the Lutheran tradition. Rather, he was sharply critizing those Lutherans in the 1930s who had used Lutheranism's doctrine of the twofold rule of God to justify Hitler and National Socialism.

Actually Barth was criticizing the *misuse* of the teaching. Instead of a highly dialectical and paradoxical view of God's twofold rule, the misusers sunk into a dualistic approach. According to this dualistic model, which is a Lutheran heresy, there are two completely separate spheres, one having to do with earthly society and the other having to do with the salvation of our souls. Moreover, this dualism is often given a spatial twist. The secular world and the world of the church are the two separate realities. The secular world in this view is autonomous. It runs according to its own principles and rules, and the Christian must simply submit to them. The church preaches the gospel, which then affects only the internal souls of Christians and perhaps their intimate relationships. As one Lutheran jurist put it, the issues of public life "should remain untouched by the proclamation of the gospel, completely untouched." A well-known nineteenth-century Lutheran theologian, Christian Luthardt, put it this way:

> The gospel has absolutely nothing to do with outward existence but only with eternal life. . . . It is not the vocation of Jesus Christ or of the gospel to change the orders of secular life and establish them anew. . . . Christianity wants to change the person's heart, not his external situation.[13]

Such a dualistic approach was used to argue that Christians as Christians had no grounds for resisting tyrannical governments, be they that of Hitler, Pinochet, or Vorster. This approach leads to the infamous political quietism that Lutherans have sometimes fostered. As with all heresies, this

13. Both of these sources are used in Carl E. Braaten, *Principles of Lutheran Theology* (Philadelphia: Fortress, 1983), p. 124.

dualistic approach has an element of truth in it, but that element is magnified so as to push out the other elements that make it a genuinely useful doctrine.

The doctrine of the twofold rule of God is more than useful, however. It is deeply biblical and Christian; it is not a Lutheran oddity. Paul writes of the two aeons in Romans—the new era that Christ is bringing into the world and the old aeon that is under the rule of law and sin. The same eschatological tension is present in other biblical sources. The new order of Christ is in tension with the old order, yet Christians must live in both. Jesus said we must give Caesar what is his and God what is God's. There is a duality but not a dualism at the heart of the Christian vision. It cannot be flattened into one dimension. We are caught in two realities that must be taken seriously.

Carl Braaten puts the essence of the doctrine succinctly:

> This doctrine of the two kingdoms marks out the identity of the church within the global horizon of the politics of God and the divine governance of this world. This doctrine draws a distinction between the two ways of God's working in the world, two strategies that God uses to deal with the powers of evil and the reality of sin, two approaches to human beings, to mobilize them for active cooperation in two distinctly different kinds of institutions. One is created as an instrument of governance seeking justice through the administration of law and the preservation of order, and the other as an instrument of the Gospel and its sacraments announcing and mediating an ultimate and everlasting salvation which only Christ can give in an act of unconditional love and personal sacrifice.[14]

This biblical and Christian perspective arose when the kingdom expected by the followers of Jesus did not come. The kingdom had come in Jesus—the preacher had become the preached—but the full realization of that which was announced and experienced in the Christ event did not take

14. Ibid., p. 135.

place. Nevertheless, Christians believed that the world they were given to live in and to follow Christ in was not abandoned by God. The Old Testament witness to God's creating, sustaining, and judging activities was not discarded. Indeed, it was affirmed in the face of heresies that tried to split the Creator from the Redeemer God.

Surely the God who in Jesus suffered on a cross and died for all and who rose again approaches humans differently in the gospel than he does those same people in their worldly life in society. There is a twofoldness in God's action in the world, a twofoldness that both generates and reflects a real tension in the individual and corporate lives of Christians. All major Christian religious traditions recognize in some fashion this tension between Christ and the ongoing societal necessities of the world. They are aware that following Christ and living in the world is no easy task. Those who are unaware of that understand neither Christ nor the world.

However, Christian religious traditions handle this tension in very different ways. H. Richard Niebuhr's *Christ and Culture* is a classic analysis of how they handle this tension. The "Christ against culture" (sectarian) tradition escapes the tension by withdrawing from the world. The classic "Christ above culture" (Roman Catholic) tradition aims to manage the tension by forging Christ and culture into a grand synthesis presided over by the church. The "Christ transforming culture" (Reformed) tradition seeks to convert the culture toward the will of God as it is discerned by the church and carried out by its laity. The "Christ of culture" (liberal religion) tradition escapes the tension by absorbing Christ into the enlightened culture of the day.[15]

The "Christ and culture in paradox" (Lutheran) tradition handles the tension in a paradoxical way through its teaching on the twofold rule of God. Thus it is not the tension of Christ and culture that is a contentious issue; it is rather how that tension is handled. Of the five possible ways of managing

---

15. Niebuhr, *Christ and Culture*.

it suggested by Niebuhr, the Lutheran way comes closest to living with an unresolved tension. The other traditions move more vigorously toward resolution, and that can often be problematic and perhaps unbiblical.

In the paradox tradition Christians live in two realities at the same time. Each reality is under the governance of God but in sharply different ways. God governs the "kingdom on the left" with his law and the "kingdom on the right" with his gospel. God's aim in both modes of rule is the same, to overcome evil and recall the disobedient creation to himself, but God uses very different means in each "kingdom." Let us examine God's rule of the world through law first.

God's Rule through Law

The world has been created and sustained by God the Creator. As such it is characterized by a moral guidance system, God's law. God's law is expressed in orders of creation—state, economy, family, and church. Under conditions of innocence, the law would be willingly and naturally followed by the whole creation. With the Fall, however, the law became a coercive power, operating through the orders of creation that God preserves for our benefit. The law coerces through conscience, custom, and positive law backed up by force. The law also operates amid the dynamic interactions of life in a less formal and intentional way. While it has been codified in the Ten Commandments revealed to Moses, it also operates as the "unrecognized" or "anonymous" demand that arises in all encounters that call for responsibility. While the law in this view includes what the Catholic tradition has termed "natural law," the modern Lutheran view of the law is more dynamic and less rationalistic. Awareness of the law arises from the real dynamics of life. The law guides all sorts of relations, from the richness of mutual love to the harshness of a balance of power. It includes all the ways that God maintains the worldly order, from natural forms of love to the use of force in the relations among nations. Law is the instrument God uses to shore up the fragile covenantal structures of creation.

The state—legitimate government—is one of these special covenantal structures, along with the family, the economic sphere, and the church. All are ordained by God from the Creation to give order to human life, to give us a place to be and work to do. All are also accountable to God's will, whether they recognize that or not. This is a particularly important point to make with regard to the state, for it above all has pretensions to divinity and is likely to make its powerful claims into a false gospel. This has happened frequently with the rise of the nation-state; the nation has claimed to be the church. On the contrary, the state has a subordinate, but nevertheless, important, function—to establish a peaceful and just order. As it pursues that function, it is accountable to a transcendent order beyond itself, the law of God. One of the important roles of the church is to make that clear to the state. However, the church is not the state, which has a tentative autonomy based on the role given it by God. The church does not have a set of specific blueprints derived from the Bible or tradition to offer the state for the execution of its duties. But the church does remind the state that its autonomy is indeed tentative, its authority delegated by God.

In earlier Lutheran formulations, particularly with regard to the state, the law tended to be viewed as mainly negative and rather static. It was looked upon primarily as a "dike to sin." The negative action of the law prevents the wolves from eating the sheep. It certainly has that function, but it has positive features, too.

Recent Lutheran scholarship, especially that led by Scandinavian theologians, emphasizes the constructive pressures in God's action.[16] God, through many agencies, cajoles the world toward more expansive and fulfilling relations among beings. Love is developed, justice is extended and refined,

16. See, e.g., Wingren's *Creation and Law* and Aulen's *Church, Law, and Society.*

and the world is made a better place to live. God operates through "masks" to get this work done. Many of these masks are not recognizably Christian or even religious. Secular persons, with their capacities for civic righteousness, can work behind the mask of God to promote his law. Thus, the operation of the law in both its negative and positive aspects can be performed through unlikely agencies. The church and individual Christians have no corner on the capability of being the vehicles of God's intentions for basic peace and justice in the world. Christians are called to cooperate with all persons moving with the direction of God's law.

Further, Lutheran theology now sees the law as dynamic. Older formulations had it as eternally defined. The relations of ruler to ruled, of husband to wife, of parents to children were seen as part of an eternal and unchanging order. Recent Lutheran scholarship sees the law, to use Gustaf Wingren's words, as "the dynamic Law of Creation." While the law is objective and outside us, our appropriation of it is not infallible. God's energies break down the distorted conceptions of law that have resulted in oppressive social structures. New arrangements ensue. Democracy replaces tyranny. More equality between the sexes emerges. While there is no automatic progressive movement in change, there is the possibility of God pressing for new forms of love and justice among his creatures. One of the duties of the church and of individual Christians is to discern which changes move with God's will and which move against it.

The law of God operates in all dimensions of our earthly existence. All humans are surrounded by its demands as they live out their lives in family, work, education, friendship, citizenship, and in religious communities. At times they are buoyed up by the positive impact of this dynamic law of creation; at other times they are sorely pressed by its strictures. Their lives are caught up in a boiling mixture of possibilities and limitations. Sometimes the boiling mixture becomes a fiery cauldron that burns up peoples, nations, and empires. The judgment of God rains down upon guilty and innocent alike. The Almighty has his own mysterious and awesome ways. God is not a toothless grandfather in the sky. God is the terrible Judge of our sinful ways and uses the law in awful judgment. The law is the "alien" and "hidden" work of God.

"Battle" is an apt metaphor for what is happening in the world of God's law. Satan is at work in the world, trying to disrupt and break the covenantal structure that God intends. We often succumb to the temptations of Satan. God uses weapons of conscience, law, and force to counter Satan's designs. So a battle has been going on since the Fall, and we all are caught up in it. Existence is a jagged affair, penetrated by Satan's and our own willfulness on the one hand, and God's sustaining and judging law on the other. And it is a mysterious process. We humans cannot always discern what God is willing from what Satan is doing. So many events are caught up in ambiguity. Nevertheless, we are not without clues as to what makes for a modicum of the order and justice that God intends for this world.

A final set of reflections will be useful before we move to God's rule as gospel. The action of the law in the world is nonredemptive. We are not saved by the energies of the law, no matter how positive they might be. The law, operating as God's political instrument, creates, sustains, and judges human life but does not redeem it. It makes the world a better place to live but does not complete or fulfill it. Yet life in this world means inescapable responsibility for Christians. God has not abandoned the world, and the Christian calling is certainly not to reject responsibility within a world that God intends to preserve. While the world is not the final home for the Christian, it is an abode that God wants us to care for. This will mean that all people, Christians included, will be involved in some worldly responsibilities that will not appear directly as works of love. Christians may have to be soldiers. Luther thought they could be hangmen. Worldly responsibility will mean coming to terms with the finitude and fallenness of the world.

God's Rule through the Gospel

At the same time that God sustains the world through law, he also offers salvation through the gospel.[17] The New Testament witnesses to the in-breaking of the kingdom of God in Jesus as the Christ. This is God's saving Word to us. The Word is addressed through the church to all human beings, no matter where they are located in the world's structures or when they live in the world's history. All are equally distant and equally close to this address.

The gospel—as Word and Sacrament—is addressed to and received by individuals through the power of the Holy Spirit. This "vertical" encounter is between an individual and God's good news. No other person or group can respond for this person, though he or she can be supported and nurtured by others. As individuals receive the grace of God in Christ they come under God's "right-hand rule." Through the Spirit, faith, love, and hope are generated in their hearts. They, with others who have received the good news with faith, become part of God's present but invisible kingdom. Further, their reconciliation with God in Christ means that they will participate in the complete realization of that kingdom in God's future.

Yet they remain sinners and therefore remain in the dialectic of judgment and forgiveness before God, and remain subject to the demand of the law in their worldly existence. Insofar as they are empowered in faith, love, and hope by the Spirit, they live in grateful trust before God and in faithful obedience to their calling in the world. They live simultaneously in both kingdoms.

---

17. It should be mentioned that God's law functions in this "vertical" relationship to God as well. It functions as a teacher; this is the pedagogical use of the law, distinguished from the political use, which we have just discussed. The individual person stands before the judgment of God's law at every moment of life. The law is sharp-edged and radical. It pierces every defense and presses deeply into the motivations of the person. Its withering gaze leads conscientious persons to a repentance in which they throw themselves upon the grace and mercy of God. So the law teaches each person their sin in preparation for their redemption.

In this Lutheran view, the law should not be turned into
the gospel. The demands of the law before God (vertical) or
within the world (horizontal) do not save. They are demands,
not a gift. No one can claim redemptive powers for them or
for our responses to them no matter how noble our responses
might be. If we humans make such claims for our responses,
we dishonor Christ. Conversely, the gospel should not be
made into law. The extravagant love revealed in the gospel
cannot become the guiding principle for ordering life in the
rough and tumble of this world. The world must remain
under the law, not the gospel. If it pretends to be under the
direct guidance of the gospel, it makes itself vulnerable to
the most willful agencies of evil. It dishonors God the Creator.

While the two ways that God rules the world must be
clearly distinguished (for the sake of both the gospel and the
law), they are not finally separated. God the Creator and God
the Redeemer are not separate deities. Likewise, the two kingdoms are not finally separate spatially or existentially; they
interact in creative ways. Duality does not lead to a final
dualism. There are three ways in which the twofold rule of
God comes together creatively in this world.

The first way is in the calling of each Christian person. As
faith, love, and hope are kindled by the Spirit in the hearts
of Christians, they will practice those virtues within and
through the worldly callings they have been given. These
Spirit-driven virtues will affect the responsible roles Christians have as family members, workers, citizens, and church
members. They will transform these worldly responsibilities
into authentic Christian callings. God's creative love enters
the world through the exercise of Christian vocation.

This process, however, is never uncomplicated. Christians
must take their worldly responsibilities seriously as well as
the special summons of faith, love, and hope. They will be
called to responsible risk. Christian virtue will be a leaven
that works creatively on the hard demands of worldly life.
It is the creative task of each Christian to find the fitting deed
between an adventureless acceptance of the world as it is and

an irresponsible desire to transform it. Insofar as that deed is truly fitting, it will cooperate with God's dynamic law of creation.

Second, in corresponding fashion, the church is a place where the twofold rule of God is at times conjoined, the Spirit willing. The church's proper work, of course, is to proclaim the gospel so that it, through the Spirit, might bring God's creatures into his right-hand kingdom. But the church is also responsible for addressing the world according to God's law. It is called to proclaim the whole Word of God—both gospel and law. Further, it is to claim only the power of the Word as it operates in society. Its powers are thoroughly in the realm of persuasion, not coercion. The church is not the state.

However, the church is also called to apply the insights of the gospel to its understanding of the world. The radical love expressed in the gospel is relevant, at least indirectly, to the affairs of the world, just as Christian virtues are relevant to the lives of individual Christians in their callings. These insights are to be applied carefully and realistically, avoiding the sentimentalism that is the serious temptation of those of goodwill and of unworldly temperament. The gospel cannot be made into law. Attempts at making gospel into law will destroy both law and gospel. Yet the gospel is relevant to the world's affairs in a paradoxical fashion. It is a constant judgment on whatever is achieved in the world and is a constant lure to higher achievement. It is always "out in front," just as God's eschatological future, and it cannot be captured or legislated in the present. We must never forget that the person who fully expressed that radical gospel love was crucified. The "gospel ethic" does not fit smoothly into the world.

Finally, it is in God's action itself that we confess the conjoining of the two kingdoms. The actions of God the Creator and Redeemer cannot finally be separate. According to the eyes of faith, those actions come from the same loving God and will be fully unified in the eschaton, when all resistance to God's will will be overcome and God will be all in all.

Then there will be no need for masks, coercion, and judgment. The law will no longer sting. God's kingdom will be fulfilled.

Until then, however, the twofold nature of God's rule must be affirmed. But this affirmation must be held with humility and openness, for our human constructs cannot hold God hostage. God's ongoing redemptive events may indeed erupt spontaneously in the midst of worldly affairs. At times we might even be able to identify them. While they may not be full manifestations of the final kingdom of God, they may be seen as signs and anticipations of the eternal shalom for which the whole creation strains. But these will have to be consistent with the only clear anticipation we have of that kingdom, Jesus as the Christ.

4. THE PARADOX OF HISTORY

"The kingdom of God is in the midst of you" (Luke 17:21), Jesus proclaimed, even as he warned, "My kingship is not of this world" (John 18:36). The kingdom has come in Christ, and it will come in the future. These paradoxes condition the Christian view of history.

The kingdom of God has obviously not come in its fullness. That is one of the Jewish objections to belief in Jesus as the Messiah. He didn't bring the kingdom. The world goes on its jagged path, perhaps positively conditioned by Christian influence, but no one should mistake that Christian influence for the kingdom of God.

The stubbornness of human sin remains in history. The fact that the man who Christians believe is the Messiah of God wound up on a cross is a telling testimony to the stubbornness of sin. He was crucified by the "brightest and best" of the political and religious authorities of the time. For Christians, the cross blocks all optimistic readings of human possibility.

Humans in their finitude and sin cannot complete history. There is simply no room for utopian expectations in the paradoxical vision. Historical, anthropological, and theological wisdom confirm this dictum. Human efforts have distinct limits. When humans attempt to overstep these limits, they self-righteously make themselves man–gods and bring untold misery to the earth and its peoples. Judgment upon these efforts is and will be a persistent characteristic of our historical existence, culminating finally with the great judgment at the end of history.

Yet this judgment on human sin is only one side of the paradox, for God has also given us hope. First, we have a hope that transcends history, the promise that God's love will finally be triumphant over all that resists it. The resurrection of Jesus is an anticipation of what is in store for the whole creation on the other side of judgment. Second, we have the possibility of historical hope. God has given humans the capacity for civil righteousness. Because God's dynamic law of creation operates in the historical process, good things can happen. Improvements are possible, though certainly not guaranteed. Christians are obligated to participate in good efforts.

God is patient. He allows history to go on in spite of human rebellion. The City of God and the Earthly City comingle throughout history. Each moment given is additional time for the gospel to continue its work and to make the world a better place. But God holds history in his hand, offering opportunity and meting out judgment as he sees fit. The "how" and "when" of the movement of God's sovereign will are beyond us. Yet Christians are called to make the most of every opportunity, encouraged by hope in God and chastened by their knowledge of human sin.

THE LUTHERAN DIFFERENCE

The four themes outlined above mark the paradoxical vision. They are related to one another and overlap. Together they provide a framework for doing public theology. Here I will summarize their relevance for public theology and their difference from the Reformed themes that have so dominated American religious, and to a great extent, secular life. I will also contrast them with Catholic themes, especially because Catholic public theology is coming increasingly to the fore in American public discourse. To keep this summary section concise, I will make only general comparisons and use only a few illustrative examples.

God's Twofold Rule

The paradoxical vision affirms a permanent (this side of the eschaton) duality in God's relation to the world and history. God's twofold rule will not be overcome by human efforts that will make it obsolete. This view stands in contrast to Reformed views in which God relates to the world and history in essentially one way: God's redemptive actions run through all events. The Christian community's responsibility is to discern God's saving intentions and to act with them for the redemption of the world. According to such views, the kingdom of God can and will come in history.

THE LAW BECOMES GOSPEL

The error of Reformed views opens history to the possibility of salvation through political or social transformation. While the Reformed vision may insist on God's involvement—perhaps even God's sovereignty—in this process, history has the possibility of becoming the kingdom of God, and humans have the chance to participate in the transforming energies of that kingdom. Indeed, that is their salvation. Thus there is, from the paradoxical viewpoint, an undue hope for history. Historical liberation is nearly equated with salvation. The Reformed attitude expects too much from this worldly process, and it moves too easily toward a crusading mentality. When it is disappointed in what happens, it turns away in despair from its latest hope and tries to fasten onto some new emergence of liberation in history.

The Catholic attitude leads to similar problems through a different route. Catholics believe that the duality in history can be overcome by humankind, directed by the synthesizing capacities of the church. The church in its wisdom and power aims at a synthesis of culture. The whole of humanity, lifted to the fully human level by the liberating praxis of politics, economics, and culture, will be completed by the supernatural gifts of the church. Finally detached from the ancient synthesis of the church and medieval culture, many Catholic bishops and theologians in recent years have openly flirted with the synthesis of Marxism and Christianity in liberation theology. Even when the partner is changed, the Catholic thirst for synthesis is there, so that the intolerable duality of Christian life in the world might be overcome.

In Lutheran parlance, these tendencies violate the twofold rule of God by making the law into the gospel. The creative, sustaining, and judging actions of God are mistaken for the gospel, a mistake that distorts both law and gospel. Such an error loads too much onto worldly processes. Highly ambiguous realities are claimed to be salvific. At its worst, those "on the right side of history" claim God's saving power for their endeavors. This is fraught with the kinds of hazards manifested in any sacred legitimation of human work. Even now there are too many instances of such dangers at work in the world. Making the actions of God's law—or human distortions thereof—into the gospel is a perilous enterprise.

At a less dangerous, but nevertheless troubling level, Dennis McCann and Max Stackhouse, a Catholic ethicist and Protestant theologian respectively, wrote a stirring "Postcommunist Manifesto" that illustrates the tendency to confuse law and gospel.[18] These two authors had a most laudable

18. Max L. Stackhouse and Dennis P. McCann, "A Postcommunist Manifesto," *The Christian Century,* 16 January 1991, pp. 44-47. The editors of the journal then asked a number of ethicists to respond to the manifesto. My response, entitled "A Little Less Enthusiasm, Please, I'm Lutheran," conveyed my sense that the authors were confusing a good historical project—democratic capitalism—with the salvation of God. I believed

intention to persuade Christian ethicists to give up their doctrinaire rejection of democratic capitalism for a more constructive engagement with it. But in affirming the possibilities of democratic capitalism, they used words like "salvation," "holy vocation," and "redemption" to refer to human actions within that political economy. Conversely, they argued that a refusal to engage democratic capitalism constructively is a "betrayal of the gospel." The confusions here are obvious, at least from the Lutheran viewpoint. No political economy saves and no betrayal of the gospel is involved when churches neglect a constructive encounter with democratic capitalism.

While the confusion of law and gospel in this instance seems somewhat harmless, a deeper and more perilous tendency is revealed in both Catholic and Reformed approaches. The confusion of law and gospel is a very serious threat to the Christian mission in the world. If the law is mistaken for the gospel, the gospel loses its character as grace offered freely to all. Repentant individuals are not offered salvation through Christ alone. Rather, they must work within the liberating praxis of certain very specific groups. They must be on the right side of history. This thinking contradicts the uniqueness and universality of God's saving action in Christ. It is truly another gospel.

Sometimes confusion of law and gospel does not lead to the exclusion of persons from the gospel, but rather exclusion of the gospel of Christ as God's uniquely chosen way of salvation. In a good deal of what is going on in mainstream Christianity, human religious strivings in all religious traditions are seen as equivalent pathways to God. Such beliefs

they were subtly confusing the works of the law toward human betterment with something quite different, the gift of salvation in Christ. In their response to that symposium of ethicists (23 January 1991, pp. 77-85), the authors criticize me for detaching salvation from the ethical works that should follow. They concluded their response to me with a cute, but revealing, remark. "But we do not want to rub this in. It is difficult enough being a Lutheran ethicist—if one always has a bad conscience for speaking of good works" (p. 83). But it was not good works that bothered me, it was conflating them with the gospel.

cut the nerve of Christian missionary activity. Instead of the classic affirmation that God acted decisively and uniquely in Christ for the salvation of the whole world, the theological pluralists in both Protestantism and Catholicism are seeing God's saving work in all the great religions of the world. They presume that human religious efforts can be salvific. They reject the classic Christian conviction that Christ is *the* way God has chosen to move toward us, that Christ is a liberation from religious striving itself.

THE GOSPEL BECOMES LAW.

The failure to distinguish adequately the two ways in which God relates to the world can lead to another major problem of which Reformed traditions are vulnerable. Instead of making human activity into the salvation of God (making the law into the gospel), the gospel, with its radical theme of agape love, is made into a law. The radical love that God shows humans in Christ becomes a direct principle for guiding life in the public world. Further, the intense personal responses to the gospel—faith, love, and hope—are directly applied to the ambiguities of the fallen world.

This is the error of sentimentalism. The radical love of God in Christ, which ended in the cross, is viewed as something that can be used to rule successfully in the "left-hand kingdom," the realm of coercive power. Agape becomes a simple possibility in the world. The realms of politics, even international relations, economics, and social life are considered amenable to the guidance of agape love. In the sentimentalist view, Christian virtues are not only believed to be unambiguously present in Christians, but can also be expressed directly into the worldly roles they play.

This inapproriate supplanting of the law by the gospel is one of the major mistakes behind the sentimentalism in mainstream Protestantism's public theology. In its view of international relations, there is a constant drift toward pacifism. Forgiving love that underestimates the destructive intentions of the enemy, turning the other cheek, refusing to use coercive power against evil, unilateral disarmament, and unilateral freezes of weapons development have been persisting commendations of sentimental Protestantism. Even a number of Catholic bishops have indulged in such misjudgments.

In domestic politics, the trajectory is similar. Agape love demands the expansion of the welfare state without insisting on individual accountability. Forgiveness means an ever-expanding sympathy for the wrongdoer and never-ending expectations for rehabilitation. Christian tolerance means withholding judgment about individual behavior but demanding that society pick up the pieces when that behavior leads to self-destructive or socially damaging effects. The unconditional acceptance of the gospel translates into the refusal to make judgments about personal behavior, be it in the realm of sexual relations, family life, or public life. The law is simply cancelled out as a firm guide to personal life in the world.

Further, sentimentalism overlooks the hard demands associated with worldly roles. Business life is expected to be run by altruistic motives, not the motives of economic efficiency. (Thus we have the tired maxim: the needs of people, not profit.) Political life is expected to express mercy directly. (We aim for a compassionate society.) National life is required to manifest a full-orbed community. (We can't keep the nuclear family together, but our society ought to be like a family.)

Unfortunately, when sentimentalism expects too much of worldly life, it cannot appreciate the relative achievements of the good that do ensue in the realm of law. It tends to denounce the partial good that is achieved in hopes of something much more. Or it turns away in despair and looks for the "gospel ethic" to be realized elsewhere, generally far from home where the ambiguities are all too clear.

The problem with all this is that the "gospel ethic" is not fit for the challenges of the world. The cross reminds us of that. The world cannot be directly run by gospel love or the Christian virtues that are elicited by it. The world is run under the law, the "left-hand kingdom of God." The law must and does account for the fallenness of the world. It demands and coerces. It holds persons responsible. It judges. It aims at the better amid a choice of worsts. Responsible policies are trade-offs between what justice demands and what is possible in an intransigent world; irresponsible policies are often those that are mistakenly shaped by the assumption that love can become a direct principle for public ethics.

Does this Lutheran insistence on the twofold rule of God lead to religious mysticism far removed from the public world and political cynicism about that world? Far from it. The dynamic law of creation constantly presses for higher achievements of a realistic justice. Christians, along with other persons of goodwill, are called to work toward those higher achievements. Further, the calling of each Christian, including public figures in economic and political life, is an occasion for the dynamic interaction of that twofold rule. True enough, the pressures of the law make each worldly role ambiguous at best. Public roles take account of the fallen world. Good ethics may not always make good politics, just as noble religious and moral persons may not make the best politicians. Nevertheless, the Christian virtues of faith, love, and hope interact dialectically with these roles, creating a lively tension that opens those roles up to new possibilities.

The tension that arises from this creative duality in the Christian life cannot be escaped. The Reformed expectation of full conversion of the world, the Catholic hope for synthesis, and the sectarian withdrawal from the ambiguities of worldly roles are not fully accurate descriptions of Christian life in this world. The Lutheran attitude needs to temper them.

Christian Sanctification

In contrast to the Lutheran paradoxical view (simultaneously justified and sinner), Reformed ethics envision much more. The Spirit can overcome the recalcitrance of the old Adam. The "new person in Christ" can make visible, progressive steps toward perfection. This means both perceiving and doing the will of God. Reformed traditions have generally affirmed a third use of the law in addition to the two uses that Lutheranism accepts. The third use is meant to guide the life of the redeemed. It derives from biblical principles that guide the covenanted community of the Old Testament as well as from New Testament teachings of Jesus and the apostles. Given knowledge of these sources, Christians who are truly converted can know the will of God for their lives and quite possibly for the world. Furthermore, the Spirit gives the discipline to conform life to the new law.

This attitude is both creative and dangerous. It is creative because it gives Reformed Christianity great clarity about what it means to live the Christian life as well as the strengthened will to do it. It additionally gives Reformed Christianity more capacity to organize around a common cause. If the new law is discernible to the Christian community, it is possible to structure life in accordance with that discernment. Because of this theological affirmation, Reformed Christianity has indeed been capable of "constructive Christianity."

Unfortunately this Reformed view claims too much. Such confidence can quickly lead to self-righteous arrogance. Self-righteousness is a peril because it can blind the Christian to the continuing fallen condition of the soul. Its perfectionism mistakes sins, which in many cases are manageable, for the real problem—sin, which is not manageable. A more profound Pauline-Lutheran interpretation of sin insists that the ontological problem of sin cannot be overcome completely and that every achievement of the Christian life is ambiguous. The Reformed attitude is sometimes blind to the continuing tug of the old Adam in individual life.

Individual self-righteous arrogance, though irksome, is not as threatening as when it gets translated into corporate action. Reformed Christianity becomes threatening when it claims that its interpretation of biblical principles or its discernment of God's will turns into a crusading mentality, as it sometimes does. What else can account for the utter clarity mainstream

Christianity has claimed for itself in pronouncing on matters of foreign policy? Or for right-wing Protestantism's penchant for identifying "Christian" legislation? Or for the crusading zeal with which new movements—feminism, ecology, revolution—are taken to be new emergents of the divine will in history? Or for the totalizing fervor by which biblical texts, hymns, liturgy, and theological writing of all sorts are thoroughly and systematically purged of "exclusive" language? Certainly the root of these exaggerated claims is an overly strong view of sanctification, which is then applied to church and society.

A further "nudge" in the Lutheran direction would lead to a bit more skepticism about whether the Bible or the social ethics of the church gives that much clarity about worldly issues. Two-kingdoms thinking would argue that secular people have important insights into the creative workings of the law, perhaps surpassing even those of Christians. Christians simply do not have all the answers to these matters, either for their own community or for the world. Further, there would be no grounds for the totalizing fervor of the zealots. Such enthusiasm simply overlooks the persisting ambiguity of individual and corporate life. A bit of Lutheran diffidence is called for.

The Role of the Church in Society

Evangelical church historian Mark Noll has characterized the American posture toward church involvement in society in the following way.

> The dominant pattern of political involvement in America has always been one of direct, aggressive action modeled on Reformed theories of life in the world. Like the early leaders of Calvinism on the Continent and the English Puritans, Americans have moved in a straight line from personal belief to social reform, from private experience to political activity.

It has assumed the necessity of moving directly from passion
for God and the Bible to passion for the renovation of society.[19]

Certainly such a propensity is born out in the actions of the
Protestant mainstream in recent decades. They and their ecumenical offspring, the National Council of Churches and
the World Council of Churches, have made every effort to
"renovate society" through their statements and actions.
Their statements are certainly more numerous than their actions, though that would most likely not be the case if they
had the economic and political wherewithal to do more than
they have. These organizations have been extremely busy in
making pronouncements on the major and minor issues of
our time. They follow up their pronouncements with many
kinds of "advocacy" activities in national and state legisla-
tures. They have been particularly busy in the area of foreign
relations, an area in which they inevitably seem to find themselves in opposition to the policies of the West.

These "aggressive" and "direct" tendencies follow from
the theological commitments we examined in the sections
immediately above. "Transformist Christianity" should be
expected to try to transform society. (Whether such efforts
are successful is extremely doubtful, as I argued in chapter
2; however, such a result is not from lack of trying.) These
tendencies have been reinforced in these last decades by another factor, the underlying loss of confidence in the specifically *religious* mission of the church. I contended earlier that
that mission has been rocked by many challenges over the
last several centuries. Churches that have been deeply involved in their surrounding culture have been most affected,
and one of the symptoms of waning belief is the tendency to
substitute ethics, particularly social ethics, for religion.[20]

19. Noll, "Lutheran Difference," p. 37.
20. I offer an anecdotal example to support this general contention. As
I write this I am living in England. Each morning on the BBC a five-
minute section is given over to "Thought for the Day." Clergypersons of
various faiths are invited to make their contributions. Almost without

Practically speaking, the central headquarters of the mainstream Protestant groups and their ecumencial agencies are absorbed in social ethics. A content analysis of their various communications would bear out an overwhelming commitment to social ethical concerns over specifically religious concerns. Commenting on the recent trajectory of the World Council of Churches, respected ecumenical commentator George Lindbeck asserts:

> From the 1960s on, the service of humanity, reconceived in liberationist and politically progressive terms, increasingly became the motor driving the ecumenical train. It now dominates the World Council agenda in the form of Justice, Peace, and the Integrity of Creation initiatives. However good these JPIC programs may be, they are more than questionable to the extent they become the goal and motive rather than fruit and by-product of Christian life together. When it is work not worship which unites, human need rather than God's glory becomes central, and justification by service replaces justification by faith.[21]

---

fail, the clergy step forward to give their opinions about the social and political issues that are much discussed in the news programs surrounding this little feature. They rarely call forth distinctly spiritual insights from the Bible or their theological tradition to illuminate the more universal predicament of human existence in the world, perhaps illustrated in one of the issues of the day. Invariably their opinions are of the sentimental sort and fall far short of what is offered by their secular counterparts. When these religious figures are given a chance to draw upon specifically religious wells of wisdom, they quickly move instead to the secular playing field. At worst, religious notions are used to legitimate highly partisan political opinions. A Methodist pastor contributed my favorite example thus far. Amid controversy over how vigorously Great Britain should enter the European Community, this Europhile ended her political commentary by challenging her audience: "God has set before us a fork in the road: We are called to choose God's way." There was little doubt about what was God's way. Such frenetic efforts to be influential in worldly affairs led Richard John Neuhaus to make this memorable comment: "It has been said of mainline Protestantism today that it is embarrassed to make any religious statement that does not possess redeeming social merit" (*The Naked Public Square* [Grand Rapids: Eerdmans, 1984], p. 215.)

21. George A. Lindbeck, "Tilting in the Ecumenical Wars," *Lutheran Forum* 26, no. 4 (November 1992): 23.

A part of this displacement of the religious by the ethical is the affixation of dogmatic certainty not to religious doctrine but to social ethical positions. Within Protestant mainstream official circles, it is anathema to disagree with prescribed positions on South Africa, Central America, development in the Third World, capitalism, ecology, feminism, and multiculturalism. At the same time there is a highly latitudinarian attitude toward theological formulations, as well as toward the ethics of personal life in sex, marriage, and family matters. A noticeable drift away from foreign missions confirms suspicion that the promulgation of the gospel around the world is a waning emphasis. Indeed, much of foreign missions is now given over to social service and developmental concerns. At home, frantic efforts at evangelism become an attempt to compensate for dwindling numbers.

Catholic tendencies toward direct and aggressive action in society have been noticeably revised since Vatican II. The age-old willingness of the church to wield the secular sword is much diminished. But the longing for synthesis of Christ and culture under the guidance of the church still remains. Catholics are, with their mainstream Protestant compatriots, still likely to be the most willing to commit funds and staff power to political causes, from antiabortion groups to community organizations. Moreover, the American bishops, taking perhaps too much encouragement from the attention given to several major social statements, seem intent on giving their advice on many more issues. Indeed, one gets the impression that mainstream, Catholic, and also fundamentalist churches would really like to direct the country if the broader society would give them the chance.

The Lutheran difference has been clear here. The Lutheran tradition has been more focused and limited in its definition of the mission of the church. The church is called to proclaim the gospel in both Word and Sacrament. That is its central calling. When churches teach and preach the gospel purely and administer the Sacraments properly, that is enough to identify the essence of the church. That does not mean, of course, that the church is not concerned about a lot of other things. But those other things are not essential to its identity.

This means that the priority of the church is to attend to and proclaim what I earlier called its "core vision." This means forming persons in its central religious and moral vision. Its other activities, including its political role in society, belong definitely to the outer concentric circles. The church properly has a sense of limits. As it moves out toward concern with social issues and public policy, its warrant for speaking and acting with dogmatic certainty becomes weaker.

The paradoxical vision also leads to a preference for indirect modes of the church expressing itself in society. Its primary function is to proclaim the gospel and pray that the Spirit forms a people in response to Word and Sacrament. Its calling is not constantly to advise, let alone direct, society. Its primary calling is to nurture its members' callings. Reliance on more direct modes tends to confuse the church's central mission and to damage its integrity. It is then tempted to be something it really is not. Therefore, the church should only infrequently comment on social affairs, at least in relatively "normal" times. Moreover, the Lutheran view has historically held that the church should prefer influence (persuasion), not power (coercive or semicoercive) in its dealings with social actors in the broader society. God has given the church only the power of the Word, not the sword. In part 3 I will examine in more detail the kinds of indirect and influential means available to the church as it witnesses in society.

Finally, the paradoxical vision draws no straight line from personal conversion to social transformation. Personal conversion can lead only to a limited sanctification. Christians remain both justified and sinner until their dying day. Perfection in this life is not possible, so Christians cannot assume a personal perfection to project further into strategies of social perfection. But there is an even stronger reason for this reluctance to move in a straight line from personal belief to social transformation. That is the conviction concerning the twofold rule of God. God rules the repentant heart with his gospel, but he rules the world of public affairs with his law. It is a theological error to assume that the gospel can govern the world.

Thus we have the Lutheran difference. In the following chapters we will examine how it has been articulated in official Lutheranism and how it has surprisingly been quite influential in recent American public life through individual voices. The paradoxical vision has made a difference through several important and effective public theologies.

4

▼ ▼ ▼ ▼

THE PARADOXICAL VISION
IN MODERN AMERICA:
OFFICIAL LUTHERANISM

In order to reiterate my twofold argument formulated in chapter 3, let us rehearse its main points: first, that the paradoxical vision provides a crucially important framework for doing public theology, and second, this vision has been articulated effectively in recent American history in both official and unofficial ways. The major portion of chapter 3 was given to elaborating the paradoxical vision and its ensuing framework, as well as to pointing to the differences provided by this framework from Reformed and Catholic "attitudes." The task of this chapter is to examine the official formulations of American Lutheran public theologies informed by the paradoxical vision and its framework of operation. Further, I will assess these formulations according to my definition of public theology. In other words, I will attempt to identify the examples and assess the impact of the "Lutheran attitude" as it has been articulated by the American Lutheran churches. I will try to point to the actual "nudges" made in the Lutheran direction by these official practitioners of the paradoxical vision.

Earlier I defined public theology as the corporate and individual engagement of a religious tradition with its public, social environment—politics, economics, and culture.[1] This

---

1. For a full explication of our definition see the beginning of chapter 1.

engagement involves both knowledge and action. Intellectual tasks include those of interpretation and persuasion. Action involves decision-making according to the religious vision. Further, for public theology to be genuinely public, it must possess the virtues needed to make an impact on the public world—intelligibility and credibility. Finally, the world must allow it free access to the marketplace of ideas and action in the public sphere.

Let us now delve into the efforts made to express publicly the paradoxical vision. We will begin with those of American Lutheran churches and then in the next chapter move to those of individuals.

AMERICAN LUTHERANISM UNTIL 1960

As mentioned above, Lutheran history up to the 1930s was characterized by a valiant attempt to missionize and care for the masses of northern European immigrants who came to American shores, particularly in the last decades of the nineteenth century. Lutherans came from many different ethnic and language backgrounds, as well as from varied confessional traditions. Lutheran missionary organizations in Europe and the indigenous American Lutheran churches worked hard to educate pastors and send them to the far-flung groups of immigrants of Lutheran origin. Besides gathering them into churches, Lutherans also created an enormous number of "inner mission" charitable institutions—orphanages, hospitals, homes for the elderly, deaconess houses, homes for the mentally and physically handicapped, seamen's missions, and hospices.[2] The major social issue that was addressed publicly by the early Lutheran gatherings was that of temperance,

2. Christa Klein and Christian von Dehsen, *Politics and Policy: The Genesis and Theology of Social Statements in the Lutheran Church in America* (Minneapolis: Fortress, 1989), p. 10. This book is an excellent resource for learning about the development of public theology in the Lutheran churches, particularly the Lutheran Church in America (1962–88). It reports on the processes that went into the formation of the body of social

a relevant issue for immigrant populations under serious threat from drunkenness and/or alcoholism. Sporadic anti-slavery sentiments were also voiced.[3]

But by and large Lutheranism steered clear of public theology. This hesitancy stemmed mostly from the practical necessity of avoiding unnecessary conflict, but also from a theological rationale that tended to reinforce the political quietism of their European Lutheran forebears. Two-kingdoms doctrine was used to separate spiritual and earthly concerns. This inactivity on the public front led Walter Rauschenbusch, the major American articulator of the social gospel, to remark, "Thus far Lutheranism has buried its ten talents in a tablecloth of dogmatic theory and kept its people from that share in the social awakening which is their duty and right."[4]

At least one or two talents appeared from under that "tablecloth" in the next decades. The twenties saw the beginnings of a formal social issues committee within the United Lutheran Church, the largest, oldest, and most indigenized of the Lutheran bodies. It grappled throughout the 20s, 30s, and 40s with two main issues: marriage and war.[5] The incidence of divorce had risen rapidly in those decades, and the

---

statements of the LCA and includes all of the statements themselves. It also does an important task of interpreting the meaning of those documents for American Lutheranism. In the following pages I have relied on Klein's study, though the value judgments are my own. Other excellent studies on the development of Lutheran social thought are available, e.g., Reginald Dietz, "Eastern Lutheranism in American Society and American Christianity 1870–1914" (Ph.D. diss., Yale University, 1943); Paul P. Kuenning, "American Lutheran Pietism: Activist and Abolitionist" (Ph.D. diss., Marquette University, 1985); Edward Schneider, "An Examination of the Social Statements of the American Lutheran Church from 1961 to 1972 from the Perspective of Luther and the Augsburg Confession" (Ph.D. diss., University of Iowa, 1978); and Lloyd Svendsbye, "The History of a Developing Social Responsibility among Lutherans in America from 1930 to 1960" (Th.D. diss., Union Seminary, 1967). An important general work about the Lutheran churches' history in America is E. Clifford Nelson, ed., *The Lutherans in North America* (Philadelphia: Fortress, 1975).

3. Ibid., p. 4.
4. Quoted in ibid., p. 11.
5. Ibid., pp. 21ff.

church returned again and again to concern for the stability of Christian marriage. As regards war, the United Lutheran Church tended to follow the mainstream Protestant drift toward pacifism. There was not much distinctively Lutheran in its approaches.

The Augustana Synod appointed a professor of Christian ethics at its Rock Island Seminary in the early 1930s who strongly swayed that Swedish-background church toward involvement in social issues. However, that professor, A. D. Mattson, was also heavily influenced by the social gospel movement. Therefore, while Augustana became active on social-ethical issues, it did so out of a framework that was not distinctively Lutheran. The other sizeable American Lutheran churches—the Evangelical Lutheran Church (Norwegian), the Missouri Synod (German), and the American Lutheran Church (German)—remained relatively uninvolved, though the last mentioned established the Board for Christian Social Action in 1948.

The Lutheran churches had not yet found a Lutheran public voice on American soil. In the absence of their own perspective, they either remained silent or tended in social thought to emulate their older and larger Protestant siblings. Lutherans were still much more interested in articulating confessional theology on the one hand and developing social welfare institutions on the other. But change was soon to come.

From 1948 onward the American Lutheran Church's Board for Christian Social Action, under the direction of layman Carl F. Reuss, developed a tradition of helping its members wrestle with social questions.

By the end of its life in 1960, the ALC Board for Christian Social Action had a collection of 50 studies and statements, many of them developed cooperatively through the American Lutheran Conference or National Lutheran Council processes. Statements on six topics—including marriage/divorce, race relations, church and state, and public schools—had been approved by ALC conventions. The ALC materials were addressed to members of the church as aids in the development of their own thinking and as a basis for their individual actions as citizens. Speaking directly to government or endorsing specific public policy proposals was not part of the pattern.[6]

Efforts at public theology were ready to blossom more profusely in the United Lutheran Church, too. A new generation of Lutherans found their way into the major interdenominational divinity schools in the fifties. Their teachers in Lutheran seminaries were beginning to break away from a rigid classical pattern of seminary education and encouraged their young students to get their Ph.D.'s in the larger world of American theological learning. Up to that point students had either done graduate studies within Lutheran seminaries or made educational forays back to the old country.

Union Theological Seminary in New York City was a place of great creative ferment in postwar America. Reinhold Niebuhr, Paul Tillich, and Wilhelm Pauck were powerful intellectuals who had something of a love-hate relationship with

6. Charles P. Lutz, *Public Voice: Social Policy Developments in The American Lutheran Church, 1960–1987* (Minneapolis: American Lutheran Church, 1987). This is a useful summary of the ALC's official efforts at public theology. The author also reflects critically on the strengths and weaknesses of the ALC efforts. I will not be summarizing the public theological efforts of the various cooperative Lutheran councils that have been active in American Lutheranism. While they produced a number of important studies and statements, and for a long time were the main vehicle of the Lutheran churches' connection to national government, they rarely affected the life and opinion of the sponsoring churches. Nor did they attract much attention from either the religious or secular world. Also, the LCA and ALC participated in the National Council of Churches, as does the ELCA presently. The LCA was, and the current ELCA is, a member of the World Council of Churches. Further, the American Lutheran churches under discussion, with the exception of the Missouri Synod, were and are members of the Lutheran World Federation. All these ecumenical bodies are involved in public theological efforts that have been under considerable debate in recent years. While they provide a tempting subject for comment in this study, I will resist that temptation.

Lutheranism. At their feet a number of Lutherans came for graduate study who would go on to become the shapers of American Lutheran public theology—William Lazareth, George Forell, Harold Letts, and Rufus Cornelsen. Besides their American studies, these students also drank deeply of the new Luther research of European origin.

Franklin Clark Fry, the highly visible president of the United Lutheran Church in America, facilitated these theological ethicists' efforts to formulate a distinctively Lutheran public theology. This band of theological ethicists was instrumental in putting together a Lutheran perspective on social ethics for the United Lutheran Church in America. It was systematically articulated in a series of studies entitled *Christian Social Responsibility.*[7]

THE LUTHERAN CHURCH IN AMERICA (LCA)

When the 1962 merger of the United Lutheran Church in America, the Augustana Synod, the American Evangelical Lutheran Church, and the Suomi Synod formed the Lutheran Church in America, the stage was set for the articulation of a specifically Lutheran public theology. First the LCA's Board of Social Ministry and then its Department of Church and Society in The Division of Mission in North America became the loci for the formulation of a number of Lutheran statements on the issues of the day.

The person who most decisively shaped official Lutheran public theology was William Lazareth, whose influence can be traced in almost every committee, commission, or document having to do with social issues. As a Lutheran seminary professor and active participant in the various expressions of the church, and then as the director of the Department of Church and Society, Lazareth labored effectively to shape a public theology formed by the paradoxical vision. The "evangelical ethic" he promoted was challenged at times by theological visions more influenced by sectarian, Reformed, and

7. Klein, *Politics and Policy*, pp. 32ff.

even Orthodox perspectives than by Lutheran perspectives, but by and large the vision survived and flourished in the social statements of the Lutheran Church in America.

Lazareth certainly did not articulate this Lutheran perspective on social ethics by himself. Many other key Lutheran pastors, laypersons, and theologians joined in the task. Among them, George Forell, professor of religion at the University of Iowa, and Richard Niebanck, Lazareth's student and fellow imbiber of Niebuhrian realism, were perhaps the most prominent. Niebanck, in fact, had the most decisive hand in shaping the specific formulation of LCA documents over its twenty-five years of existence.

It is interesting to note that Niebanck is virtually unknown beyond Lutheran circles and is not a household name even within the Lutheran family. Lazareth, though very prominent in the denomination and well known among the Lutheran laity (so prominent that he came within a few votes of being elected bishop of the LCA), has lesser reputation beyond church circles. His writing was almost always exclusively aimed at his own church, and he published little beyond its official needs. Later he had great impact on the World Council of Churches Faith and Order Commission as its director. That was followed by his becoming bishop of the Metropolitan Synod of New York in the new Evangelical Lutheran Church in America.

Forell has written for extraecclesial readers more than Lazareth, and a number of his books are used widely in college and university circles. His interpretation of the paradoxical vision has had a major impact on students attending the University of Iowa. Even Forell, however, has had little influence on public opinion on economic, political, and social matters beyond the parameters of his own church. He follows, as do Lazareth and Niebanck, the pattern of Lutheran theologians who have largely confined their public theology to the Lutheran church. Perhaps this is one reason why Lutheran public theology has not made a stronger impact on the world than it has. Its theologians have concentrated on being *church* theologians. The practitioners of a Lutheran public theology for the larger world had to come from beyond official Lutheranism, as I demonstrate later on in chapter 5.

The Lutheran Church in America, however, did have the benefit of these theologians' considerable gifts. Nineteen social statements were produced in the quarter century of its existence. They range from "Aging and the Older Adult" to "World Community: Ethical Imperatives in an Age of Interdependence."[8] All are exercises in Lutheran public theology; the imprint of the paradoxical vision is clearly discernible.

It is important to note the process by which these statements were shaped. Many were developed in response to requests from the synods (regional organizations) of the church and a number by the governing council of the national church. A department or division then geared up to develop the first draft. Sometimes this was done after study conferences were organized by the church. Sometimes, too, a special commission was formed; it then, with staff assistance, studied an issue and developed a draft. This draft then went through a long process of feedback. (As the LCA went forward, more participation by various elements in the church was demanded and granted. The initial drafting, nonetheless, was done by trained Lutheran theologians.) Opinion in the church was carefully measured. Revisions were made in response to these various feedback processes. Finally the statement was taken

8. The statements and the dates of their adoption by the LCA are: (1) Aging and the Older Adult (1978), (2) Capital Punishment (1966), (3) The Church and Social Welfare (1968), (4) Church and State: A Lutheran Perspective (1966), (5) Conscientious Objection (1968), (6) Death and Dying (1982), (7) Economic Justice (1980), (8) The Human Crisis in Ecology (1972), (9) Human Rights (1978), (10) In Pursuit of Justice and Dignity: Society, the Offender, and Systems of Correction (1972), (11) Marriage and Family (1964), (12) Peace and Politics (1984), (13) Poverty (1966), (14) Prayer and Bible Reading in the Public Schools (1964), (15) Race Relations (1964), (16) Religious Liberty in the United States (1968), (17) Sex, Marriage and Family (1970), (18) Vietnam (1966), and (19) World Community (1970).

to a biennial convention where it was subject to long debate and then to revision, rejection, or acceptance. Many statements were significantly revised on the convention floor.

An important small volume, *By What Authority? The Making and Use of Social Statements*, spelled out the authority and role social statements had in the church after it had acted in convention:

> First, social statements teach and thereby provide the conceptual framework within which church members and agencies can grapple with issues and choose appropriate action. Second, the statements provide authoritative policy for the regulation of denominational institutions and for addressing other social and political bodies. Finally, the statements represent the church body's public witness on specific issues and therefore contribute to the formation of the public conscience.[9]

This approach—wherein statements are teaching documents that do not bind the individual conscience but do bind the internal behavior and external witness of the church—persists in the new Evangelical Lutheran Church in America. Thus its statements continue to constitute much of the ELCA's public theology and to shape its behavior. Later we will reflect on whether those statements continue to be shaped by "the Lutheran attitude."

It would be far too lengthy to survey the nineteen documents. A preferable strategy is to look more carefully at one illustrative statement and show how the paradoxical vision provides the crucial framework for the statement. We will briefly look at "Peace and Politics," the very last statement made by the Lutheran Church in America.

"Peace and Politics"

The statement was brought to the 1984 convention after a long period of development. That year was a Reagan-era year

9. *By What Authority? The Making and Use of Social Statements* (Philadelphia: Division for Mission in North America/LCA, 1977). Richard Niebanck was the primary author of the document.

when a hot debate raged in the United States concerning the ethics of nuclear weapons deterrence. A number of mainstream Protestant statements moved in a pacifist direction—condemning the United States weapons buildup and calling for a unlilateral freeze on weapons development, production, and deployment. The "peace churches" pressed hard for unilateral disarmament. The Catholic bishops, in "The Challenge of Peace" (United States Catholic Bishops, Washington, D.C.: Origins, National Catholic Documentary Service, 1983), gave grudging approval to the policy of deterrence, but only in the interim before we would disarm. The letter effectively diminished the moral legitimation of American foreign policy. This issue was definitely a challenge for the "Lutheran attitude."

Christa Klein summarizes the document's main thrust, which survived several days of serious challenge from the convention floor:

> Divided into three major sections, it begins with a careful analysis of the policy of deterrence, noting both the possibility that deterrence has contributed to the absence of a major war since World War II, and the risks, including a "flexible response," inherent in the presence of nuclear weapons. Next the statement considers theological principles on such points as the state's authority to use force to maintain peace and the applicability of the just war theory to nuclear conflict. The final section supports the peace movement as an independent expression of popular concern and recognizes political realities which commend a policy of deterrence.[10]

But what about the effect of the paradoxical vision on the document? That is a more important issue for our purposes here than where the document actually ends up, though there is certainly a relation between the two. Let us consider the four themes that make up our framework.

10. Klein, *Politics and Policy,* p. 164.

1. THE QUALITATIVE DISTINCTION BETWEEN GOD'S SALVATION IN CHRIST AND ALL HUMAN EFFORTS.

"Peace and Politics," as almost all the other social statements of the LCA, fully expresses the qualitative distinction between God's salvation in Christ and human efforts. In so doing it preserves the gospel's radicalism (God's salvation is pure grace) and universality (it is offered to all repentant hearts, no matter on what side of the world's fault lines they find themselves).

This statement's way of doing this is to distinguish between eternal and temporal peace. "The Peace of God's reign, infinitely surpassing the peace of creation, is the *shalom* of Christ's triumph over the present age, the Sabbath-rest of the people of God (Heb. 4:9-10)."[11] "Peace with God is a gift that is not of this world (John 14:27), which the world can neither give nor take away. Yet those to whom it is given are sent into the world (John 20:21; Matt. 28:19-20), not removed from it (John 17:5)."[12] Thus Christians receive saving grace through Christ but are at the same time called to care for the world and its people. They are free lords of all because of the gospel and at the same time are servants of all.

The document further affirms the importance, to God and therefore to Christians, of temporal peace. The Creator's presence is clearly discerned in the political work of peace. "The human longing to build peace is evidence that the Creator has not abandoned the creation."[13] The gift of eternal peace does not nullify the duty of Christians to work for temporal peace. Further, not only Christians but all people of goodwill have the longing for peace; "the divine law is written on their hearts, and their consciences testify to God's creative 'yes' (Rom. 2:15)."[14]

11. "Peace and Politics," in ibid., p. 248. One of the helpful features in Klein's book is the inclusion of all the social statements. The references to "Peace and Politics" are numbered according to Klein's pagination, not that of the original document.

12. Ibid., p. 249.

13. Ibid., p. 250.

14. Ibid.

Yet these human efforts for peace are not salvific. They are the preserving action of God, not his saving action. The statement rejects the tendency of all human efforts to claim redemptive significance for their actions. Indeed, it recognizes a great danger in a "national messianism in which a particular nation-state pridefully declares it to be its historic calling to 'save' the world from political, social, or religious 'error,' making the world over into its own likeness."[15] Those in the peace movement can likewise become arrogant in their claims.

This sharp distinction between the ultimate salvation of God and human efforts at penultimate solutions does not absolve us from making important relative distinctions between earthly efforts, however. "Honest comparative moral evaluation of the character and behavior of political regimes is called for."[16] It is clear in the document that the West has more political legitimacy than the Soviet Union.

"Peace and Politics" also distingishes between the core of Christian religious and moral conviction and the outer concentric circles of political analysis, socioethical principles, and policy recommendations. The theological section, which obviously carries more consensus and moral weight, is clearly marked off from "judgments and tasks" and "enabling resolutions." Further, there is no claim that the church in its wisdom has any blueprint of God's will for the world on these matters. The sanctification of the Spirit in individual Christians or the church does not provide a clear revelation on these ambiguous matters.

> Although we have no special authority as a church to advocate particular policies as if they were divinely sanctioned, our political stewardship . . . obligates us to contribute to the ongoing debate. . . . This we must do both boldly and modestly—boldly in the freedom for which Christ has set us free; modestly, in view of our sin, limited vision, and the everchanging character of the world."[17]

15. Ibid., p. 252.
16. Ibid.
17. Ibid., p. 251.

2. THE PARADOX OF HUMAN NATURE.

The document certainly drives home the sinfulness of humankind. Instead of blaming the development of nuclear weapons on some external cause (communism, capitalism) or some relatively superficial internal cause (ignorance, psychological insecurity), "Peace and Politics" locates sin at the root of war. Violence in corporate human affairs is the result of sin and is the "deadly expression of the sinful lust for domination and the compulsion to self-justification."[18]

Yet, "while conflicts and violence are abiding features of this sinful world, war is not inevitable."[19] The document shows no political cynicism about or resignation to the inevitability of a nuclear conflagration. Nor is it hysterical, like many of the antinuclear documents of the time were. Humans of goodwill can manage to avoid such a disaster. There are effective, though not guaranteed, activities of peacekeeping (nuclear deterrence at the lowest level of risk), peace-building (positive measures nations can take to expand common interests and cooperation), and peacemaking (love of enemies and strategies of reconciliation). Politics, far from being merely negative, can facilitate all of these processes so there can be a reasonable hope for temporal peace. Humans have capacities for justice as well as for sin.

3. GOD'S PARADOXICAL RULE.

Our treatment of the first theme already has indicated the presence of this third theme as a guiding principle in the statement. Here it is important to note that the doctrine of the twofold rule of God prevents the document from falling into the trap of sentimentalism.

The peace of the world, to paraphrase Augustine, is based on strife. The principle of the balance of power—even the balance of terror in nuclear deterrence—is a relevant guideline for governing the relations of nations in the realm of the

18. Ibid., p. 250.
19. Ibid., p. 251.

law—God's left-hand rule. The gospel and the ethic of radical love that follows from the gospel are not directly relevant to the rough and tumble world of politics. They cannot be the guiding principles for relations among nations.

"Peace and Politics" thus avoids the sentimentalist snare so prevalent in mainstream Protestant documents of the time, where agape love, with its forgiving, nonviolent, and self-sacrificial motifs, was pressed forward as directly relevant to the ethics of nuclear deterrence. Such a move obviously led toward unilateralist disarmament or thorough-going pacifism. Nuclear pacifism was certainly a tendency of the time.

Neither is the law made into the gospel in the Lutheran document. The task of maintaining temporal peace is a very important human task, but "saving" the earth from nuclear destruction is certainly not the same as God's saving his lost creation through Christ.

The rule of God's law is carried on through secular politics. "Politics is the task of protecting and caring for the common life. Thus peace is the basis, sense, and goal of politics. The Creator is present in the politics of peace."[20] Further, these politics need not be carried on solely by Christians, though Christians are summoned to make their contribution. The criteria for the use of force are accessible to secular people as well as Christians, as the document makes clear in its use of the just war theory.

Moreover, the state can use coercion in its pursuit of a just peace.

> The legitimate use of deadly force stands under God's command of love for the weak in the deterrence of aggression, and love for the enemy in the case of hostilities. The discernment of love in such cases is full of ambiguities, and requires the full participation of the citizenry in critical reflection and moral discourse.[21]

20. Ibid., p. 250.
21. Ibid.

God's work in his left-hand kingdom may proceed through means that certainly do not on the surface accord with agape love.

The statement's argument, like most of the LCA's social statements, distinguishes the descriptive from the normative and regulative. The descriptive is an analysis of the main features of the issue under discussion. The normative is derived from biblical and theological sources, not from some "prophetic" discernment of the "signs of the times." The regulative takes seriously both the normative and the descriptive, so that its prescriptions fall neither into a superficial pragmatism that disguises a hidden ideology, nor into a utopianism. In other words, it is a serious argument from those committed to the paradoxical vision.

The argument leads to what I believe is a persuasive conclusion, particularly in the light of the epochal changes from 1989 onward. Using the paradoxical vision's framework of theological and practical insights, the statement concludes with a qualified endorsement of nuclear deterrence: "Yet insofar as aggression (one's own as well as the other's) is restrained by the possession of nuclear weapons (which includes the threat to use them in retaliation), nuclear deterrence remains at the present time the lesser of evils. Yet evil it is and remains."[22]

However, nuclear deterrence is terribly unstable and dangerous and should not be viewed as a permanent policy. All our peacekeeping energies ought to aim at "deterrence stabilized at the lowest possible level of risk."[23] The statement was prescient about the eventual success of deterrence and the path that the United States and Russia have taken; they seem to be stabilizing deterrence at the lowest level of risk. However, it seems unlikely that nuclear deterrence will ever be only a temporary policy. The statement is a bit too enthusiastic in its judgment that we can or ought to do away with nuclear weapons completely.

22. Ibid., p. 253.
23. Ibid.

The two ways of divine rule—through the law and the gospel—are not left on separate tracks by the document. Those who receive the gospel are called to hold the state and its war-making capacities accountable to a higher law insofar as they are given wisdom to discern it. Their calling as Christians is to work for peace in all the locations of their callings. The twofold rule of God intersects creatively and painfully in the lives of Christians living in a balance-of-terror world.

4. THE PARADOX OF HISTORY.

The "Lutheran attitude" denies that history can or will be fulfilled through human effort. It awaits God's kingdom to come in his own time and through his decision. Considering the intractability of human sin and evil, the end will not come smoothly or without judgment. Nevertheless, God's kingdom will come. God's sovereignty will finally be completely realized in a kingdom that has been anticipated in the coming of Jesus as the Christ. History, then, is an interim in which God struggles with the forces of darkness. Hints and parables of the future kingdom of God may appear in history, but they will not triumph completely until God brings in his future. The kingdom has come and it will come.

> Our theology of the cross of Christ forbids illusions regarding the possibility of establishing permanent peace and a perfect society in this age. Confident, however, in God's promise of peace, the church proclaims this hope so that all may persist in the politics of peace, trusting in the loving Creator's presence, and looking forward to the unveiled reign of God.[24]

That is how "Peace and Politics" puts it. There are no illusions about the potentialities within history or within humans to bring the kingdom. Nor is there bitter disappointment that comes when illusions are dashed. Yet there is confidence in God's steadfast love at an eternal level that drives Christians into God's actions for temporal peace.

24. Ibid., p. 251.

Assessment

We can say many positive things about the LCA's total accomplishment. The consistency by which the theological themes of the paradoxical vision were articulated is impressive. Theology counted. The "Lutheran attitude" made a difference in these documents: the statements affirmed and protected the radicality and universality of the gospel; they were realistic but not cynical or sentimental; they were not captured by a political ideology that led in ever-more predictable directions; they argued persuasively from biblical and theological grounds; they took feedback seriously; and they were clear about what the churches can and should contribute to the public discussion.

Klein summarizes this legacy of public theology nicely in her epilogue:

> In its quarter century, the Lutheran Church in America developed an admirably coherent tradition in theological ethics. Taken as a body, the social statements exhibit an approach to social issues that is identifiable and that reflects Lutheranism's confessional heritage. The "evangelical ethic," as it was called, was present from the outset.[25]

As a historian of American Christianity, she believes the LCA's approach "gives the denomination unique standing in the history of American Lutheranism and of American Christianity."[26] Indeed, it would not be brash to conclude that the LCA produced the most impressive array of official Lutheran public theology up to this point in American history.

There were shortcomings, however. Why haven't these statements found more of a hearing in the public world? Why didn't they give public discussion more of a "Lutheran nudge," as the Catholic statements no doubt have given it a Catholic nudge. Obviously, the size of the church makes a

25. Ibid., p. 173.
26. Ibid., p. 174.

difference, as does the level of authority and attention given Catholic bishops by the broader society.

But that is not the whole answer. An additional reason for their relative obscurity lies in the fact that the key Lutheran theologians had little public voice outside Lutheran church circles. They did not seek that voice nor were they given it. There were no coattails for the statements to ride upon.

Further, Lutherans as a church body in this country continue in anonymity. On the one hand, Lutherans have been ignored because they do not belong to the more familiar and established Anglo-Saxon heritage and its churches. Nor are they Catholic, part of a huge and vaguely "threatening" church, at least in the eyes of the secular media. Lutherans have shared in the treatment accorded all religious groups by the secular elite—uninterest or lightly disguised contempt. On the other hand, they themselves are a diffident lot, not particularly aggressive in calling attention to themselves or their accomplishments.

Several other problems emerged in the latter days of the LCA. The church opted strongly for direct approaches to express its public theology. It focused heavily on social statements at the expense of indirect ways of cultivating the laity to be more active in their efforts at public theology. The LCA eschewed the role of becoming a mediating institution. (I say more about these two approaches in part 3.) It began involvement in what it called "advocacy," the effort to influence legislation in national and state government. It began to use its financial clout to affect corporate decision-making. Here it followed the path laid out by its Protestant mainstream compatriots. Perhaps in its desire to become more "prophetic," it ignored some of the gifts the Lutheran tradition has had—more indirect ways of expressing its public theology. This move toward direct influence and action was to bring conflict to the ELCA later on when a number of protesting voices charged that such direct strategies raised questions about the mission and integrity of the church.

Finally, the LCA's last years saw a strong movement toward what has been termed "interest group liberalism." This is the notion that the interests carried by the dominant group—white, male, straight, middle class, European—are so weighty that they blind persons of that group from recognizing or understanding the interests of any other group. All people of the dominant group, so the argument goes, are so caught up in group identity and interest that they cannot transcend them. The dominant group has arranged everything for its own benefit, and it keeps other groups at the margins. Reinforcing this "hermeneutic of suspicion" was the continuing worry about the overwhelming white, middle-class, and northern European composition of the LCA.

Following from this analysis, the only way of improving the situation is to strengthen the hand of groups "at the margin." Thus, one must build in quotas or construct "representation" schemes along group lines. In this view theologians, particularly white male theologians, are viewed as just one more interest group that must be countered with other interests. This, of course, erodes the authority of the theological tradition. Thus, as the LCA became more enamored of this interpretation, it developed a particular doctrine of "inclusiveness" that later went on to penetrate the new ELCA. In its later days, the LCA's statements were increasingly affected by the politics of interest groups. The paradoxical vision came under escalating pressure.

THE AMERICAN LUTHERAN CHURCH (ALC)

In 1961 the American Lutheran Church was formed from three smaller Lutheran bodies—the German-background American Lutheran Church, the Norwegian-origin Evangelical Lutheran Church, and the Danish-heritage United Evangelical Lutheran Church. These churches were generally more Midwestern, ethnic, and rural than the United Lutheran Church, the dominant church in the new Lutheran Church in America (1962). These characteristics are important in understanding the extent and kind of public theology done in the ALC. While one of its predecessor bodies, the American Lutheran Church, did have a formal organization for articulating its public theology (see above), the other two gave little attention to social thought.

In its twenty-seven years of existence the ALC had only two executives of the units charged to do public theology on behalf of the denomination. The organizational unit changed names during those years but ended up being called the Office of Church in Society. Interestingly enough, both executives, Carl F. Reuss and Charles P. Lutz, were laymen. The former earned a Ph.D. in sociology and the latter had a theology degree with graduate study in journalism and political science.[27] The background of the two leaders presents an interesting contrast with that of the LCA leaders. Reuss and Lutz brought many gifts to their work but did not manifest the same kind of theological interest and acumen shown by key figures in the LCA.

The composition of the ALC boards or commissions responsible for social statements changed dramaticly from predominantly clergy and male to predominantly lay and female. Staff members of the units were predominantly female from 1981 onward. The one professional theologian on the ALC board was Larry Rasmussen of Union Theological Seminary in New York, whose theological position, it would be fair to say, was and is not classically Lutheran.

The process for initiating and shaping social statements was very similar to that of the LCA. Many efforts were made to encourage discussion and feedback so that members of the ALC would have "ownership" of the statements. Some statements went through as many as ten drafts before being accepted. Besides the social statements, the ALC provided its presidents/bishops opportunity to speak in the name of their office on social issues. This opportunity was used several

27. Lutz, *Public Voice*, p. 6.

times—on peace, Central America, and the poor—by a group
of presidents/bishops.[28]

The ALC had a very interesting set of distinctions to distinguish levels of authority for and application of its statements. Three levels required different percentages of convention votes to be accepted:

1. Statements of comment and counsel required a simple
majority for adoption and were addressed primarily to the
members of the church as guidance for their own reflection
and action.

2. Statements of judgment and conviction required a 60
percent majority for adoption and were considered a contribution to the broader societal discussion on the subject as
well as guidance to members.

3. Statements of policy and practice required 66 percent of
the votes for adoption and were binding on the ALC as an
institution, in addition to contributing to the societal debate
and speaking as guidance to church members.[29]

This approach, as well as the reminders of it in many of
the statements themselves, made clear that the ALC recognized the difference between its core religious and moral vision, where there should be strong consensus, and its opinions
on social and political policy issues. As the authority of a
statement increased, so did the need for the number of affirmative votes in convention. Interestingly enough, the ALC
turned down several initiatives in the 1970s to endorse the
Equal Rights Amendment and the boycott of Nestle products
during the debate over Nestle's marketing of infant formula.[30]

Thirty-six statements were formulated by the ALC. Twen-
ty-four were statements of comment and counsel, only five
were statements of judgment and conviction, and nine were
statements of policy and practice.[31]

28. Ibid., p. 16.
29. Ibid., p. 11.
30. Ibid., p. 6.
31. Ibid., p. 12. The five in the middle category were "Environmental
Crisis" (1970), "National Service and Selective Service Reform," (1970),

The last director of the ALC Office of Church in Society, Charles Lutz, observed that the general direction of the statements moved from indirect education of the ALC laity to direct address and influence of the broader society, from attention to "personal ethics" (what I earlier called the core moral vision) to social ethics, from domestic to foreign policy issues (particularly issues pertaining to Southern Africa), and from moderate to "progressive" political orientation.[32]

As with the LCA statements, it would be far too tedious to survey the many ALC statements. But it may be helpful to compare and contrast the ALC statement on peace with that of the LCA. Both were developed in roughly the same time span—1982 for the ALC and 1984 for the LCA—and both addressed a controversial issue, the so-called nuclear arms race.

"Mandate for Peacemaking"

In general there is little sustained theological or ethical argument in this document, let alone *Lutheran* theological and ethical argument. At the beginning it lists a loosely related set of affirmations pertaining to the "nuclear arms race," and moves after five pages of these affirmations to recommendations that are binding upon the actions and public witness of the ALC. Let us examine the statement according to the four criteria of our paradoxical vision.

1. THE QUALITATIVE DISTINCTION BETWEEN THE GOSPEL AND ALL HUMAN ACTIONS.

This hallmark of Lutheran theological thinking is present in the document, but in a muted way. "The gospel proclaims

---

"Violence in Television Programming," (1970), "Abortion" (1980), and "Mandate for Peacemaking" (1982). The nine that were given most authority were "National Service and Selective Service Reform," (1970), "Role of the Pastor in the Community," (1970), "Women and Men in Church and Society" (1972), "Racism in the Church," (1974), "Christian Social Responsibility" (1978), "Nature of the Church and Its Relationship with Government," (1980), "Mandate for Peacemaking" (1982), "Teaching and Practice on Marriage, Divorce, Remarriage" (1982), and "Human Law and the Conscience of Believers" (1984).

32. Ibid., p. 10.

reconciliation between God and rebellious humanity. We have confidence in the redemptive activity of God, whose will and work includes peace for all humanity. The cross of our Lord is the culminating point of the kingdom and the place of utter reconciliation."[33] Human action for peace is then seen as basically a response to this reconciling activity of God. But, unlike the LCA's, this statement does not make a clear distinction between the peace that Christ brings in the gospel and the temporal peace that we are called by the gospel to pursue. Shalom (peace) is of one piece; individual and churchly human work toward peace are constitutive of God's salvation.

Another problem concerns the statement's distinction between Christian unity based on the gospel and the likely diversity on sociopolitical issues. (This refers to what I have termed the distinction between the core religious and moral vision and the outer concentric circles of social teachings and public policy.) The statement leaves little room for those who agree on the gospel but disagree on public policy. Those who do not believe in the ALC version of peacemaking are given little comfort that they are also part of the Christian community. It is amazing that the statement was passed with an overwhelming majority, 94.6 percent.[34]

2. THE PARADOX OF HUMAN NATURE.

The statement has a number of references to our "fallen, sinful world." It contains a series of confessions in which Christians are charged with not extending the peace brought by the gospel to international relations. However, the statement exudes confidence that Christians grasped by the gospel can now overcome these tendencies of our fallen world. Christians are a new humanity, and the "false pride and pretenses of the old humanity are abolished."[35] Christians' security in

33. The American Lutheran Church, "Mandate for Peacemaking," (Minneapolis: Augsburg, 1984), pp. 1-2.
34. Lutz, *Public Voice,* p. 11.
35. "Mandate for Peacekeeping," p. 2.

the gospel can enable them to give up the quest for national security.

Moreover, the estimation of the goodwill of the enemy of the time, the Union of Soviet Socialist Republics, is palpable. We need not countervail Soviet aggressiveness with formidable power. The document assumes that "inviting" the Soviet Union to pursue arms reduction with us is a matter of persuasion, not hard negotiation based on a balance of power.[36] Indeed, the main visual aid for the statement is the statue "Swords into Plowshares" given to the United Nations by the Soviet Union, thus suggesting that the Soviets actually had those intentions.

A serious lapse into an undue optimism about human nature is represented by the statement's lack of ambiguity in assessing the motives and effects of anyone calling themselves "peacemakers." Everyone, including those involved in "mass movements of social change," are peacemakers who are automatically on the side of God's will for peace. Christian peacemakers seem particularly immune to the continuing distortions of human sin.

3. THE TWOFOLD RULE OF GOD.

It is in this area that the ALC statement fails most dramatically in making a Lutheran argument, in sharp contrast to the LCA statement. First, the two ways that God rules are simply conflated; the two kingdoms are confused. The radical ethic of the gospel is directly applied to the rough and tumble world of international relations. The Beatitudes are suggested as a direct guide to the relations of nations. The gospel's call to trust in God is used to suggest that we trust our earthly enemies.[37]

The love ethic of the transformed Christian becomes the guiding principle of the larger society. The statement easily extends the reconciling capacity of Christian love in "primary

36. Ibid., p. 8.
37. Ibid., p. 2.

relationships" to the life of nations. The risk-taking, self-sacrificing capacity of Christian love should free our nation to take unilateral steps in reducing the nuclear danger.[38]

This tendency to make the ethic of the gospel directly applicable to international relations leads the statement toward a strongly pacifist posture. We might emulate the early Christians, who, the statement claims, were predominantly pacifist. More likely, it suggests, we might adopt a nuclear pacifism.[39] The statement gives repeated support for conscientious objection and selective conscientious objection, but little comfort or attention is given to those who reject pacifist arguments.

Making the gospel into the law in this fashion not only leads to personal pacifism and a sentimental stance toward international relations; it diverts the statement's attention from the kind of strategies in the left-hand kingdom that actually kept the peace. In contrast to the LCA statement, it gives no extended attention to the possibilities—and the limitations—of deterrence. It has no category of "peacekeeping," under which the LCA document made a qualified argument for deterrence.

The ALC statement has only one sentence devoted to the policy that turned out to be successful. "Our ethical dilemma is that weapons whose use cannot be justified are needed to sustain the balance of fear in which nuclear warfare has been prevented for more than three decades."[40] But the rest of the statement has little use for such a strategy. The money going to armaments should be diverted to redress the economic injustices of the world. Our present approach to national security vis-à-vis the Soviets is too militaristic.[41]

While the just war doctrine is mentioned, it is used only to warn us against "unthinking compliance with whatever

38. Ibid., p. 8.
39. Ibid., p. 5.
40. Ibid.
41. Ibid., p. 9.

policies a nation's political and military leadership happens to be offering the people at a given time."[42] Rather, we should listen to the voices of those in the peace movements in Europe and Japan, and especially in the developing world, but presumably not those of the French bishops or the German Protestant Church who were not so pacifist.

If the statement tends to make the gospel into the law, it also approaches the converse danger of making the law into the gospel. A particular interpretation of the will and action of God (the law), that God is on the side of the peace movement of the early eighties, is almost made into the good news. This is not explicitly said, but the statement's enthusiasm for a highly controversial movement is eagerly legitimated by the highly selective biblical and theological resources it employs.

Thus the paradoxical tension in the life of the Christian is diminished in this document. The Christian is not caught in the anguishing position of being summoned by a radical love that is in serious tension with a policy of deterrence that fits and is effective in a fallen world. The tension is reduced by adopting a sectarian rejection of those instruments of power that actually kept the peace and then prevailed against an implacable enemy.

4. THE PARADOX OF HISTORY.

The statement has an appendix provided to stimulate group discussion. (This appendix was not adopted by the general convention.) The group is asked to design a "strategy for moving the world toward the goal of abolishing nuclear weapons."[43] It envisions a world where funds for defense concerns can be dramatically turned to economic development. It calls for a U.S. policy devoted to "the elimination of nuclear weapons from the earth."[44] In short, we have a mildly utopian vision for the world coupled with sentimental means for getting there.

42. Ibid., p. 4.
43. Ibid., p. 11.
44. Ibid., p. 7.

Assessment

The ALC document "Mandate for Peacemaking" does not fare well in comparison to the LCA statement "Peace and Politics," both in its theological/moral argumentation and in its substantive conclusions. It lacks the framework of the paradoxical vision, and its conclusions seem naive in retrospect. All of the ALC's statements were not so weak theologically and so ideological politically. A number—"Human Sexuality and Sexual Behavior," for example—have extensive biblical and Lutheran theological foundations. But by and large the ALC statements were not characterized by sustained theological argument of a Lutheran sort. Indeed, it is revealing that, when the last director of the Office for Church in Society reflected on the strengths and weaknesses of the ALC performance, he listed only procedural and methodological problems, not theological problems. He simply assumed that the statements were informed by Lutheran theological convictions, an assumption that was not always warranted.

A number of strong points emerged from the ALC involvement in public theology, however. As mentioned above, several statements deserved wider attention than they received. The classification of statements according to three levels of authority was very helpful. Great efforts were made to gather feedback. Most of the ALC efforts were aimed at informing the laity on important issues. Finally, it was quite unusual and salutary that Charles Lutz, the last director of the Office of Church in Society, engaged in public critical reflection on the ALC's venture in public theology. That reflection is contained in the volume entitled *Public Voice* (cited above), which is unusual in its honesty and candor.

Nevertheless, many deficiencies were evidenced in the ALC work. The most serious was its weakness in maintaining the paradoxical vision. Its public theology was not strong in theology per se, but when it did work from a theological vision it was sometimes not explicitly Lutheran. The ALC did not provide for the same level of theological engagement that the LCA in fact did. Like the LCA's statements, the ALC's statements did not gain much attention from the church's laity, let alone from the larger world to which a number of statements were directed. Such failures are attributable to the same kinds of problems that plagued the LCA. Again, like the LCA, the ALC strained mightily for "inclusiveness" in its final years, an effort that probably diminished its capacity to express the paradoxical vision and at the same time increased its tendency to reflect a liberal political orientation in a denomination that was not particularly liberal.

THE LUTHERAN CHURCH–MISSOURI SYNOD

The Lutheran Church–Missouri Synod is unique in several senses. It is the most persistingly ethnic of the Lutheran bodies. After flirting with the merger process and other sorts of cooperation with the other Lutheran churches, it has withdrawn in recent years. This withdrawal is partly due to ongoing internal conflict within the church, but also partly due to its commitment to what it believes is a beleaguered classical Lutheran orthodoxy. It follows a more conservative theological, ecclesiological, and political path than its Lutheran compatriots.

The Missouri Synod also stands alone in its commitment to indirect methods of affecting the public order. Except for public "advocacy" against abortion and for the support and protection of its schools, the Missouri Synod makes few attempts to directly address or influence public policy. Until very recently, it did not even have those public outlets. The Synod's statements are called "reports" and are designed as aids to form the conscience of the laity and to lead to informed participation in the public order. They do not have binding authority, and Synod conventions do not adopt them as guides to public policy. Thus the Missouri Synod's history in America is marked by fewer ventures in direct public theology than that of other major Lutheran bodies.

It is important at this point to examine the method and content of the official theological ethics of the Missouri Synod. The Synod formed the Social Concerns Committee as part of its Commission on Theology and Church Relations. That committee no longer exists. Whatever theological ethics are now being done are done by the Commission. The parent commission, though, issued a number of reports on public issues—abortion, capital punishment, euthanasia, and human sexuality—which for the most part were the work of the ill-fated Social Concerns Committee.

The Missouri Synod is not nearly as responsive to the pressures of "inclusiveness" and "participation" as the ALC and LCA were and the ELCA currently is. While women and "persons of color" serve on Synod commissions and committees, they are not allocated their places on the basis of quotas or formulae. Nor is there a propensity to run the Synod reports through a variety of feedback processes with the general membership. Synod conventions, however, are often the scene of spirited debate on the reports. The over-riding criterion for participating in the authorship of the statements seems to be the capacity for classical Lutheran theological articulation. The work of the astute Missouri Synod moral theologian, Gilbert Meilaender Jr., is evident in most of the early documents.

Perhaps because of this more traditional mode of operation, the Synod reports are less obviously the product of compromise among various viewpoints. They mount consistent and impressive theological and moral arguments.

The reports are cogent exercises in Lutheran theological ethics. They measure up well to the four criteria of the paradoxical vision. They sharply distinguish between the gracious gift of salvation in Christ and all human actions. They maintain a view of human nature as both radically fallen but yet capable of civil righteousness. They distinguish carefully the two ways that God rules, and they reveal neither utopian nor cynical attitudes toward history. Moreover, theological and moral argument is by far their dominant feature. For the most part, they actually offer the insights that a particular religious tradition can and ought carefully to express, not the ideological propensities of a task force or an assembly convened for several days. The reports on sexuality, euthanasia, and abortion are exemplars of Christian ethical reflection.[45] Contrary to the general opinion that the Missouri Synod is intellectually isolated, these statements also show serious engagement with current secular analysis of the issues under discussion.

The reports address subjects close to what I have called the core moral vision of the church. Except for the capital punishment report, which reaffirms the Synod's qualified approval of that practice, the reports deal with issues close to the Christian's personal existence—marriage and family life, death and dying, and abortion. Foreign policy issues are assiduously avoided. Further, the reports speak authoritatively about Christian theological and moral presumptions but allow for diverse opinion about how those presumptions might work out in public policy.

Each report ends with general principles for guiding Christian conscience. The only exception is the report on abortion, which endorses strong and specific "pro-life" measures in both church and society. Indeed, the Synod's stance on abortion has led it to transgress its tradition of not participating in direct public "advocacy" activities.

There certainly are problems with the reports. They are not the product of a high degree of participation among Synod members, nor are they discussed widely in congregations. They are scarcely noticed in the larger public world, religious or secular. While the reports allow for diversity of Christian opinion on public policy, they strongly manifest predictably conservative implications for public policy. They sometimes get enmeshed in biblical literalism, as can be seen in the painful

45. "Human Sexuality: A Theological Perspective" (1981), "Report on Euthanasia with Guiding Principles" (1979), and "Abortion in Perspective" (1984) (St. Louis: Social Concerns Committee of the Commission on Theology and Church Relations, Lutheran Church–Missouri Synod).

discussion of headship in marriage in the human sexuality report.[46] Nevertheless, they are important exercises in working from the paradoxical vision. Unfortunately, they are not very public, and, further, the Social Concerns Committee has been abolished. Given the ongoing internal conflict in the church, it is unlikely that any ambitious new effort at public theology will be forthcoming.

THE EVANGELICAL LUTHERAN CHURCH IN AMERICA (ELCA)

In January 1988 the American Lutheran Church, the Association of Evangelical Lutheran Churches (a protesting movement that left the Lutheran Church–Missouri Synod in the late 1970s), and the Lutheran Church in America joined to form the Evangelical Lutheran Church of America, a church of slightly more than five million members. A number of small bodies, but only one sizeable Lutheran church, the Lutheran Church–Missouri Synod, remain outside that effort to bring all Lutherans into one church.

The merger involved many challenges. The American Lutheran Church, the Association of Evangelical Lutheran Churches, and the Lutheran Church in America came with very different practices and traditions regarding polity, the role of the Lutheran confessions, ministry, the status and role of bishops, and ecumenical relations. Each church was declining in membership, and the loss of denominational loyalty that often accompanies mergers exacerbated that trend.

Another challenge was an intense desire on the part of many to be "new." The most decisive—and controversial—new element was its particular approach to "inclusiveness." This approach built on the LCA's tendency in its later years toward interest group liberalism, and it led toward formal and informal quotas for leadership positions in the church. Moreover, the late eighties and early nineties brought an atmosphere of distrust of all sorts of large organizations, and this

46. "Human Sexuality," Part II on Marriage and Its Purposes.

distrust was particularly focused on their headquarters. Shortfalls in funds have plagued the church from its beginning.

Nevertheless, the ELCA began with a strong desire to express itself publicly. Its Department for Studies of The Commission for Church in Society—now subsumed under the Division of Church in Society—proceeded vigorously to produce social teaching and practice statements under the new strategy of inclusiveness. Thus far it has brought a foundational document and two social statements to the ELCA Churchwide Assembly for action. It is preparing at least three more—on sexuality, ecology, and race and ethnicity. It has also released a large number of "resources" on other issues, including conscientious objection, South Africa, Namibia, Central America, the Middle East, peace, world community, the Columbus Quincentenary, race relations, hunger, and many more.

In addition to its development of statements and "resources," the ELCA moved vigorously to set up other instruments for the more direct expression of its public theology. It set up a Lutheran Office for Corporate Social Responsibility to advocate for its policies with private corporations in which it has financial involvement. It also established Lutheran Offices for Governmental Affairs in Washington and in a number of state capitals, as well as a Lutheran Office for World Community at the United Nations.

This is quite a burst of activity in a stretch of less than five years. Without going into undue detail, let us try to make a report and assessment of these recent Lutheran initiatives to "go public." The social statements are a good place to begin.

Social Statements

The 1991 Churchwide Assembly of the ELCA adopted two social teaching statements, "The Church in Society: A Lutheran Perspective" and "Abortion," as well as one social practice statement, "The Death Penalty." As indicated, the new church makes a distinction between social teaching and social practice statements, though both are considered social statements. Social teaching statements

> provide an analysis and interpretation of an issue, set forth basic theological and ethical perspectives related to it, and offer guidance for the corporate Evangelical Lutheran Church in America and its individual members. They also illustrate the implications of their teaching for the social practice of this church. In their use as teaching documents, their authority is persuasive, not coercive.[47]

Social practice statements

> focus on policy guidelines for the ELCA's responsibility in society. They are especially important in defining and developing priorities and directives for this church's advocacy and corporate social responsibility practices. In their use as teaching documents, their authority is persuasive, not coercive.[48]

Interestingly enough, while practice statements are not binding on the consciences of individual members of the ELCA, they are binding (coercive?) on the corporate behavior of the ELCA.

"The Church in Society: A Lutheran Perspective"

The most important social statement of the ELCA is "The Church in Society: A Lutheran Perspective," since it is the foundational guide for the church's participation in society. Curiously enough, this foundational document was not

47. Addendum to the social statement "Abortion," The Evangelical Lutheran Church in America, 1991, p. 11. This addendum quotes "Social Statements in the Evangelical Lutheran Church in America," adopted by the 1989 Churchwide Assembly. That assembly also specified that an addendum be added to those statements that "elicit significant division in the Churchwide Assembly, summarizing dissenting points of view."

48. "The Death Penalty" (Chicago: ELCA, 1991), p. 6. The explication of the meaning of a social practice statement is contained in the 1989 document on social statements in the ELCA. (See note above.)

adopted prior to the new church's numerous involvements in society—providing many "resources" on social issues, establishing advocacy offices, and even setting forth two new social statements, which were selected and formed before, and adopted at the same time, the foundational document itself was accepted. Several carts came before the horse.

The "affirmations" section of the statement articulates the familiar themes of the paradoxical vision. The distinctiveness of the gospel and the church's mission are affirmed. The twofold rule of God through law and gospel are again upheld, as is the paradoxical view of history. Human sinfulness is emphasized but along with an affirmation of the human possibility for achieving a modicum of justice and peace.

A new emphasis is on the *way* the church is to affect society. It affirms the more indirect modes of influence—the forming of the character of the church's members and the heightening of their sense of calling in their various places of responsibility. In addition, it calls for more serious attention to the church as a locus of moral deliberation. Informed by God's revelation, reason, and the guidance of the Holy Spirit, the church is called upon to discern the will of God for the world.

The document asserts that moral deliberation should deal openly and creatively with conflict. (Social statements, in fact, provide space in an addendum for strongly expressed minority opinions on the issue at hand.) Then the statement fatefully lays out guidelines about how diversity of viewpoint will be assured. These categories of people should deliberate together: "those who feel and suffer with the issue; those whose interests or security are at stake; pastors, bishops, theologians, ethicists, and other teachers in this church; advocates; and experts in the social and natural sciences, the arts and humanities."[49] Note that those whose responsibility it is to bear the theological heritage are one among a number of categories and that they come third on the list. Heading the list of deliberants are those who "feel" and "suffer" with the issue and those whose "interests" are at stake.

49. "The Church in Society" (Chicago: ELCA, 1989), p. 6.

The "commitments" section of the document promises that the church will sustain the vocations of its members, witness as an institution, and deliberate on social questions. These commitments embrace both indirect (sustaining vocation, moral deliberation, institutional integrity) and direct means (social statements, advocacy) for affecting the social order. No preference is stated for either means; both seem of equal importance and risk.

"The Death Penalty"

"The Death Penalty" statement follows the direction of earlier statements of the ELCA's predecessor churches. It judges the dealth penalty to be ineffective and unjust, and calls for its abolition.

Lutheran themes are expressed but with more qualification. The twofold rule of God is not explicated with clarity. For instance, the statement holds that the gospel should lead human practice toward "restorative" justice rather than the retributive justice associated with the law. Restorative justice holds open the possibility of conversion and restoration, which will make the community safer for all.[50]

Besides the possible exception just mentioned, the statement breaks no new—or, in the above case, dubious—theological ground nor proposes original arguments or strategies. Furthermore, the statement seems aware that a majority of the ELCA's members support the death penalty. It takes pains to remind its readers that the statement's intention is not "to end such diversity by 'binding' members to a particular position."[51]

"Abortion"

The "Abortion" statement provoked far more discussion before and during its adoption than that on capital punishment.

50. "The Death Penalty" (Chicago: ELCA, 1991), p. 3.
51. Ibid., p. 2.

The moral and legal issue of abortion is under more intensive and extensive debate than the death penalty, which seems to be a relatively settled practice in spite of the churches' protestations.

The statement begins with an affirmation of unity "in our confession that we are justified by grace through faith in Jesus Christ." This unity based on the core of the Lutheran vision "gives both the freedom and obligation to engage in serious deliberation on moral matters," on which ELCA members "have serious differences."[52]

The statement aims at transcending the usual "pro-life" versus "pro-choice" language in discussing abortion, as well as the pervasive interpretation of the abortion issue as one of "rights." For the most part, the statement is successful in that intention.

The "Abortion" statement's success in using the major themes of the paradoxical vision is rather more limited. The paradox of human nature is mentioned but is not as fruitfully explored as it might have been on an issue as ambiguous and tragic as abortion. The writers of the statement could not bring themselves to call abortion a sin. The language of law and gospel is not very evident in the statement, nor is there reference to the twofold rule of God, which might well have been useful in distinguishing between what is expected in the Christian's calling from what can be demanded under the civil law.

Particularly apt might have been a reference to the two kingdoms intersecting in the life of the Christian in such a way that agape love becomes applicable in relation to the unborn child. It would seem more appropriate to apply Christian love directly to the innocent developing life of the unborn fetus, or baby, than to that of the criminal, as the statement on the death penalty does. This negligence in enlisting themes of the "Lutheran attitude" is part of the more general weakness in relating theological themes to the main moral arguments of the document.

52. "Abortion," (Chicago: ELCA, 1991), p. 1.

Nonetheless, the argument of the document is relatively clear and persuasive. It proposes a developmental view of fetal life. It affirms that the unborn's claim to life increases as it moves toward viability and becomes almost unassailable at that point, except in the case of lethal fetal abnormalities that would bring a very early death. The moral claims of both the mother and her developing fetus are taken seriously. Abortion ought to be an option only of last resort. The statement encourages women with unintended pregnancies to continue the pregnancy, and it supports adoption as an alternative to abortion.

The presumption for life is qualified by a threat to the life of the mother, serious fetal abnormalities, pregnancies caused by rape or incest, and, more debatably, pregnancies where "dominated and oppressed" women have little choice regarding sexual intercourse or little access to contraceptives. After viability only the most severe threats to the mother or the fetus are allowed to challenge the presumption for life.

The public policy section urges private and public actions to prevent unintended pregnancies and to support life after birth. Moreover, it argues that the state has a legitimate role in the regulation of abortion and commits the church to "support legislation that prohibits abortions that are performed after the fetus is determined to be viable, except when the mother's life is threatened or when lethal abnormalities indicate the prospective newborn will die very soon."[53] At the same time, it contends that the government should fund abortions for poor women under the conditions it earlier outlined.

While the statement presents a reasonable and persuasive argument, one that a majority of Lutherans could accept, its flaws are disturbing. The most serious is the dissipation of the theological themes of the paradoxical vision. A second is closely connected with the first: the biblical and theological principles enunciated in the first part of the statement play little part in the important judgments made later on. Bible

53. Ibid., p. 10.

and theology are detached from the heart of the reasoning. This weakness points to a number of underlying problems in the ELCA attempts at public theology, which I will shortly address.

ASSESSMENT OF OFFICIAL LUTHERANISM

There is little need to say much more about the Lutheran Church–Missouri Synod than I have said above. It has limited its social statements and advocacy efforts to a small number of issues about which it has traditionally been concerned. This is partly due to its continuing theological resistance to direct public theological efforts by the church and partly due to its persisting internal conflicts. Its theological vision is under considerable pressure from repeated attacks from the quasi-fundamentalist theological right. It is unlikely that these dynamics will change soon.

What the Synod has done, however, is of high quality. The Synod needs to find ways to make its own membership more aware of its moral reflection and to project its voice into the broader discussion. It especially needs to again find ways to use the talents it tapped in its Social Concerns Committee. Indeed, it might be important to resuscitate that committee or create something similar. However, the current conflicted state of the church renders a new, effective initiative unlikely.

Much in the early efforts of the ELCA should be applauded. There seems to be continuity in its commitment to the basic themes of the paradoxical vision, particularly in its foundational document. The quality of the two ratified statements is good, with higher marks going to the document on abortion. The process used to encourage deliberation on the proposed statements has elicited much debate; feedback from various constituencies in the church has been taken seriously. Indeed, given the variety of constituencies intentionally built into the deliberative process, it is well-nigh miraculous that relatively coherent and persuasive statements have been forged. On the other fronts of advocacy and the provision of social-ethical "resources" for the church, the ELCA has been vigorous indeed. Besides the Department of Studies of the Division for Church in Society, other divisions and commissions are busy "resourcing" the church.

However, serious deficiencies exist in the ELCA approach. The most threatening has to do with the processes of representation so indebted to the "interest group liberalism" begun in the predecessor bodies. While there is no doubt that this approach has brought new voices into the church, it has also resulted in schemes of representation that amount to formal and informal quota systems. Except for the election of bishops and the calling of pastors, most leadership positions are appointed or elected according to strict classifications of group membership. These schemes simply discriminate by the wrong criteria; they do not take seriously the need to select leadership that knows and is committed to the Lutheran construal of the Christian faith. They undermine genuine authority.

Another problem is that those who "feel hurt" or whose "interest" is damaged with regard to an issue are ushered to the center of the discussion. The paradoxical vision becomes one more perspective to be represented among a number of others, and not the most interested or interesting, at that. This is a formula for the gradual erosion of not only the ELCA'S public theology, but also theological continuity in everything the ELCA does.

This flawed process accounts for several additional problems. One has already been mentioned: the failure to connect biblical and theological notions to the central threads of the argument of social statements. If theologians represent only one interest among a number, there is no reason why the whole argument should be permeated with theology. Indeed, theologians come under suspicion as an "interest group" for those who have nontheological agendas.

Another deficiency has to do with the fragmentation of the statements. When many interests are intentionally brought into the deliberation without their sharing much of a common vision, a coherent statement becomes less likely. Such a situation can lead to a chaotic pluralism where steady progress toward a coherent statement is impeded, thereby introducing an air of panic and hurriedness as the statement comes due for consideration. Such an air was present in the concluding sessions of the task force on abortion.

Perhaps one root of this problem is a confusion about the issue of unity and diversity. If those responsible for the public theology of the ELCA do not have a firm grasp of and commitment to its core religious and moral vision, diversity on social issues will simply tear the church apart. The center cannot hold because there simply isn't one. Unfortunately, the official centers for Lutheran public theology possess a diminished grasp of and commitment to the paradoxical vision. The key staff generally do not approach the theological acumen of the Lazareths, Forells, and Niebancks of an earlier day. Indeed, several of the key ELCA officials have manifested a theological orientation far removed from the paradoxical vision. When diversity at both the core and periphery abound, it will be difficult to maintain the vision.

Diversity at the core tempts the church to gather persons of like ideological persuasion on social issues to disguise the lack of interest in or unity on fundamental convictions. Such, it seems, is the case with regard to those who engage in the advocacy activities of the church, as well as to those who provide "resources" for the church's reflection on many other social issues. These actors are not held accountable to the feedback processes that writers of social statements must face. Thus advocates have lobbied for legislation on which the church has no direct position, if it has a position at all. Certainly the fact that advocacy centers were going full-force before the ELCA had any official social teaching or practice statements is a telling indictment. Further, advocacy with private sector corporations goes far beyond anything warranted by the public theology of the church, both in terms of content and frequency.[54]

54. I gained such an impression at a meeting of the Advisory Committee

Further, the ELCA has given undue attention to social statements and advocacy. Too many social statements have been initiated and too much advocacy activity has been generated. Its commitments to nurture the baptismal vocation of Christians, to use the expertise of its key theologians and elite laity, and to become an institution for mediating conflict have not come to much. Even its encouragement of moral deliberation, which has been considerable, has been flawed by exaggerated attention given to "voices from the margin," who often do not share the paradoxical vision.

Perhaps much of this is simply the travail of a new church. Things will get sorted out, excesses will be corrected, and the sharp sounds of critical voices will diminish. Or, more ominously, these flaws may be symptoms of the deep malaise experienced by mainstream Protestantism. Is Lutheranism losing its theological soul, as have a number of mainstream Protestant bodies? Has the ELCA, as Mark Noll has put it, launched "its ecclesiastical ship into a mainstream that had almost run dry?"[55]

As for the Lutheran Church–Missouri Synod, Noll's words are as insightful as one could expect, although they address the general condition of the Synod more than they do its social statements.

---

on the Church's Corporate Social Responsibility at ELCA headquarters in Chicago in January 1991. The composition of the committee was predominantly made up of lawyers, minorities (several of whom were lawyers), consultants on socially responsible investment, and church officials. One businessperson was present; another was absent. The disposition of the group was what I would term "actively interventionist." Business was presumed to be guilty if managers and employees did not represent the proper percentages of women and minorities. Stockholder resolutions were freely and quickly arranged for these offenders. Further, a boycott of coffee beans from El Salvador was endorsed on the strength of a recommendation from the Interfaith Center for Corporate Responsibility, against the pleas of the Catholic bishops of El Salvador. My impression was that interventions were far too frequent and easy and that the interventions were almost always according to the agenda of the left.

55. Noll, "The Lutheran Difference," p. 36.

When its discord of the 1970's brought Missouri greater national attention, it did so in terms that seem to come straight
out of the history of the fundamentalist movement. Did Missouri under C. F. W. Walther escape nineteenth-century American evangelicalism only to reemerge a century later as wood-
enly biblicistic, anti-intellectually creationistic, defensively
patriarchialist, and conventionally rightist in politics—just
when it was becoming increasingly clear how much these
fundamentalist positions depended on quirks in American
Protestant history rather than main traditions of classical
Christian faith?[56]

So what of the future of official American Lutheran public
theology? The ELCA may lose its soul to the deep secularizing
currents of modern life that have already nearly eviscerated
older American Protestant traditions. The Missouri Synod
may lose its soul to a primitivist reaction to those secularizing
currents. Will this indeed happen and Lutheran public theology be left to individuals rather than churches? As Noll
says, no outsider can hope to answer that question. "The
Lutherans must answer for themselves."[57]

56. Ibid.
57. Ibid., p. 40.

▼ ▼ ▼ ▼

5

THE PARADOXICAL VISION
IN MODERN AMERICA:
INDIVIDUAL EXPRESSIONS

The proposition that creative theology or ethics can be done only by individuals is eminently plausible. Church committees are likely to produce compromised and piecemeal efforts that head toward deserved oblivion. Their virtue, of course, lies in the fact that they are revised and accepted by corporate bodies, which lends them more authority.

The most creative and effective theology and ethics, however, are formulated by individuals who have been molded in rich traditions. These individuals then use their creative capacities to articulate those traditions in new ways or apply them to new situations. So it has been in the Lutheran tradition, as in many other religious traditions. The paradoxical vision has proved to be a rich resource for theologians and ethicists throughout the Christian ages. And, given the strength and numbers of the Christian community in America, it would be odd if such a powerful vision had not had its effective proponents on American soil.

I have already shown how the paradoxical vision has been expressed in official American Lutheranism. Sadly enough, even high quality elaborations of official Lutheran public theology have not had much public effect. However, the same cannot be said about those individual public theologians inspired by the paradoxical vision. Those individuals have often

146

gained the attention of the public and made important contributions to public debate.

I have chosen three individuals to illustrate my contention that the paradoxical vision has had a significant effect on the public theology of this Reformed-shaped nation. The first to be discussed, Reinhold Niebuhr, was arguably the most important public theologian of this century. He was certainly the last theological figure to have had a broadly based impact on secular America—its politics, economics, and intellectual culture.

In relation to our present project, however, the fact of Niebuhr's importance is not the most debatable thing. What is more debatable is that he is being claimed for the paradoxical vision. True, he was quite critical of Luther's social ethic and never identified himself formally with institutional Lutheranism. Nevertheless, it seems obvious to me—and I hope it will seem clear to the readers of this ensuing chapter—that Niebuhr was clearly a practitioner of the paradoxical vision. Indeed, I believe he was the best proponent in modern religious history of the doctrine of the twofold reign of God.

I will justify my other two choices, Glenn Tinder and Richard John Neuhaus, as well, since there are competing voices who could just as well have been heard. Glenn Tinder is a practicing Episcopalian, although in his important book, *The Political Meaning of Christianity*, he explicitly identifies himself with the "Reformation tradition."[1] Moreover, it is clear as he unfolds his argument that he is closer to Luther than Calvin. Tinder has written a number of books that are permeated by the paradoxical vision. *Against Fate: An Essay on Personal Dignity* and *Community: Reflections on a Tragic Ideal* are further examples.[2] His textbook, *Political Thinking—The*

1. Glenn Tinder, *The Political Meaning of Christianity* (Baton Rouge and London: Louisiana State University Press, 1989), p. 3.

2. Glenn Tinder, *Against Fate: An Essay on Personal Dignity* (Notre Dame, Ind.: University of Notre Dame Press, 1981), and *Community: Reflections on a Tragic Ideal* (Baton Rouge and London: Louisiana State University Press, 1980).

Perennial Questions, which has gone through many editions, is strongly conditioned by the paradoxical vision.[3] Moreover, that book continues to raise philosophical questions in the field of political science, which is often in danger of being dominated by statistical analysis.

Tinder is interesting for our purposes because he is willing to bear Christian intellectual witness in a secular academy that has not been hospitable to religious themes, to say the least. Further, he is a layman who is obviously respected and competent in a secular field of endeavor. His influence in the secular academy is more pronounced than it is among religious intellectuals.

Another voice that could well be included in addition to or in place of Tinder is that of Peter Berger. In many ways, Berger is more influential in his field of sociology than Tinder in his political science. In addition, Berger is read widely by theologians. However, I have chosen Tinder because his recent Christian apologetic work in political philosophy has been more vigorous in pressing the Christian case than Berger's recent work in the sociology of economics. Finally, Berger is a close colleague of our third individual practitioner of the paradoxical vision, Richard Neuhaus, whom I wish to include as a neoconservative public theologian. Since I want to include several different ideological orientations among proponents of the paradoxical vision, Tinder seems more appropriate at this point than Berger.

Other possible representatives of the paradoxical vision in the secular academy are Martin Marty and Jaroslav Pelikan, whose reputations in higher education equal Tinder's, or for that matter, Berger's. Indeed, Marty is one of the best-known and most respected public religious figures in America. He is a great interpreter of past and present Christian churchly existence to the world. Marty, like Pelikan, however, attempts to stay clear of public battles in economics, politics,

3. Glenn Tinder, *Political Thinking: The Perennial Questions,* 4th ed. (Glenview and London: Scott, Foresman and Co., 1986).

and culture. Both seem to believe their vocations call them to more scholarly detachment. In contrast, Tinder seems willing to challenge his field more directly with the paradoxical vision.

My third choice is Richard John Neuhaus, whom I include for several reasons. His presentation of the paradoxical vision is the most straightforward of the three selected. Indeed, he was a highly visible Lutheran clergyman and theologian up to his move to Catholicism in 1990. Moreover, perhaps more than anyone since Niebuhr, Neuhaus has pressed his paradoxical vision right into the midst of American economic, political, and cultural debates. An indefatigable writer, organizer, and conversationalist, his polemics have arguably enlivened public debate more than any other serious theological thinker. In concert with Berger, he has probably had more effect on practical economic and political life than any other American religious figure; their book *To Empower People* has affected governmental thinking and policy.[4]

All three public theologians were or are devotees of the paradoxical vision as individuals, not as communicants of Lutheran churches. Niebuhr was a member of the Evangelical Synod and then of the Evangelical and Reformed Church, both of which had elements of the Lutheran heritage. The Evangelical and Reformed Church later was merged into the United Church of Christ. Tinder remains an Episcopalian though his son is a Lutheran pastor. Neuhaus, albeit an ordained Lutheran pastor until he became a Catholic priest, was always outside formal Lutheran church and society offices. His polemics were often directed at those Lutheran offices, and he was kept at arm's length throughout his life as a Lutheran.

Another factor in choosing these three is that each heads in somewhat different political directions from within the framework of the paradoxical vision. Niebuhr was an activist

4. Peter L. Berger and Richard John Neuhaus, *To Empower People* (Washington, D.C.: American Enterprise Institute, 1977).

reformer, identifying for the greater part of his life with the vigorous left wing of American liberalism. Tinder calls himself a "hesitant" liberal. He believes in the great liberal ideals but also is convinced that the fallenness of humanity tragically limits our capacity to reach them. Neuhaus is an energetic neoconservative who has been influential in initiating and shaping that important movement in American public life.

Yet while each goes his own way in political life, the paradoxical vision qualifies and conditions his Christian apologetics. His particular Lutheran "attitude" deeply affects the way he thinks about secular and religious life in America. My primary purpose here is not to claim these three as crypto-Lutherans, as if I were trying to enhance the reputation of Lutheranism by adding a few luminaries to its legacy. Rather, it is to show how the paradoxical vision expressed by these three has had significant effects on their public theologies. Their use of the paradoxical vision protects the universality and radicality of the gospel, views human nature accurately, avoids both sentimentality and cynicism in social ethics, and assesses the historical process with the right mixture of realism and hope. Let us now turn to the particular ways that this happens in each of the thinkers.

REINHOLD NIEBUHR: CHRISTIAN REALIST

It is not necessary to go further into Niebuhr's role as an important public theologian. Niebuhr studies are experiencing a rebirth that pays tribute to his enduring stature.[5] Nor

5. An important recent biography of Niebuhr is that of Richard Fox, *Reinhold Niebuhr: A Biography* (New York: Pantheon, 1985). Although the book is weak in understanding Niebuhr's theological work and flawed in unduly psychologizing his motives, it is a thorough record of his many-faceted accomplishments as a public theologian. More books on Niebuhr have appeared since Fox's biography, among them Ronald Stone, *Professor Reinhold Niebuhr: A Mentor of the Twentieth Century* (Louisville, Ky.: Westminster/John Knox Press, 1992), and Charles C. Brown, *Niebuhr and His Age: Reinhold Niebuhr's Prophetic Role in the Twentieth Century* (New York: Trinity Press International, 1992).

is it necessary to say much more about the centrality of paradox in Niebuhr's thinking. Richard Fox summarizes Niebuhr's life and thought in the following way:

> The uniqueness of Reinhold Niebuhr lay in the energy and zeal with which he pursued paradox and irony in both life and thought. Truth could only be expressed in paradox, he believed, and life lived as a succession of pregnant contradictions.[6]

But is the paradox to which Fox alludes the same paradox we have been elaborating? Does it represent that important Lutheran nudge in American public theology?

The Gospel and Human Works

We can begin to answer that by examining Niebuhr in relation to our first criterion—the important distinction between the gospel and all human efforts. I have argued that such a distinction is crucially important to preserve the radicality and universality of the gospel, as well as to guard against persistent human claims that we can save ourselves in some new program of personal or social transformation.

In reflecting on the cross as God's way of combining perfect goodness and power, Niebuhr emphasizes the unique and radical offering of grace to us for our salvation. This is the work of Christ for us. God in Christ takes into himself the wrath brought on by our sin. Christ acts alone, refusing "to participate in the claims and counterclaims of historical existence."[7] This saving work is done for us out of the mercy of God, and we can do nothing to add to this divine deed of reconciliation; we merely receive it by faith. God's grace in Christ is prevenient, unmerited, objective, and offered to all

6. As cited in a review of Fox's book by Richard Neuhaus, *Commentary*, March 1986, p. 62.

7. Reinhold Niebuhr, *The Nature and Destiny of Man*, (New York: Scribners, 1949), 2:72.

with repentant hearts. Further, Niebuhr emphasizes that even repentance is the effect of the power and wisdom of God encountering us.[8]

Niebuhr approvingly cites the apostle Paul's articulation of the profundities of the biblical doctrine of grace. "The final peace of the soul is gained on one hand by the assurance of divine forgiveness; and on the other by faith. The Christ who is apprehended by faith imputes his righteousness to it. It is not an actual possession except by faith."[9] And again, "So we are saved by faith and not by works, which is to say that our final peace is not the moral peace of having become what Christ defines as our true nature, but is the religious peace of knowing that a divine mercy accepts our loyalty to Christ despite our continued betrayal of him."[10]

It is true that "ideally the doctrine of justification by grace is a release of the soul into action."[11] But Niebuhr never makes the claim that such action is redemptive for human beings— either for the subject or recipient of such action. Only God in Christ saves.

Besides Niebuhr's emphasis on the divine source of saving grace, he is far too profound in his analysis of human sin to assign salvific significance to either individual or corporate action. Indeed, humans are caught in such a vicious cycle of sin that salvation must strike them from beyond themselves. Moreover, on the other side of justification, humans always remain sinners. One of Niebuhr's famous distinctions is between the "equality of sin and the inequality of guilt."[12] All humans are equally sinful before God and are not capable of saving themselves or others, although they are capable of hurting each other unequally.

Niebuhr spends several chapters of volume 2 of *The Nature and Destiny of Man* showing how sanctification is a dialectical

8. Ibid., p. 100.

9. Ibid., p. 103.

10. Niebuhr, as cited in *Reinhold Niebuhr on Politics,* ed. Harry R. Davis and Robert C. Good (New York: Scribners, 1960), p. 207.

11. Niebuhr, *Nature and Destiny,* 2:188.

12. Ibid., 1:219ff.

process. Humans have and do not have the truth. Humans, even the most "sanctified" of them, never escape the sinful ambiguities of their actions. When they act they express both their sinful and "righteous" dimensions. Such limitations prohibit humans from claiming redemptive significance for their own actions.

Such strictures are doubly true of the life of groups. From his stark analysis in *Moral Man and Immoral Society* to his last written efforts, Niebuhr argued that groups magnify the perverse and sinful tendencies of individuals. Politics, one form of collective action, simply cannot save. They can make important improvements in history, but they cannot save. This is not only due to the sinful propensities of human corporate action, but also to the self-transcending capacities of the individual human spirit. Group life in history, no matter how alluring, simply cannot satisfy the longing of free human self-transcendence.

Furthermore, group action can be far more dangerous than individual action because it has larger historical consequences. Indeed, an even greater human danger is to sacralize corporate human actions, claiming them as the embodiment of the will of God. "One need not be a secularist to believe that politics in the name of God is of the devil."[13]

Niebuhr maintains the qualitative distinction between the saving work of God in Christ and all human attempts at salvation. He closes off all the schemes of self-liberation as well as those of political salvation. Authentic Christian conviction starts with the emphasis on salvation through Christ and through nothing else.

Human Nature

As regards Christian teaching about human nature, Niebuhr has arguably developed the most profound and extensive interpretation of that doctrine since Augustine. His theological anthropology in volume 1 of *The Nature and Destiny*

13. Niebuhr, *Niebuhr on Politics*, p. 203.

of Man is unsurpassed in the twentieth century in its systematic power. Against every ancient and modern error in assessing human nature, Niebuhr proposes his interpretation of the biblical, Christian view of human nature, which he believes alone can do justice to the paradox of human nature, to the heights and depths of the human predicament.

Humans stand at the juncture of nature and spirit.[14] This fact of creation sets off the dialectic of human life. It issues in anxiety that is the occasion for sin. Humans deal with their anxiety by sin of pride or sensuality, which infects all of their lives. Yet the capacity for love and justice is not totally lost to humans. The pressure of their essential being nags their actual existence. Their original justice is not totally defaced. Thus, even without the special grace of Christ, humans can ascend to great heights of creativity, though they are more likely to descend to great depths of evil, or, perhaps even more commonly, to live out ambiguous mixtures of good and evil.

This paradoxical view of human nature is the foundation of Niebuhr's analyses and theories of human collective life, the political process, and history itself. One of his most famous aphorisms reflects this paradoxical view: "Man's capacity for justice makes democracy possible, but man's inclination to injustice makes democracy necessary."[15]

Indeed, Niebuhr mitigates the more pessimistic Augustinian-Lutheran view of human nature. He certainly does not downplay human sin but at the same time gives a higher estimation of the human capacity for "civil righteousness" in collective life than either Augustine or Luther. On the other hand, he vigorously denounces all theories of human nature that either overlook human sin by attributing human misery to ignorance or that locate sin outside the self in human institutions or social processes.

14. Ibid., p. 17.
15. Niebuhr, *The Children of Light and the Children of Darkness* (New York: Scribners, 1944), p. xi.

Such a paradoxical assessment is doubly significant in an era when the denial of human sin excuses humans from every sort of responsibility and when the affirmation of human innocence leads to naive belief in the harmlessness of human self-interest or expressiveness. Even religious communities have fallen prey to viewing some segments of humanity, for example, the oppressed, as free of sin and have seen their revolutionary praxis as salvific. Or, if less politically inclined, religious groups have too often viewed self-liberation through psychological or spiritual exercises as a simple possibility.

The Twofold Reign of God

It is Niebuhr's expert but implicit use of the twofold reign of God that makes him such an effective proponent of the paradoxical vision. We have already established above that Niebuhr insists on the sharp distinction between the saving gospel and all human work. That is an important working assumption in his further use of the law/gospel distinction so central to two-kingdoms thinking. First of all, it guards against the law being made into the gospel. That is, it insists that the gospel of Christ's redeeming mercy is what saves, not any kind of human action, no matter how righteous that appears. (On careful analysis, the action is never completely righteous even though it might outwardly conform to the demands of God's law. More likely it falls far short of the stringent demands of God's law, even in its outward expression.)

Niebuhr, however, spent most of his ammunition on those who would make the gospel into a law, that is, would take the radical religious and moral norms of the gospel as direct guides for human action in a fallen world. His protestations against Protestant liberalism were about just that. They constantly made "the impossible possible," the radical norm of agape love manifested in Christ, a "simple possibility" in human relations, especially human group relations. This led them, erroneously, he believed, into pacifism in international relations and sentimentalism in domestic affairs, particularly in industrial relations.

In short, Niebuhr believed that one could not take the highest principle of the Christian religious and moral vision and make it into a law or norm to guide human affairs. What is applicable in the kingdom of God, agape love, is not directly applicable in human affairs. Its transcendent character, for one thing, obviates such a strategy. The fallenness of the world, for another, makes such moralism ineffectual and finally irresponsible.

On the contrary, Niebuhr argued, principles of justice—equality and freedom—are more fit for guiding a fallen world than agape love. Those principles are likely to be partially achieved more by balances of power than by pious exhortations to love. But the human capacity for justice, commanded by conscience or original justice, plays an important role. It can achieve a modicum of disinterested justice in the welter of competing interests so that legitimate claims are recognized and redressed.

Thus can humans achieve a relatively more just order than before, even though such progress is neither assured nor permanent. Any partial achievement can well break down in the dynamic interplay of interests.

Niebuhr was a master in recognizing the dynamic character of God's law, though he did not use that language. The pressure for a higher degree of justice comes from a number of sources. It arises from the demands of groups that are oppressed. Their essential being claims more just treatment than has been accorded them. It also arises from those in more favored groups whose conscience is pricked by the claims of the oppressed for justice. It arises when codified laws of justice are used to redress imbalances that were unrecognized until some "prophetic" group noticed them. God uses all these means to exert the demands of his law.

But above all, at least for Christians, the pressure for dynamic reform of human structures comes from the norm of agape love itself. It is precisely on this point that Niebuhr advances the paradoxical vision's capacity for envisioning and pursuing a more expansive notion of justice. He insists on relating the norm of agape love more effectively to the struggle for justice than anyone before him in the paradoxical tradition. Yet he does not fall into the Reformed trap of making that norm, or God's law for the redeemed, into a direct blueprint for a transformed society.

Niebuhr certainly does see that the two ways that God reigns in the world, through the coercive ways of the law and through the agape love of the gospel, are related in important ways. He elaborates the encounter of love with justice in a dialectical way. Agape love, the "impossible possible," is related to the rough and tumble of the earthly search for justice in four ways: (1) as indeterminate possibility and obligation, (2) as indiscriminate criticism and judgment, (3) as the standard for discriminate decisions, and (4) as contrition and forgiveness.[16] This dialectical work of love applies not only to the struggle for justice in corporate affairs, but to all human relations. Agape love judges, summons, critiques, and allows forgiveness in all the manifold relations of earthly loves. (This is another way of saying that the summons of agape operates in all Christian vocations. It acts as the yeast that leavens the lump.)

It is important to note the third point listed above in the account of how love relates to justice. Love operates as a source of discriminate decisions. It helps to discern the proper direction when assessing competing goals and means of pursuing justice. The principle of love helps to make proximate decisions between the greater and lesser of goods and evils. It does not operate alone, for we humans have sources from reason and experience that help us make such proximate choices. This movement from the central convictions of Christian faith through the proximate principles of justice to judgments on particular policies must be done with both boldness and humility. Judging the relative merits of competing policies, however, is a matter of prudential wisdom

16. Niebuhr, *Niebuhr on Politics*, pp. 154-59.

and should not fracture the unity that Christians ought to have on the ultimate principle.

For Niebuhr, this obligation to make relative distinctions between the shades of gray in this fallen world is essential to genuine responsibility. If we do not take such an obligation seriously, we will end up missing the proximate good that is reachable in our search for illusive perfection. Such is the danger of soft utopians (sentimentalists) and hard utopians (fascists and communists) alike. The highest good can be the enemy of the relatively better.

What is extraordinary about the way Niebuhr handles the paradoxical vision is his ability to be steadfastly committed to the pursuit of a higher justice without becoming either bitterly resigned to or sentimentally naive about the resistance to that pursuit. There is nothing static in Niebuhr's thought to discourage social reform. This capacity of his thought was no doubt anchored in the conviction and temperament of the man himself. Regardless of its source, its effect is to make Niebuhr's Christian realism the finest exemplar of the paradoxical vision in American history.

History

This brings us to Niebuhr's paradoxical conception of history. It follows as a corollary to all that has gone heretofore. On the one side of the paradox is the conviction that history does indeed have meaning. It has been revealed in the whole biblical story in general and in the event of Christ particularly. God's will for a kingdom of uncoerced love is the end and meaning of history. God's sovereign power will assure that that meaning will prevail in the end. This unity of meaning, however, is grasped by faith and not by sight. Christians are reminded that the fullest revelation and demonstration of love ended on a cross, crucified by the 'best and brightest' that humanity had to offer at the time. So the love revealed in Christ cannot be triumphant in history. Yet, because history cannot completely contradict its underlying meaning and norm, love will not be fully tragic in history either. Human actions toward love and justice can have real historical effect.

On the other side of the paradox lies the stubborn reality of human sin and finitude. This means that history cannot be redemptive out of its own resources, cannot be its own Christ. It has no order of progress that will eventually expunge human sin and finitude. Indeed, Niebuhr sees that some of the greatest evils in history are the result of efforts to overcome its limits by imposing human solutions on it. This is the tendency of soft and hard utopians alike, though the former are less dangerous because of their reluctance to use coercive methods to achieve their goals, while the latter will not stop short of the most horrendous methods to arrive at their totalitarian goals.[17]

So humans in history are caught between having the truth and not having it, between achieving justice and falling far short of it. Those who believe in the objective values of goodness, truth, and beauty are tempted to claim too much. Those who do not believe in them are likely to acquiesce in their skepticism to historical evils. Genuine tolerance is most likely to be practiced by those who grasp these paradoxes of history.[18]

This paradox means further that our end (as chronological time) will come before our end (as purpose) is reached. All things move toward fulfillment of meaning and death.[19] Therefore, hope is necessary if we are to bear the burdens of history. All human efforts toward the kingdom are diminished by sin and finitude in history, but they are given meaning by their transcendent source and fulfillment beyond history. Each deed of love is related to its transcendent source and therefore is an approximation of the kingdom of God. Yet it is only an approximation to be fulfilled beyond history. The kingdom constantly impinges upon history but cannot be realized within history.

17. Ibid., pp. 12-37.
18. Niebuhr, *Nature and Destiny*, 2:235ff.
19. Ibid., p. 287.

History exhibits growth, such as technological development, but not progress. The capacity for evil grows alongside the capacity for good. The magnification of human powers through technology merely writes the possibilities for both catastrophe and triumph in larger script. Therefore, history cumulates rather than solves the problems of history. This means that a final clash between good and evil is inevitable. Humans will not be able to avoid that final conflict, after which the final judgment will occur. Thus will history be brought to a close and its full meaning disclosed and realized. Only the sovereign power of God will bring the kingdom to fruition.[20] Christian hope is in God.

> Such 'otherworldliness' is not an escape from history. It gives us a fulcrum from which we can operate in history. It gives us a faith by which we can seek to fulfill our historic tasks without illusions and without despair.[21]

Summary Reflections

Niebuhr's method of proceeding in life and thought was as paradoxical as their actual substance. He proceeded dialectically, playing off one polarity against another and finding his judgments somewhere in the complex interplay of those polarities. That is why theologians of both the political left and right can authentically claim him as a mentor. Both Robert MacAfee Brown on the left and Michael Novak on the right have grounds for claiming to be genuine students of Niebuhr. Moreover, Niebuhr's own judgments about particular issues evolved over his lifetime. He was willing to admit that he had changed his mind. But the basic framework of the paradoxical vision remained solid from the mid-thirties onward.

The particular way that Niebuhr worked through that framework has been immensely important for American public theology, both for his own and for that of the many who

20. Ibid., p. 318.
21. Niebuhr, *Niebuhr on Politics,* p. 208.

were taught by him. He interpreted American history in *The Irony of American History* through the prism of irony, an interpretative category closely related to the paradoxical vision.[22] He employed the framework in a way that awakened American Lutherans from their earlier quietism. He strongly chastened a liberalized Reformed tradition that had degenerated into a sentimentality that tended toward soft utopianism even as it sympathized with harder varieties. He brought the insights of classical Pauline-Augustinian-Lutheran thinking to bear on the secular thought of the day. Christian realism has had wide effects on many of the secular elite who have in turn influenced American life deeply.

Niebuhr's thinking remains one of the major paradigms for doing public theology, even though his vision went into partial eclipse for a time. Because his legacy is enduring, however, it is enjoying a marked revival. It is currently being employed to critize the temptations that beckon so alluringly in the liberation theologies of our day. It continues to provide a paradoxical nudge to American theologies that too easily forget its vital lessons.

Few can summarize the crucial contributions of the paradoxical vision better than Niebuhr did in these words:

> Reformation insights must be related to the whole range of human experiences more "dialectically" than the Reformation succeeded in doing. The "yes" and "no" of its dialectical affirmations: that the Christian is "justus et peccator," "both sinner and righteous;" that history fulfills and negates the Kingdom of God; that grace is continuous with, and in contradiction to, nature; that Christ is what we ought to be and also what we cannot be; that the power of God is in us and that the power of God is against us in judgment and mercy; that all these affirmations which are but varied forms of the one central paradox of the relation of the Gospel to history must be applied to the experiences of life from top to bottom.[23]

22. Niebuhr, *The Irony of American History* (New York: Scribners, 1952)
23. Niebuhr, *Nature and Destiny,* 2:204.

GLENN TINDER: HESITANT RADICAL

Tinder presents a sharp contrast to Niebuhr. A layman, he came to the Christian faith without prior involvement in a church. He has not been an activist caught up directly in the causes of the day. He has not until recently gained the attention of the churches or religious intellectuals. He is not brash and bold in the public presentation of himself. On the contrary, he has quietly plied his trade as a political philosopher. Over the years he has become influential among American political scientists and has carved a place for his thought in national journals. His major work, *The Political Meaning of Christianity*, constitutes his most extended argument about the engagement of Christianity and the public world. It is a more systematic treatment of themes he explored in earlier books.

The Political Meaning of Christianity is a fresh, contemporary application of the paradoxical vision to political matters. Its author leaves little doubt that he is self-consciously operating from that vision. "My attitudes are more Lutheran than Calvinist," he says as he identifies himself with the "Reformation" tradition.[24] Kierkegaard, that intrepid interpreter of the sharper edges of the Lutheran vision, is a particular favorite of Tinder. He begins his textbook, *Political Thinking*, with this quote from Kierkegaard:

> The paradox is the source of the thinker's passion, and the thinker without a paradox is like a lover without feeling: a paltry mediocrity. The supreme paradox of all thought is the attempt to discover something that thought cannot think.[25]

In developing his argument, he not only recasts the classical Lutheran themes in fresh concepts and language, but develops his own interpretation of what the Christian life should look

24. Tinder, *Political Meaning*, p. 2.
25. Søren Kierkegaard, as quoted in the frontispiece of Tinder's *Political Thinking*.

like in the light of those themes. He calls that interpretation "the prophetic stance," which we shall explore presently.

Before we can treat that subject adequately, however, we must begin with Tinder's assessment of the paradox of the human predicament, which necessitates the paradox of God's saving action.

The Paradox of Human Nature

"All are sacred and none are good," is the truth of the matter.[26] All humans are sacred because of being created with a destiny. They have an earthly destiny, which is the "free and temporal unfoldment of their essential being."[27] Earthly destiny includes, among many other glories of becoming human, the use of one's talents for the service of others. Human destiny does not end with earthly history though. The final destiny of humans is an eternal one in which they share the life of God. Both dimensions of human destiny, however, can be refused. We are not compelled by God to embrace them.

Further, humans are sacred because God has exalted them in Christ. Christ's work of salvation lifts them into God's kingdom, which is peopled exclusively with royalty. God's agape love in Christ joyously accepts them; it refuses to judge. All humans, then, are invited into that kingdom, though they may decline the invitation. Therefore, all have great worth and dignity by virtue of their creation and redemption.

At the same time humans are fallen. They refuse to accept their earthly destiny; they fritter their essential being away. Moreover, they resist their exaltation by Christ. They demand their own self-exaltation. In doing these things, which stems from an inevitable and persisting "determination to stay inside the world," they ironically insure their debasement.[28] Their lives become encumbered by troublesome and

26. Tinder, "Can We Be Good without God?" *Atlantic Monthly,* December 1989, p. 76.
27. Ibid., p. 72.
28. Ibid., p. 78.

death-dealing fate (the untoward, cumulative effects of sin) instead of destiny.

Perhaps even more than Niebuhr, Tinder views the actions of groups as more radically fallen than individuals. Solitary individuals can accept the exaltation of God, but groups cannot.[29] They cannot respond to authentic transcendence; they are too bound up in their own survival and power. Moreover, in pressing their own self-interest, they inevitably use coercive means, which to Tinder is always evil. Indeed, Tinder is so skeptical of institutions that a number of critics think he sees no possibilities for corporate human existence. On this point he reminds one of the Niebuhr of *Moral Man and Immoral Society*. But, also like Niebuhr, he does not reach quietistic or cynical conclusions about possibilities within history, as we shall soon see.

Tinder believes that this Christian view of human nature is far wiser than its secular and religious competitors. Their mistaken notions of human nature do not hold the paradox together. They deny human exaltation and become cynics in their negative evaluation of the general run of humanity. Without historical and eternal destinies given by God, humans are judged by cynics according to their intensity and quality. Since only a few humans possess those qualities in superlative degree, most humans are viewed from this viewpoint with disgust. There is but a step or two from that judgment to cruel injustice for much of the human race.

If many estimations of human nature deny human dignity, others tend toward what Tinder calls "idealism." Idealism finds in humans the capacities for self-exaltation. If the God-man (Christ) is rejected as the ground of our dignity, the man-god rushes in to take his place. The man-god most often takes collective form. Tinder thinks that the twentieth century is bloodsoaked with the historical repercussions of the idealistic self-exaltation of the man-god. Marxism, Nazism, and Freudianism are all destructive efforts of man to become God.

29. Ibid., p. 82.

In recent decades, the "universal disaster of revolution" continues to press the case for the self-saving capacities of the man-god.[30] Tinder believes that history bears out the dangers of destroying the paradox of the Christian view of human nature.

God's Exaltation of Humans

Given the deep tendency in humans toward self-obsession, there is little that humans can do to present themselves acceptable to God. However, they refuse to accept their condition. They constantly strive toward self-exaltation, which results in a continual round of judging. As humans try to find some place above the common herd, they constantly judge each other. They find each other wanting, and secretly find themselves falling short in this eternal cycle of judging. The judging further results in injustice toward those thought to be inferior or evil. "The archetype of sin is the reduction of a person to the thing we call a corpse."[31]

The predicament of human sin can only be assuaged by a love that in the final instance does not judge. This is the love of God revealed and expressed in the God-man, Jesus Christ.

> The agape of God consists in the bestowal of a destiny, and that of human beings in its recognition through faith. Since a destiny is not a matter of empirical observation, a person with a destiny is, so to speak, invisible. But every person has a destiny. Hence the process of mutual scrutiny is in vain, and even the most objective judgments of other people are fundamentally false. Agape arises from a realization of this and is therefore expressed in a refusal to judge.[32]

Thus salvation has to do with what God does for us in the God-man. Before God our posture is totally receptive. Any

30. Ibid.
31. Ibid., p. 78.
32. Ibid., p. 72.

move toward self-justification through our own acts spoils the gift that God has given us and gets us involved again in the terrible round of judging, which we are bound to lose. In Tinder's interpretation there can be no claim on our part that we participate in our own salvation. It is pure gift. Further, as we shall see, the Christian life that follows exaltation through Christ is characterized by a peculiar hesitancy. Humans ought not claim too much for their sanctification either.

The Twofold Rule of God

As we have seen, Tinder carefully avoids one of the great dangers of failing to distinguish the twofold reign of God through law and gospel. He insists that the gospel is really gospel. "Any relationship between man and God must be established by God. Given our incapacity for entering into God's life, God must enter into ours."[33] It is not a religious or moral activity of the law that humans can accomplish. Tinder does not make the law into the gospel.

On the other hand, Tinder does not make the gospel into a law. The radical love of the gospel cannot become a direct guide for life in the fallen world, though it has powerful indirect effects. Tinder's view of the fallenness of both individuals and groups, but particularly of groups, prevents any lapse into sentimentalism. He does not believe that "constructive Christianity" can transform the public world. Christians inhabit an alien world that is far from the City of God. That should be clear from his analysis of sin outlined above.

But the earthly kingdom, the realm of God's left-hand rule, is a dynamic world in which real change can take place. Contrary to the more robust activism of Niebuhr, however, Tinder is likely to see that change as the mysterious product of God's sovereign will rather than human achievement. It is precisely here where Tinder seems more akin to H. Richard

33. Tinder, *Political Meaning,* p. 84.

Niebuhr than to Reinhold Niebuhr. We must await "the leadership of God in history."[34] Christians must simply have faith that God is in charge and not be too bumptious with their own prideful acts. Above all, an aggressive ethic of responsibility in which humans claim control over the direction of history is anathema to Tinder. Such pride will lead to the tragedies that accompany any attempt at self-exaltation.

Because God obviously cares for all human creatures by giving them both a temporal and an eternal destiny, this world is precious even though fallen. Therefore Christians must be responsible in this world even though they are not responsible for it.

Tinder thinks that the twofold rule of God has been fruitfully conjoined in Western history. The gospel has had powerful effect in the realm of the law. Surprisingly, after his pessimism about the world, Tinder can say that "the idea of the exalted individual is the spiritual center of Western politics."[35] He knows that this idea is often forgotten and violated, but without it politics would "become altogether what it is at present only in part—an affair of expediency and self-interest."[36]

Under prodding by the noble idea of the exalted individual, governments in Western society have moved toward policies that treat humans considerately (above all that means respecting their liberty) and equally and that recognize that these values should be applied universally.[37] Tinder believes that these values are supported by other noble humanistic philosophies but that none of them can supply the grounds and motivation for adequately maintaining and extending these values. Only the Judeo-Christian tradition can do that.[38]

That these values came to affect Western politics seems to be the joint product of Christian coercion, Enlightenment

34. Ibid., p. 14.
35. Ibid., p. 33.
36. Ibid., p. 34.
37. Ibid., pp. 31-35.
38. Tinder, *Can We Be Good?* p. 70.

application of Christian values, and, above all, the mysterious beneficence of God. But if Christians were once coercive in imposing their values on a recalcitrant world, that time ought now to be over. Tinder believes that the "prophetic stance" of Christians ought not involve them in the application of coercive power. This is an obvious difference from the Lutheran willingness to involve Christians in the exercise of power in their calling. It presents likewise a sharp contrast with Reinhold Niebuhr's conviction that involvement in power is an important ingredient in seeking a fuller justice. Perhaps it is not that Tinder rejects power for everyone, but, in an almost sectarian way, he discourages it for Christians, as well as for the church.

Rather, the prophetic stance means "offering one's own weakness as a medium for the sovereignty of God in history."[39] This involves political suffering, not striking back, and solidarity with the suffering people of the world.[40] Suffering of this sort is quintessentially an individual act. Groups or institutions are not capable of it. Just as Jesus was crucified alone, so the solitary Christian follows his or her master.

Christians should make no efforts to pursuade the state to give coercive muscle to their explicit religious values. The church's calling is to bring people into the presence of God through the gospel, not exerting power in the world. Religious coercion is the route to intolerance and incivility. Nevertheless, Christians should demand and receive attention. If and when they get it, they then must speak with integrity and power. They must enter into free discussion where their ideas might gain acceptance by those who do not believe. Tinder places strong emphasis on careful speaking and listening, for that sort of serious interchange is the way we accord each other the respect befitting creatures with destinies given by God.

Christian participation in the public realm is shaped by the prophetic stance. It means waiting for God in history, solitude

39. Tinder, *Political Meaning,* p. 9.
40. Ibid., pp. 211ff.

and reflective inaction, attentiveness, and then availability for acting when the fitting time has come to fill the opening God has given.[41] "The prophetic stance might be characterized simply as the personal and political bearing of one who accepts without illusions, but also without despair, the hard liberation offered by the far country."[42]

The Paradox of History

All the human goods we long for—true freedom, equality, and especially community—are unreachable in our fallen history. They are tragic ideals. They are realizable only in God's kingdom, which will come when God wills it. But these values are present proleptically in our history. We are called to strive for them in the way I outlined above. "To practice love is to be allied with the deepest currents of life."[43]

So we live in two cities and in two aeons. We cannot ignore or fail to respond to either. But our lives in this world are not filled with illusions about what is possible in history. To believe in Christian eschatology, Tinder says, is to refuse historical idolatry. "Eschatology relativizes history. It does this by saying that the meaning of history does not lie in history itself."[44]

Christians are called out from nations, parties, and political movements to live between the contemporary age and the end time. Paradoxically, they can live as good citizens in the world only if they are able to live in faith, hope, and love as what they inescapably are—strangers in the world.[45] Their responsibility is "to be attentive to God, or transcendence, to the deepest necessities of history, and to human beings everywhere; and to be available for the future that is given us."[46]

41. Ibid., pp. 68ff.
42. Ibid., p. 96.
43. Tinder, *Can We Be Good?* p. 84.
44. Tinder, *Political Meaning*, p. 89.
45. Ibid., p. 98.
46. Ibid., p. 243.

Summary Reflections

Tinder's Christian personalism, which he believes is close to Luther's own view and is certainly akin to Kierkegaard's, accentuates his pessimistic assessment of the possibilities of social history. Institutions are crude and brutal in comparison to individuals. True community simply cannot be realized by political effort; a good society is one that allows room for true community to develop on a much smaller scale and in a more spontaneous manner. This attitude, in addition to his conviction that coercion is always evil, presses him more toward Augustine than Niebuhr among representatives of the paradoxical vision. Moreover, his interpretation of Christian discipleship as "political suffering" disallows vigorous Christian participation in the power struggles that Niebuhr believes are necessary for the achievement of a greater justice.

Yet Tinder is a political philosopher who strongly endorses the increase of liberty, equality, and social care. Christians as individuals must speak out strongly for these things. But the management of history is up to God, not to Christians, nor to other humans, for that matter. Tinder combines a Reinhold Niebuhrian concern for just goals with a Richard Niebuhrian distrust of human power as the means to those goals. Like Richard Niebuhr, Tinder believes we must wait on God in history. This is not too far from Luther's belief that he had very little to do with the unfolding of the Reformation. He believed it was divine work. "While Melanchthon and I sat drinking good German beer, God struck the Papacy a mighty blow."

So, in spite of certain eccentricities in his view of the calling of Christians, Tinder works from a profound understanding of the paradoxical vision. His "hesitancy" may be a far cry from the robust activism of Reinhold Niebuhr, but he, like Niebuhr, proceeds from a penetrating grasp of the guiding themes of the paradoxical vision.

RICHARD JOHN NEUHAUS: NEOCONSERVATIVE

An obvious difference between Neuhaus and our other two representatives of the paradoxical vision is that he is not an academic, though he is certainly an intellectual. He does not have an academic doctorate, which has prompted him to remark that his honorary degrees are not like academic degrees. "Mine are earned," he says. Such acerbic wit is very characteristic of this intellectual gadfly.

Neuhaus, raised in Canada in a strong Missouri Synod Lutheran tradition, has experienced a number of major changes of direction in his life—from left-wing radicalism to neoconservatism, from parish life in a Brooklyn ghetto to cosmopolitan life as a nationally known author and activist, and from Lutheranism to Catholicism. What has remained constant in all this, at least up to this point, are his theological commitments.

It is unnecessary to work systematically through Neuhaus's theology. It is classically Lutheran in its radical doctrine of grace, its view of the mission of the church, its paradoxical view of human nature and history, and its dedication to the twofold rule of God.[47] It is rather the application of these themes to contemporary life—both church and society—that is most interesting.

In the following pages I will organize my reflections around three ongoing tasks that have occupied Neuhaus's attention: his criticism of liberal Christianity for its inability to distinguish between the gospel and human work, as well as its

47. Neuhaus has spelled his paradoxical vison out in many places over the years, but a most compressed summary of his view can be found in "To Serve the Lord of All: Law, Gospel and Social Responsibility," which appeared in *Dialog* 30, no. 2 (Fall 1990), pp. 140-49. Interestingly enough, this was one of his last writings before he moved to Catholicism. In it, however, he makes clear that such a move does not mean a rejection of the paradoxical vision. Rather, it means for him that the Catholicism of the day may be a more hospitable context for that vision than that of official Lutheranism (pp. 148, 149). Neuhaus's Lutheran theology has been influenced by his long intellectual and personal friendship with Wolfhart Pannenberg. Pannenberg's emphasis on eschatology has meant a more dynamic view of history than was typical of classical Lutheran theological ethics. Also, Pannenberg's insistence that revelation and reason not be sharply opposed has also entered into Neuhaus's presentation of the paradoxical vision.

deficient understanding of the mission of the church; his argument for the connection of the Christian view of human nature and democracy as a political arrangement; and his polemics against both secularism and sacred politics as violations of a proper understanding of the twofold reign of God.

The Gospel and Human Work

Like Niebuhr in his day, Neuhaus has focused much of his criticism on the Christian liberals of his time. He fervently believes that they have neglected the gospel in their search for salvation within history through human work. Enlisting Bonhoeffer in his criticism of the Reformed churches' propensity to crusade for some 'redemptive' earthly cause, Neuhaus cites him: "This means that the essence of the gospel does not lie in the solution of human problems, and that the solution of human problems cannot be the essential task of the church. Of course, it does not follow that the church has no tasks at all in this direction."[48]

Neuhaus has exerted great intellectual energy in combatting the notion that social movements will bring salvation, whether those movements are fueled by political expectation (revolution), ecological fervor, the hope for cultural transformation (feminism, multiculturalism, gay liberation) or for psychological deliverance (therapy). What is doubly infuriating to him is that these notions are often supported by the churches, particularly what he calls the "old-line," or more recently the "side-line," churches of the former Protestant establishment.

Not only are these social movements generally commended by church bureaucrats whose political biases are pervasively left-wing, they are not essentially what the church is about. The church's unique mission is to proclaim the gospel that bestows a "spiritual righteousness that is entirely the gift of God in Christ Jesus."[49]

48. Neuhaus, quoting Bonhoeffer in "To Serve," p. 144.
49. Ibid., p. 141.

Unfortunately, through a diminished belief that leads to misplaced emphases, the old-line churches have been tempted to let "the world set the agenda for the church." This then allows the world to crowd out the gospel and encourages the church to replace the gospel with various sorts of "prophetic" statements and actions. These "prophetic" works are generally against the so-called status quo and for the sorts of movements we listed above.

If such misplaced emphases neglect the essence of the gospel they also deflect attention from the core moral commitments and practices of the Christian faith toward an obsession with social and political policy. Neuhaus strongly believes that Christian moral convictions lead directly to a reverence for human life. This reverence, based on our creation and redemption by God, is under attack on issues dealing with both the beginning and end of life. Neuhaus has been a stalwart in efforts by Christians to protect and cherish unborn life. He has also supported efforts to resist active euthanasia. On these two fronts he believes Christian insight is clear for Christian behavior, though he is more circumspect about what social policies should be enacted.

Likewise, Neuhaus believes that the church must continue to affirm classical Christian teachings on sexual ethics. He argues for heterosexuality as God's intention for human sexual relations and holds that marriage is the only place for those relations.

Above all, Neuhaus believes that core Christian moral values lead Christians to works of charity. These works are hands-on efforts to feed the hungry, give drink to the thirsty, clothe the naked, harbor the stranger, visit the sick, minister to the prisoner, and bury the dead. Christian communities have been and continue to be the largest network in Western societies for such caring. When they perform these works they demonstrate agape love.

Unfortunately several trends have appeared that undercut these traditional works. Churches diminish their commitments to direct deeds of love for the sake of a more political role. They devote too much time and money to searching for "root causes" (which always turn out to be defined from a left-wing perspective), making statements, and "advocating" in a directly political manner. Individual and corporate good deeds give way to politics.

Further, the government continues to expand its role in funding and regulating voluntary institutions devoted to works of charity. The support is good, as Neuhaus and Berger argue in *To Empower People*, but the regulation often is not. As it becomes more detailed and intrusive, it tends to deracinate those institutions. They lose their character as Christian institutions.[50]

The churches, Neuhaus believes, have neglected their unique mission in this rush toward politics. His major objection concerns the relinquishment of vigorous proclamation and evangelism, but he believes their misplaced priorities have other untoward effects. "Thus political contests are moralized and even theologized in a manner that is detrimental to democracy and to the internal life of the churches."[51]

Neuhaus objects to the politicizing of the church's mission not merely because such a process inevitably is organized around the sacred topics of the left. Rather, he objects to direct involvement in principle. In a most surprising move, he argues that even social statements are by and large illegitimate, especially if they are prescriptive. All direct, prescriptive incursions into economic and political life involve the church in a false claim of authority and competence in that realm. Moreover, the direct use of power is contrary to the church's calling to rely solely on the Word. Such incursions make the church just another political agent among the many operating in God's left-hand kingdom, which is a betrayal of the constituting mission of the church. They deflect the church from its calling to support many vocations so that Christian laypeople will take their proper political role.

50. Berger and Neuhaus, *Empower.*
51. Neuhaus, "To Serve," p. 146.

The only time the church should speak directly is in matters of *status confessionis*. These are instances in which a social practice is clearly contrary to the Word of God, that is, it goes counter to the very essence of the gospel. Such occasions are of great solemnity and should not be proliferated to include mere ideological disagreements. On genuine matters of "confessional status," the church should speak only under the pressure of necessity and then only negatively. On other matters of social and political disagreement "where it is not necessary for the church to speak, it is necessary that the church not speak."[52]

Above all, Neuhaus rejects any claim to "Christian politics." The straightline connection between core Christian religious/moral claims and any political program is anathema to him. Such a connection legalizes the gospel and sacralizes the civil realm, a severe confusion of the twofold rule of God.[53] Nevertheless, as we shall see later, there should be important and fruitful *indirect* interactions of the two kingdoms.

Human Nature and Democracy

Some of Neuhaus's most controversial actions involve his important role in establishing the Institute for Religion and Democracy (IRD), based in Washington, D.C. That institute was selected by the "Third World Christians" who produced *The Road to Damascus: Kairos and Conversion* as the epitome of "right-wing heresy."[54] Such rage was partly stimulated by the institute's staunch anticommunism, which the "Third

52. Ibid., p. 145.
53. Ibid., p. 141.
54. *The Road to Damascus: Kairos and Conversion* (Washington, D.C.: Center for Concern, 1989), p. 22. This "Christian-Marxist" document, produced months before the collapse of Soviet communism, is a caricature of the danger of conflating the twofold reign of God. "The Reign of God is this world completely transformed in accordance with God's plan" (p. 12). Further, it is clear that the writers know God's plan, which is to transform the world through revolutionary socialism.

World Christians" branded an impediment to progressive change.

Neuhaus drafted the institute's statement of principles. Besides affirming that the church's task is first of all to be the church, it encourages Christians to resist totalitarianism at every opportunity and to promote the development of democracy everywhere in the world. There is, Neuhaus argued, "a necessary linkage between Christian faith and human freedom." Respect for God's creatures means respect for their freedom, both public and private. At that moment in history (early eighties), he contended, American democracy was the main bearer of respect for human freedom, especially religious freedom, and Soviet communism was the primary bearer of the totalitarian alternative.[55]

Neuhaus increased the pressure by arguing that many people in the mainstream Protestant bureaucracies, especially those in the ecumenical agencies, did not share this "understanding of democracy and America's role in the world." Some, tempted by the this-worldly promises of revolutionary socialism, became "apologists for oppression."[56]

These charges, of course, set off quite a response from the mainstream churches, although the accusations in retrospect seem pretty much on target. However, the IRD itself was not able to transcend political alignment. It became a center for neoconservative thought done by Christians. Nevertheless, James Reichley asserts that the "IRD at least performed the worthwhile function of offering on some issues a moderate conservative alternative to the liberal-left policies that have generally held sway since the 1960s within mainline Protestantism."[57] Since the end of the Cold War, the institute has devoted itself to defending religious liberty wherever it is threatened.

55. "Christianity and Democracy" (Washington, D.C.: Institute on Religion and Democracy, 1981), pp. 4-10.

56. Ibid., p. 12.

57. Reichley, *Religion and Political Life* (Washington: Brookings Institution, 1985), p. 338.

The Twofold Rule of God

We have already examined in some detail Neuhaus's critique of Protestant mainline churches for confusing the two kingdoms. They neglect the church's divinely appointed calling to proclaim the gospel and make it an agent in the left-hand kingdom instead. In doing so they change the gospel into the law and the law into the gospel. They wind up promoting a dangerous monism.

But the church is not the only guilty party in collapsing the two realms into one. Aggressive secularism does so by denying the reality of any transcendent realm and by sealing off the secular world from any influence by values of transcendent origin. It does not uphold an honest secularity in which there is the possibility of something more than what the scientific worldview can determine. It collapses all reality into a mundane, one-dimensional plane.

Neuhaus believes that the fundamental battle going on in the modern world is a cultural one, having to do with meanings and values. Political and economic debates are reflections of deeper disagreements. There is a veritable *Kulturkampf* in our land. The most dangerous opponent of genuine democracy and ordered freedom in the West is a militant secularism that aims at a "naked public square."

The phrase "naked public square," from the title of Neuhaus's book, has now entered the American vocabulary. It points to the effort to keep all public institutions and practices free of religious or religiously based symbols, values, and expressions. Further, in its more virulent forms, militant secularism uses government regulatory power to intervene in religious institutions and practices themselves. Such secularism is the bitter fruit of making the kingdom of the left radically autonomous.

Major negative effects issue from such strategies. Most harmful is the suppression of the free exercise of religion guaranteed by our Constitution, which insures that the state recognize some measure of transcendence beyond its own actions. If such guarantees are violated, the "tyranny of the political" is right around the corner. Such suppression also impedes the proclamation of the gospel and the nurturing of Christian community, a situation which, if pressed hard, might well call for resistance or even martyrdom.

But other serious problems follow. The public realm is deprived of those substantive, religiously based moral values that give order to our liberties. Without them, Neuhaus argues, we will fall into a chaotic pluralism or a tyranny by some secular hegemonic philosophy. In either case, the basic religious commitments of the vast majority of the population will be ignored or suppressed and democracy will be seriously threatened. "The American experiment is severely and unnaturally crippled if the religiously grounded values of the American people are ruled out of order in public discourse."[58]

Summary Reflections

In recent years Neuhaus has devoted his efforts to making sure that religiously grounded values do have an outlet in public discussion. His Institute on Religion in Public Life in New York City is one of America's main locations for doing public theology. It holds conferences that always include serious theological reflection on the pressing social issues selected for attention. Most conferences result in books for public use.

The institute publishes *First Things: A Monthly Journal of Religion and Public Life*, which has become an important organ of public discussion of issues relevant to both church and society. Neuhaus himself writes regular columns and articles in national newspapers and journals. His many books deal with public challenges in the light of Christian theological and ethical wisdom. He provides an important model for relating religion to public life, for proper interaction of the two kingdoms.

58. Richard John Neuhaus, *The Naked Public Square* (Grand Rapids, Michigan: Eerdmans, 1984), p. 51.

As is obvious, Neuhaus focuses on the life of the churches, especially the Lutheran, far more than either Niebuhr or Tinder. He believes that crucial elements of the paradoxical vision have been significantly diminished in their life and thought. Therefore he contends with the churches, sometimes drawing their ire but more often earning their studied inattention. They keep hoping he will go away.

But Neuhaus's paradoxical vision also leads him to a strong critique of modern society, which he believes will become dangerously impoverished if it ignores or suppresses the religious convictions of its people. Society needs its moral wellsprings in religion if it is to flourish.

So we have three individual practioners of the paradoxical vision. A theological professor and liberal reformer, a political philosopher and hesitant radical, and a freelance writer and neoconservative activist make up our varied sample. They hold in common, however, the crucial themes of the paradoxical vision. They have borne witness to those themes in ways that have helped to correct some of the untoward tendencies of our Reformed-haunted nation. They have had more effect on public discourse in our nation than has official Lutheranism. Yet both official and individual contributions have been important. The paradoxical vision is not without its public witnesses.

PART III

▼ ▼ ▼ ▼

LIVE CONNECTIONS: HOW THEOLOGY BECOMES PUBLIC

I have argued throughout this book that the paradoxical vision ought to and in fact does engage the public world in which we live. The rule of God includes the whole creation through both law and gospel. Therefore Christians are called to make the law and gospel of God relevant to all spheres of life, not just to their own personal existence. The church is also called to address the whole Word of God—both law and gospel— to its communicants and to the world around them. The paradoxical vision indeed possesses a public dimension that cannot be repudiated without denying the vision itself.

The paradoxical tradition is not alone in its demand for the public expression of its theological convictions; the vast majority of religious traditions engage their public environments. The American scene is rife with lively interplay between religion and public life. New issues continually come to the fore; some subside while perennial concerns persist.

The continuing extent of this public expression of religious conviction surprises and irritates those who hoped the public influence of religion was in inexorable decline as modern technological civilization advanced. Even though many secularists attempt with some success to ignore, marginalize, or reduce public expressions of religion to something else, there is a discernible note of authentic religious conviction in the efforts of people to envision a public way of life grounded in something beyond mundane reality. Live connections between religion and public life simply will not go away. And, under the American Constitution, religious views certainly can legally and freely be expressed publicly. Even the strictest proponents of separation of church and state cannot make a convincing case for suppressing religiously based public argument. To what extent and in what manner the churches wish to exercise their rights of expression are other matters.

So the crucial question is not *whether* theology ought to and will become public; rather, it concerns *how* religion and public life ought to be related. More specifically, the key question before us has to do with the paradoxical vision's answers to such a question. Does the public theological framework provided by the paradoxical vision have something important to say about the *how* of religion's public expression?

In part 3 I address that question by developing a typology of possible interactions between religion and public life. As I develop it, I will also comment on the limits and possibilities of each type from the paradoxical vision's viewpoint. The exposition will thus include both analytical and evaluative elements.[1]

The typology breaks into two major parts—indirect and direct connections. Each part will provide the focus for a chapter. "Indirect" means that the church as an institution does not get involved in public theology; it does not become a public actor as an institution. Rather, it relies on indirect modes of influence and action through its laity or through independent associations organized by its laity and/or clergy. Neither individual nor associational efforts are under the control or direction of the church itself. In contrast, "direct"

1. The following two chapters are an elaboration of a typology developed in two earlier published essays. They are "The Church and Politics: Four Possible Connections" in *This World: A Journal of Religion and Public Life* (Mt. Morris, Ill.: The Rockford Institute, Spring 1989, pp. 26-37), and "Religion and Politics: Four Possible Connections" in *Discourse and the Two Cultures: Science, Religion and the Humanities,* ed. Kenneth Thompson (Latham, Md.: University Press of America, 1988).

means that the church as an institution becomes a public actor. The formal institution itself *directly* engages society—its politics, economics, and culture. The church's statements and actions vis-à-vis the broader society are controlled and directed by its formal authorities.

I have been using the word *church* to mean the formal institutional expression of a living religious tradition. It is important to limit our discussion to recognizable religious traditions and their institutional forms so that we are not confronted with the wildly profuse reality of individual religious opinions. The individual opinions of persons unconnected to specific religious traditions are far too amorphous and varied to deal with in the approach we are exploring. The individual interpretations of those persons deeply involved in churches are also varied, but that sort of variety is something that can be handled, at least formally, by my typology.

Our discussion in part 3 will not include a systematic exploration of how society affects religion. Church-society relations are a two-way street. Indeed, most sociology of religion focuses on how society affects religion. For many theorists, not much religion is left after other social factors are examined. Part 1 dealt extensively with church-society interaction. In part 3 we will see how religious communities affect their social environment.

6

▼ ▼ ▼ ▼

INDIRECT
CONNECTIONS

SHAPING HEART AND MIND: INDIRECT AND UNINTENTIONAL INFLUENCE

Before we enter into this study of "indirect connections" we need to understand several other terms. "Unintentional" means that the church has no definite, conscious intent to affect its public environment in a particular direction. It has no specific blueprints for moving society. It communicates its core religious and moral vision to its members and allows them to draw the implications of that vision for their private and public lives. Connections are not intentionally drawn between that core and the public environment of the church. The church may have the general intent to improve the world, but it leaves that task to its members to carry out on their own.

"Influence" means that the church relies on persuasion, in this case persuasion of its own members. By compelling example, by convincing narratives, by alluring rituals and practices, by preaching and teaching, and by cogent argument the church persuades its communicants to consent to the core religious and moral vision it bears. Influence emphasizes non-coercive means of enlisting people into a preferred option, be it a whole ethos or a particular practice.

"Power," on the other hand, tends toward coercion. Overt economic, political, and social pressures are employed to get people to do what one wants them to do whether or not they want to do it. Power includes a variety of strategies ranging from subtle threats to outright force. For example, a church's efforts to encourage corporations or banks to divest from involvements in South Africa by appealing to conscience is an example of persuasion. But when that same church threatens to withdraw funds from those corporations or banks if they do not divest, the church is moving toward the exercise of coercive power. Persuasion relies more upon moral and practical argument than does power, but finally there is no absolute separation between the two strategies.

I have entitled this first main approach "shaping heart and mind." This phrase points to the inward formation of heart, mind, and soul according to the core religious and moral vision of a religious community. All religious traditions seek to form the inward parts of their communicants—their dispositions, outlook, and habits of heart.

When proceeding effectively along these lines, the church as a narrative-formed community shapes people at a profound level. Their outlook and character is patterned according to the core vision of the tradition. When the church is really the church, its preaching, teaching, worship, and discipline form and transform persons so that their innermost being is powerfully fashioned.

Affecting people in this way is arguably the most fundamental and potentially the most effective way the church affects the public order—politics, economics, and cultural life. Laypeople in their various callings in the world express the core religious vision that has formed them. Through them the religious tradition spontaneously and often pervasively affects its environment. The effects are felt in private life—marriage, family, friendship—as well as in economic and political life. Further, as Christians relate their religious vision to the thought forms of the day, intellectual life is also influenced.

Many historical studies have traced this kind of indirect and unintentional influence. One of the most celebrated is

Max Weber's *The Protestant Ethic and the Spirit of Capitalism.*
In this work Weber argues that Reformed piety of a certain
sort, which he calls "inner-worldly asceticism," was crucial
to the development of Western capitalism. Those Calvinists
were not intentionally shaping a new economic order, nor
were their religious institutions coercing that order, but they
formed persons in such a way that Protestants became the
harbingers of a new economic order.[1]

In a more political vein, Alfred Lord Lindsay maintained
in his *Essentials of Democracy* that Reformation doctrines of
the equality of all sinners before God's judgment and grace
worked through the governance practices of nonconformist
sects and gradually surfaced to encourage democratic political
ideas and practices in both Britain and America. A powerful
religious ethos embodied in democratic practices affected the
political structures of the world even though the movement
itself intended no such effect.[2]

More contemporary studies in the sociology of religion
continue to trace the deep effects of religious traditions on
the character of their participants. I have already mentioned
the recent work of Robert Bellah in *Habits of the Heart.* Other
scholars, such as Phillip Hallie, Clark Cochran, David Martin,
James Hunter, and Robert Wuthnow have continued the in-
quiry into how religion deeply affects the outlook and values
of modern persons.

Indeed, the three public theologians we discussed in chapter
5 are significant examples of this mode of the church's vision
becoming relevant in the world of culture. Certainly the
churches that nurtured Niebuhr, Tinder, and Neuhaus had
no direct intention to produce public theologians. How could
they ever have known what the destiny of these three was
to be? Yet the three were formed deeply in different ways by
the paradoxical vision. They then took that vision into the

1. Max Weber, *The Protestant Ethic and the Spirit of Capitalism* (New
York: Scribners, 1958).
2. Alfred Lindsay, *The Essentials of Democracy* (London: Oxford University Press, 1948).

public world of intellectual discourse in unpredictable and creative ways.

We could enumerate many examples of strong religious traditions shaping the hearts and minds of persons who then carry their calling into the public world. Philosophers such as Alvin Plantinga and Charles Taylor come to mind. We could also move our focus of attention to the world of economic or political life and list the names of many Christians bearing witness to their values. Indeed, every area of life offers examples of individuals who have been shaped by the paradoxical vision and have powerfully affected their realm of influence.

It would be terribly short-sighted, however, to dwell only on the well-known names in each sector of society. Far more important is the daily working out of Christian discipleship by untold and unnamed millions of persons in their various callings. Religious traditions are "schools of virtue" through which masses of citizens form and maintain the "elementary republics" and "the small platoons" of our common life. They provide the possibility of ordered liberty necessary to democratic life, as de Tocqueville recognized so long ago. They supply the "moral glue" that disciplines the freedom that so easily can degenerate into license. Allen Hertzke has remarked:

> This vitality was observed keenly in the 19th century by Alexis de Tocqueville, who argued that religion and the churches should be considered the "first" of the American political institutions precisely because they avoided direct political intervention. Religion is most powerful, he argued, in its indirect, cultural influence, educating people in their obligations to the community and directing their attention away from self-interest, materialism, and hedonism inherent in a society that celebrates individual freedom. Churches, in short, made liberal democracy possible; without the inner mores they taught, the centrifugal forces of individualism would plunge society into moral anarchy, selfishness, and indulgence.[3]

3. Allen D. Hertzke, "Lutheran Political Witness," in *The Evangelical Lutheran Church in America and Public Policy Advocacy*, ed. Roy J. Enquist (Chicago: Evangelical Lutheran Church in America, 1990), p. 62.

This indirect and unintentional mode of church influence is still effective and prevalent in many places in America today. Strong religious traditions continue to form the character of millions of Americans. Indeed, most local congregations of whatever religious tradition operate according to this mode. They try to do the basics well and allow their laity to carry their convictions into the public sphere.

Among the family of Lutheran churches, the Lutheran Church–Missouri Synod represents this mode well. As we have seen, it rarely makes public policy pronouncements, it carries on few "advocacy" programs, and it certainly does not claim to have special wisdom about worldly affairs. Its theology is almost exclusively meant for the church, not for the public world. Yet it continues strongly to form the hearts and minds of its people. Diverse political figures ranging from Edwin Meese to Paul Simon are persons whose nurture in Missouri Synod piety is evident. The same tradition shaped scholars like Martin Marty and Jaroslav Pelikan, as well as authors like Walter Wangerin. In all these persons the paradoxical vision has become publicly relevant, but the church had little conscious intent in producing such an effect.

Although this type of churchly influence is still very obvious, it is under great threat from the social dynamics we discussed in chapter 1. The general Protestant culture that permeated American life is receding rapidly. What once provided positive reinforcement of the church's efforts at character formation has been replaced by a cacophony of claims on the developing young. Popular culture often promotes anti-Christian attitudes and values. The enshrinement of choice as perhaps the central American value encourages hyperindividualism. That, coupled with the formal and informal pressures to privatize religion, makes for a fragmented culture and fragmented persons.

In the face of these negative developments, the churches, particularly the mainstream Protestant and Catholic churches, seem ineffectual in shaping character. They are not nearly

intentional enough about imprinting their members, especially their young. Too many members of these churches have
only superficial knowledge of and training in their tradition,
far too little to sustain them amid the flurry of challenges
that confront them in their public lives. The story may be
somewhat different among evangelicals, fundamentalists, and
other groups, such as the Mormons. But all religious communities face trials they have rarely if ever had to face before.

Let us take note of an irony connected with this first mode
of indirect influence. It has to do with the relation of indirect
modes with the more direct approaches to be discussed in
chapter 7. Historically, it seems that when the American
churches were able to instill their vision and values in members, they were relatively quiescent as public actors. They
generally did not directly engage the public world as churches.
Now, when they are less able and willing to form their members spiritually and morally, the mainstream and Catholic
churches put heavier emphasis on their role as public actors.

When churches can no longer persuade their own people,
they make greater attempts to get their way politically
through more coercive means. When, for example, the
Catholic church cannot persuade Catholics to refrain from
abortion, it attempts to prevent them and others from doing
so through legal means. Or, as another example, when the
Evangelical Lutheran Church in America cannot persuade
more than 20 percent of its clergy to put their pension money
in "social purpose" funds, it is tempted to put all pension
money in those, or similar, funds. Such coercive measures
have predictable effects; members who have been coerced
protest vigorously.

Many persons in both church and society would like to
stop with this way of relating religion to public life. The
indirect and unintentional influence approach seems to fit the
traditional doctrine of the church's mission. It focuses on the
central calling of the church, the preaching of the gospel, and
confines its main activities to the formation of its members

in the core religious and moral values of its vision. Furthermore, this approach does not bestow authority on the church to claim more competence and spend more energy on issues peripheral to its central mission. It does society a favor by discouraging the sacralization of highly debatable policy options.

Moreover, this approach need not be conservative by any means. The formation of Christian character commended by John Howard Yoder and Stanley Hauerwas is profoundly countercultural, if not downright subversive of contemporary American political and economic practice. But even if this approach leads to a less radical posture, it has the promise, if done well, of having a far-reaching, pervasive, and long-term effect on public life. The laity can affect a complex and secular world much more than the church can. There are far more of them than clergy, and they have access to a far wider array of public roles than the church or its clergy.

This approach also has the tendency to unify Christian communities around their central convictions, not divide them over issues about which Christians of intelligence and goodwill often disagree. Many laypersons, perhaps a majority, believe that if the church really does its job of character formation well, that is all it need do. The church would do its job and then set the laity free to do theirs.

However, large numbers of Christians disagree with this limitation on the church's role. For one thing, the indirectness and unintentionality of this approach assume that laity will indeed make the connections between their religious convictions and public life, a task that we know is not always done or done well. Laypeople often dichotomize their religious and secular lives. Further, the church's lack of intentionality reduces its witness in society to spontaneous, often unconscious, connections. This approach is too long-term and general. Finally, it truncates the mission of the church by prohibiting the church from directly addressing the Word as law to the public world. Sole reliance on this approach is incomplete.

APPLYING AND EMBODYING THE VISION: INDIRECT AND INTENTIONAL INFLUENCE

The key difference between the first and this second type of indirect approach has to do with the element of intentionality. In this second type, the church does not rely completely on the spontaneous connection between the Christian laity's hearts and minds on the one hand, and the complex public world on the other. It certainly does not deny this unintentional connection, but aims to supplement it with more intentional strategies. It strives to bring its religious and moral vision to bear consciously and intentionally on the public challenges facing it and its laity.

The church fosters intentional interactions between its vision and the world. It encourages these connections, however, in the conscious reflections and actions of the laity. Stimulated and encouraged by this intentional encounter between faith and world, the laity move into the world with more self-conscious direction. Meanwhile, the church's connection to the public world remains indirect; it is not a public actor itself. Since it gives up direct control of the laity's actions, it again must rely on persuasion. It cannot coerce its members' actions in the world even though it does awaken them to its vision's relevance to public challenges.

Applying the Vision

The word *apply* is a bit wooden for my purposes here, for it implies simply a one-way street. In any genuine encounter between a religious tradition and the public challenges around it, there is real interaction. The tradition's core vision has been extended by the church into social teachings concerning sex; marriage and family life; and economic, social, and political life. While the core vision may remain relatively unchanged over time, its extension into social teachings and public policy is open to much more negotiation and change. For example, churches could at one time ignore, remain neutral about, or even approve apartheid, but no longer. The exaltation of the individual, a concept deeply embedded in the Christian religious and moral vision, finally has been extended firmly into the area of racial relations. Many churches had already made that extension long ago, but now all churches make it. Or, to use another example, Christians can only with great difficulty endorse a governmental strategy that does not have serious provisions for minimal support of its citizens.

Such extensions of the core vision are not yet firmly drawn in many areas of public concern. Communities are groping for the moral extensions of their core vision. What, for example, do Christian teachings mean for gay rights in society, particularly for the rights of gays to serve in the armed forces? The elaboration of the Christian vision is certainly not firm on this and other matters.

Moreover, as one moves toward more specific public policies, great disagreements emerge about which methods are most effective in reaching a generally agreed upon goal. For example, everyone agrees that unemployment is a bad thing, but there is sharp disagreement upon how much a society should reasonably tolerate. Further, there is little consensus about what policies make for a greater or lesser percentage of unemployment. Many Christians believe that general economic expansion is the best way to proceed. Others want government job programs. Still others support strategies that enlist both private and public sectors. There is no settled Christian social teaching on how best to mitigate unemployment. The full import of the Christian moral vision has not been drawn. It rather unfolds in the dynamic interaction of core vision and social challenge. Creative reflection by the church and its laity takes place in the midst of this interplay of vision and challenge.

Intentional but indirect approaches are used to facilitate this interaction on all levels of the church's life. Our parish, for example, carries on adult education programs on social issues. Christians involved firsthand in particular issues share how their thinking through the Christian vision leads them to particular opinions and attitudes. One memorable session was held the Sunday following the inception of the Gulf War. More than a hundred people listened to several pastors and laypersons reflect publicly on how their Christian convictions led them to their stance on the war. Needless to say, there was no unanimous position.

Such deliberations need not focus on specific issues. Another series at our parish involved laypersons from various occupations telling others how their Christian convictions affect their callings in the world. Not only were other Christians heartened by these accounts of Christian witness, but they were also stimulated to make connections between Sunday and Monday in their own lives.

In these examples, and in many others that could be enumerated, the local parish can become a locus of moral deliberation. Such deliberation can stimulate and help the laity make connections between their religious and moral convictions and their life in society. It is one important way a local community of the faithful can intentionally facilitate religion's public expression through its laity. Yet the parish does this without claiming to speak directly for its people through its own public theology.

Such a local strategy sounds easy and somewhat innocuous, but it is far from that. Many Christians avoid such efforts at connection because they are discomforting. These people come to church to find solace and spiritual nurture, not to expose themselves to sometimes painful reflection on the problems of the world. They feel they can get that on their nightly news program, though it is unlikely they would hear Christian reflection on important issues from that source.

Also, there is a serious temptation in churchly contexts to invest one's own position on specific policies with fervent religious legitimation. Partisan opinions then are given too much religious and moral weight. Those who disagree feel that their religious identity itself is being challenged, and they are tempted to fight fire with fire. Such is the stuff of which church divisions are made.

Even indirect strategies such as this can be difficult and perilous. But the potential positive effects are too important to ignore. It is worth the risk to engage in these intentional connections at the parish level. This approach, however, needs to be done carefully and well. Skilled presenters must be able to make distinctions between core religious and moral convictions and the more debatable extensions of that core into issues and policies fraught with ambiguity. Permission to disagree on the applications of fundamental values to the further concentric circles of Christian concern is necessary. A proper balance of commitment and tolerance of diversity on this score is the goal at which to aim.

Higher levels of the church's various expressions can facilitate such deliberation. Regional and national judicatories can gather the kind of expertise necessary to produce materials for the parish level. Unfortunately, churches at the regional and national level want all too often to make official statements that make clear "where they stand." This interjects the volatile issues of representation and authority into the mix and often discourages rather than encourages authentic deliberation. Further, those who put the statements together are usually activists whose biases are transparent to any perceptive observer.

The church should spend much more time, energy, and creativity on these more indirect and intentional strategies I have mentioned. Rather than rushing to judgment, the church should encourage genuine religious and moral reflection among its laity. This would take the kind of care and restraint that is rare among the churches but would be well worth the effort. It would make for a well-formed and informed laity who could make effective connections between their religious tradition and the public world.

Institutional expressions of such a strategy would also be helpful. The example of the Evangelical Academies of Germany are particularly instructive. These centers were set up by the churches after World War II so that social and political issues might never again be separated from Christian social teaching, as had so disastrously occurred during Hitler's time. The academies themselves generally have not taken positions on issues but rather bring together Christians from various, sometimes conflicting perspectives, to engage in reflection. They provide an atmosphere in which Christians who share core religious and moral convictions can debate issues about which they do not agree. The academies have, for example, a long history of bringing management and labor representatives from Mercedes Benz together for dialogue on items of mutual concern. They have become mediating institutions. In doing so they also nurture a Christian sense of vocation among the laity in their various places of responsibility.

Similar approaches have been attempted within the Evangelical Lutheran Church in America and its predecessor bodies. Laos in Ministry and the Lutheran Academy are American versions of the Academies of Europe. The Lutheran Academy continues to draw laypersons into precisely the kind of connections I have written about above. Sadly, though, these various efforts have never received the kind of support and attention needed to flourish.

My hope is that intentional but indirect influence will gain more acceptance in America's churches. The Reformation doctrine of the calling of all Christians can be strengthened among the laity by such strategies. Moreover, there is a great need for the churches to play a mediating role by providing the context for serious discussion of permissible Christian options on social issues. Conscience can be formed without the churches hastening to premature commitment to specific policy positions.

Embodying the Vision

H. Richard Niebuhr wrote that the most persuasive way that the church could exercise social responsibility was by incarnating its vision in its own institutional life. He called this "social pioneering." Instead of commending ambiguous policies to a world in which its own competence is highly doubted, the church should make every effort to bring its corporate life into harmony with its religious and moral commitments. This struggle for integrity, Niebuhr believed, is not only intrinsically appropriate for the church, it is also more effective than pronouncements in convincing the rest of society to take the church's witness seriously. Society would be open to its own creative reform were it presented with effective models constructed by the church.[4]

Social pioneering has had an impressive historical record in Western Christendom. Hospitals, orphanages, universities, asylums, kindergartens, and homes for the elderly were pioneered by the church. It sensed a need in society, created a model, and then waited for the secular society to pick up the model for its own.

We also have examples of such modeling in the contemporary world. Churches have constructed fine inner-city education programs that have then been copied at least in part by secular authorities. Churches have been crucial in pioneering hospices. Churches are engaged in serious discussions about what it means to be socially responsible with their investments. They have tried to model inclusivity with regard to women and minorities. Churches have pioneered local development projects on the mission fields. Many other examples could be called forth to show how churches have tried to be faithful to their own vision in their own institutional life. As they embody their vision in practical models, they become exemplars for the rest of society.

However, it is in a related area that churches have also been the most lax. With regard to their church-related institutions and agencies, the churches have much less of which to be proud. Church-related colleges, social service agencies, homes for the elderly, camps, and hospitals have increasingly come to appear and act like their secular counterparts. They follow every possible secular model of self-understanding and

4. H. Richard Niebuhr, "The Responsibility of the Church for Society," in *The Gospel, the Church and the World,* ed. K. S. Latourette (New York: Harper and Brothers, 1946).

guidance while they neglect the very religious factors that justified and guided their mission at their founding. Mainstream Protestant and Catholic churches have generally lost the courage and ability to make their religious and moral convictions publicly relevant in their own institutions.

Reasons for this failure abound. The modern professionalization and bureaucratization of roles in these institutions are obvious culprits. These processes tend to shape roles around pervasively secular standards. Federal and state funding add to the erosion of religious identity. With public funding comes public regulation, which often deracinates the character of church-related institutions. Extreme interpretations of the separation of church and state make it difficult for church-related institutions to embody religious values in their own institution's practices. The Enlightenment enshrinement of secular reason tends to marginalize religious convictions in the day-to-day public life of church-related organizations.

Most significant, however, is the church's own failure of nerve to take charge of its own institutions. It has acquiesced to the various pressures that have sorely challenged it. Church-related colleges often fail to take their own sponsoring body's core moral and religious convictions seriously in their curricula and campus life. Religion, at best, becomes a social ornament. Similar losses of courage and confidence could be catalogued with regard to innumerable other church-related institutions like social service agencies and hospitals.

The capacity of the church to imprint its own organizations with its values is being called into question. Such diminished capacity is not only a loss to the church, but to society as well. Instead of a flourishing private, nonprofit sector offering a variety of perspectives and practices, the sphere of civil society is increasingly reduced to deracinated agencies more or less shaped in the image of the secular state. In this scenario mass society comes closer to reality. The secular state's tendency to homogenize and control is strengthened.

It is time for the church to be honest. If it cannot summon the clarity and courage to shape its own institutions, it should admit that and get out of the business. If it is interested in retrieving the organizations it began and nurtured, it will have to become much more determined and bolder than it has been in recent years. It will need those virtues to make its vision once more publicly relevant in the lives of those private organizations.

This challenge takes on a poignance already pointed out with regard to our first approach to religion becoming public—the indirect and unintentional strategy. There I raised a question concerning the church's tendency to resort to coercive strategies when it cannot persuade its own members of the cogency of its own vision. The same sort of question is appropriate here. If the church cannot shape its own institutions, how does it have any warrant to shape the broader society? If religious communities cannot form the private organizations to which they are intimately related, why and how should those communities expect to transform public life?

Here I mention an additional example of indirect and intentional influence, though this may well fit under my "unintentional" rubric as well. I am thinking of the many independent voluntary associations that spring up from the impetus of clergy and laity who want to pursue a cause that the church itself either cannot or will not embrace. The church may or may not be involved in organizing it and giving it support. If the church is involved, it is an example of indirect and intentional influence; if not, it is closer to the unintentional approach. In either case, however, such organizations are important ways that religion becomes public.

Examples of such associations are legion. They run from Bread for the World to the YMCA, from noncontroversial services to highly inflammatory causes. Not only do they provide important services and raise significant issues, they do so in a way that keeps the church itself at a healthy distance from social conflict, which is salutary for both the independence of the organization and the integrity of the church.

Reflection on Indirect Modes

The paradoxical vision leads its adherents to favor indirect modes of public theology. There are many reasons for this preference. Most have to do with the teaching on the twofold rule of God. In that doctrine the church has a sharp focus. It is on earth to preach, teach, and offer the sacraments of the gospel. No other institution has that calling. This clarity of mission protects the church and God's gospel from the un-relenting attempts to make them into something the world and its sinners want them to be. The church is the instrument of God's proper work of the right-hand kingdom, the gospel. Indirect approaches to the church's role in the world honor that calling.

Yet the church does not abandon the world. It is called to nurture many callings—the callings of the specialized aux-iliary organizations to which it is related and the callings of its millions of individual laypersons. These are the primary links the church has with the world, and the church should not attempt to short-circuit its commission to nurture their callings by approaching the world in a basically direct mode. The two ways that God rules are conjoined in the callings of the laity and of Christian institutions. Fostering such a creative interaction is a precious obligation to which the church should vigorously fasten.

The church's ministry through its laity and institutions has the capacity to reach the deepest level of human society—the hearts and minds of its people. Economics and politics are much less able to affect the most profound guidance sys-tems of the people. If religion is indeed the substance of culture, the church is at the very front lines of the battle for society's soul. Its public role as an institutional actor has far less potential for social impact than does its indirect role as shepherd of souls.

Moreover, the indirect mode is most fit for modern society. Modern life itself is complex and specialized enough to make it impossible for the church as an institution to speak to or affect the many secular spheres that surround it. But laypersons are deployed into all areas of our dynamic and variegated society. Well-formed laity will be the ones who will be most able to make creative connections between religion and public life, be it in business, politics, education, or art. The church's theologians simply are not able to handle the encyclopedic task of relating the core religious and moral vision of the Christian faith to the diverse sectors of modern life. The laity will have that chance, particularly if the church stays faithful to its primary task of forming them in the Christian vision.

Modern society, with its penchant for autonomy, will also be more inclined to listen to articulate Christian laypersons than it will the church. Laity will be able to speak with the authority of their own disciplines and practices behind them and will more likely be able to translate the Christian vision into a language that is intelligible to the public spheres in which they exercise their responsibilities. Again, that will depend on the strength of lay formation that the church can muster. Adequate lay formation will entail far more disciplined restraint and careful commitment than the church has thus far exhibited. We can only hope that it will shift more of its resources in that direction.

Indirect approaches also are more likely to avoid the arrogance that comes when the church takes onto itself too expansive a role in the world. Indirect approaches also respect the integrity of the church as a persuasive, not a coercive, proclaimer of the Word. Such approaches distinguish properly between the Word and the sword.

Implementing the approaches we have discussed in this chapter will give a church informed by the paradoxical vision the proper attitudes of commitment to and detachment from the world. Such approaches lead the church to take the world seriously but not too seriously. By pointing to a kingdom of another quality in a dimension of another sort, the church relativizes the pretensions of the world and its politics. It ministers best to the world when it is not of the world.

7

▼ ▼ ▼ ▼

DIRECT
CONNECTIONS

The use of *direct* in this chapter means that the church becomes a public actor as an institution in society in addition to its indirect effects through its laity and its institutions and associations. The church attempts to affect society through its formal institutional statements and actions. We will explore two kinds of direct approaches to society by the church. Both kinds of direct approaches are intentional in that they aim at shaping public life in specific directions. The two different kinds of direct approaches diverge on the issue of means. The first, which we have called "Articulating Corporate Conscience," works through persuasion, initially with its own members but also with regard to the public sectors of society. The second, far more controversial, is designated "Exercising Power" and uses more coercive means to achieve its ends among its adherents and in society.

ARTICULATING CORPORATE CONSCIENCE: DIRECT AND INTENTIONAL INFLUENCE

Typical examples of this approach are the social statements we examined in detail in chapter 4. However, the foremost instances of the church articulating its corporate conscience are the pastoral letters of the American Catholic bishops. Of particular note have been their letters on the ethics of nuclear deterrence and on the American economy. Both set off a spate of public debate about the arguments they presented. These letters are excellent illustrations of theology becoming public. And in these instances the theology is articulated formally by the church and is addressed directly to society as well as to its own members.

Almost all church bodies have batteries of social statements; this is a very common way that churches try to influence the public sphere. Nearly every major church conference or assembly at the national or regional level has before it some social pronouncement that is meant to address the secular authorities on a particular issue. A large proportion of pronouncements in the 1980s dealt with economic issues on the domestic scene and foreign policy issues on the international. Especially the latter were repeatedly addressed. Statements on American political and economic policy toward South Africa and Central and Latin America were particularly numerous, rivaled only by those on American nuclear weapons strategy.

This plethora of social pronouncements on the part of the mainline churches and their ecumenical agencies have created great controversy in church and society because they have frequently tilted in a left-liberal direction, often in opposition to the rank and file members of the churches. The intensity of conflict over church statements has increased in the 1990s as the focus of statements has shifted from foreign policy issues to those much closer to the religious and moral core of Christian churches.

For various reasons, many church statements having to do with the social dynamics we discussed in chapter 1—such issues as abortion, the moral status of homosexuality in church and society, and sexual ethics—have come to the fore. These issues are not located in the outer concentric circles of our model of religious argument. They are not like foreign policy issues where there are several phases of moral argumentation to be traversed before one gets to particular policy decisions. Each phase presents an opportunity for Christians of goodwill and intelligence to disagree. Rather, these 90s issues are much closer to the heart of Christian moral existence. They occupy positions close to what I have called the religious and moral core of the Christian faith.

Because of their proximity to the center, these social statements are far more important to churchly existence than pronouncements on foreign policy. Everyone intuitively knows that churches have no real authority with regard to ambiguous foreign policy issues. The mainstream churches and the National Council of Churches can solemnly inveigh against American foreign policy all they want, but it does not take a rocket scientist to observe how few followers they have among their own adherents. Christians know that other genuine Christians often disagree among themselves on foreign policy. Thus opponents of such statements tend to ignore what they say.

But statements on sex, marriage, homosexuality, and abortion are closely related to how Christian people in fact order their personal lives. Most try to live up to traditional Christian moral teachings, which they consider normative even when they fail to live up to them. Because these teachings pertain to behavior close at hand and within the power of individual decision, they take on far more significance than foreign policy issues. I am not saying there is no ambiguity about these more personal issues, but that the church should have more clarity about values close to its religious and moral core than about the wider extension and application of those values to concrete public policy options. Laypeople sense this and are much less likely to be tolerant of extensive revision or sheer confusion on these core values than they are on foreign policy items.

This recent set of issues, because they are so important, are capable of generating great disagreement. They are high-risk issues about which people will really fight. If people lose out in the debate on such issues, they are much more likely to leave the church than if they lose out on a foreign policy issue that is several steps of argument removed from the Christian core. Thus, when Presbyterians established a committee that seemed to undercut traditional Christian teachings on these matters, a genuine row ensued, and the committee's report was rejected. A similar process is under way in the Evangelical Lutheran Church in America. The revisionist committee produced a report so vexing to general Lutheran membership that the timetable for bringing the statement to churchwide assembly was extended for more study.

Many laypersons within the church would rather the church just quit this whole business of making public statements, particularly the pretension that the church can and ought to address society. Those laypersons would rather the church facilitate a discussion within the church about these matters, in the indirect mode we discussed in chapter 6. Such a discussion, they believe, would soon tone down the revisionist line that seems invariably to emerge from task forces or church and society committees established by church headquarters.

Indeed, as I pointed out in chapter 5, critics such as Richard Neuhaus believe that "when it is not necessary for the church to speak, it is necessary that the church not speak." He would certainly apply such a limiting principle to the many statements of the churches on foreign or economic policy. He objects to the church speaking on those issues in principle, not simply because they always seem to tip to the left.

There is, so Neuhaus's argument goes, only one occasion when the church ought to speak directly to the public world, and that address should be proscriptive, not prescriptive. Such an occasion occurs when a social or governmental practice directly violates the core religious and moral convictions of the Christian tradition. Then the church must say a loud no and be willing to resist that practice. But it must not presume to commend specific public policy options. It has no warrant and little competence for such prescriptive details.[1]

1. See Neuhaus's critique of church and society efforts in his "To Serve the Lord of All: Law, Gospel and Social Responsibility," *Dialog* 30, no. 2 (Fall 1990), pp. 140-49.

Surely, though, Neuhaus would see the necessity for the church to clarify its teachings on important core issues. He would, however, limit its address to communicants of the religious tradition, not to the public world. The address to the public world would presumably be made through the church's laity and/or its voluntary associations.

It is not clear, however, why the corporate church should be limited in such a draconian manner. True enough, the practice of making social statements has been sorely misused and abused by many church bodies. But like the two-kingdoms doctrine, the direct address of society by the church should not be discarded because it has been poorly done. After all, the church is a corporate body with a coherent religious and moral identity; it is more than its deployed laity. It is responsible for stewarding the whole Word of God— both law and gospel. As the corporate body of Christ it is called to address the world directly with both law and gospel. If God has not abandoned society, surely the church should not withdraw from a measure of responsibility in and for society. One important way it exercises that responsibility is by directly addressing society.

Looking from the society side of the church-society polarity, we can discern important reasons for the church to be a public actor in society. Robin Lovin has identified three important roles for the church in society.[2] The first involves religion's capacity to be a guarantor of order. This function connects with the important effects we have listed under the rubric of unintentional and indirect influence. The church provides an underlying moral guidance system in its people and indirectly for the society. Religion and morality, George Washington said, are the pillars upon which all society rests.

The second role involves the church as a bulwark of freedom. Since religious traditions look to a transcendent order

2. Robin W. Lovin, "Religion in American Life: Three Relationships," unpublished manuscript of a lecture given at the University of Chicago Divinity School symposium on religion and public life.

for their marching orders, they provide an independent vision that cannot easily be subsumed to or tamed by the secular authorities, particularly the state. They prevent the state from monopolizing civil society.

The third important contribution of religion is its capacity to generate new social meanings. Drawing upon rich religious and moral sources, religious traditions can provide important new insights on human needs, rights and responsibilities that are all too often absent in a public sphere increasingly denuded of substantive meanings.

Thus organized religion plays an important social role in democratic societies. Even when it does not exercise direct power, it may wield considerable cultural influence.

> "Cultural influence" is the capacity to use cultural resources to affect political outcomes. These resources include symbols, ideologies, moral authority and cultural meanings. They can be used to legitimate or delegitimate political outcomes or actors, to keep some issues public and others out of the public eye altogether, and to frame the terms with which issues are discussed when they are public.[3]

Therefore, the questions concern not so much whether the church should address the public world directly, but rather how and how much. We have already examined several excellent Lutheran social statements and alluded to the influential Catholic pastoral letters. Among them we can discern some qualities that might enlighten us in our search for the proper manner of direct and intentional influence.

Guidelines for Direct Influence

1. CREDIBILITY

Credibility is one of the essential characteristics of adequate public theology, as I argued in chapter 1. But what makes a

3. N. J. Demerath III, "Religious Capital and Capital Religions: Cross-Cultural and Non-Legal Factors in the Separation of Church and State," *Daedalus* 120, no. 3 (Summer 1991), p. 31.

church's social statement credible? First, credibility increases as the frequency of church social statements decreases. I am not flippantly suggesting that this statement be carried to its logical conclusion—complete silence on the part of the church—but rather that the church should practice great restraint in addressing society. Restraint follows from two realizations: first, that the church's primary mission is not to instruct society on how it is to be ordered and, second, that its competence to do so effectively is severely limited. Keeping these in mind should prevent the church from using its sacred symbols to legitimate the ideological propensities of its current leadership, as has been so often the case with church pronouncements.

Similarly, the church should speak only when it has something unique to offer from its own theological-ethical heritage. It should be convinced that its vision has a fresh or incisive interpretation to offer or some unique judgment to make. In far too many instances, churches speak not from a coherent religious perspective but from the intellectual fads of the day. Thus their statements become second-rate social commentary and advice that is put forth far better by secular authorities or independent Christian laypersons. A further embarrassment is added when such inferior opinions are superficially invested with biblical or churchly authority.

The requirement that churches speak from their own genuinely religious-moral vision further entails that the statements are developed by those committed to and expert in that vision. The bearers of the tradition must be in charge of its corporate conscience. Our explorations of individual expressions of the paradoxical vision in chapter 5 indicate that those bearers need not be clergy or even trained theologians, but they must have clear understanding of the tradition's vision.

Certainly these bearers of the tradition must listen to expert opinion from secular authorities in the field, from those involved in the issue, and from those whose interest or person is harmed by social injustice. But the church's articulation of its conscience should not be diluted by systems of representation based primarily on sex, race, or ethnicity. Nor should that conscience be formed by those whose pain quotient is somehow claimed to be higher than others. The credibility of the church's conscience is diminished by the all-too-frequent capitulation to current "hermeneutics of suspicion." Contemporary experience, even if refracted through the eyes of the oppressed, ought not to be the norm for church pronouncements.

Indeed, a number of church statements that have been developed under the "hermeneutics of suspicion" scheme have radically departed from the moral traditions of those bodies. They appear totally out of harmony with their heritage. Ordinary members of the religious community easily detect what is going on and protest. Then it is back to the drawing boards. This vulgar dialectic raises suspicions that the church no longer has a viable religious and moral tradition, a very debilitating impression.

The church must do serious preparation when it takes up a public issue. It must devote adequate staff and time to the preparation of each statement. For most churches, that means that they will take on only a few issues and then prepare them over a period of years. The Catholic bishops have been instructive here. They spend years working on their letters, and they commit adequate staff time and energy to the task. Part of doing their homework means gathering a variety of testimony and inviting feedback. They listen to the feedback, and each successive version of their letters shows perceptible changes. A survey of the revisions that their letter on the American economy underwent in its process of development bears that out.

Finally, the credibility of statements is enhanced by the weight of authority, which may be based on a number of sources. It may be the authority of the magisterium, as is the case with the Catholic letters. It may be the authority of church assemblies who vote statements up or down after vigorous debate. In either case, however, genuine authority only accrues to a statement when the bishops or assemblies recognize and affirm the intrinsic truth of the argument made by the bearers of the tradition. They perceive that something of the light of religious and moral truth is shining through.

2. DISTINGUISHING LEVELS OF AUTHORITY

Every church statement should distinguish among levels of authority. (Here we are simply translating our concentric circles model of authority (see diagram on p. 75) into another image—that of levels rather than circles.) The highest symbols of redemption that the church holds as its very reason for being are at the apex of the pyramid. They persist in recognizable form through the ages. They may be interpreted anew for every generation, but they are not radically revised. The ethical principles that flow from those elevated symbols are also very clear and stable. Christian love (agape) is a settled moral principle, as are the Ten Commandments, teachings on Christian marriage, and Christian vocation. However, as each age attempts to restate what these verities mean in the context of the time, there is certainly room for further reflection.

As statements move to more specific formulations, they employ what ethicists have called "middle principles," often drawn from philosophical theories. Robin Lovin describes this movement:

> God's will and God's ordering of reality does not hover above the choices we make in society. It must be found in the details, or it will not govern in the generalities. . . . The Christian realist provides the generality required for public moral discourse by expressing the basic values of the faith in terms like justice, freedom, or equality, which can be understood and argued by all, and by linking those values to relatively specific claims about what, under present conditions, must be done to realize them in society.[4]

4. Robin W. Lovin, *Christian Faith and Public Choices* (Philadelphia: Fortress, 1984), p. 173.

Lovin then quotes J. H. Oldham, the originator of the "middle principles" phrase: "These principles are not binding for all time, but are provisional definitions of the type of behavior required of Christians at a given period and in given circumstances."[5]

Thus arguments of this sort allow much room for debate since different "middle principles" are held by different philosophical parties. Add to that the varied readings of empirical reality that accompany every approach to an important issue, and there is further latitude for debate.

Both Lutherans and Catholics have recognized these levels of authority and have encouraged people to disagree vigorously at the levels of both "middle principles" and policy proposals. They claim no inerrant authority at those levels.

These approaches contrast with straight-line thinking, in which judgments on particular policies are elevated to the same level as the highest religious symbols—that is, a straight line is drawn in which policy pronouncements are equated with unchanging truth. This is a formula for idolatry, for in it lesser issues are identified with the ultimate. In this situation one faction is often willing to excommunicate another from the bonds of Christian fellowship if there is disagreement.

While this straight-line thinking is obviously dangerous, it is not uncommon among the extreme right and left wings of Protestantism. A disturbing sign of tendencies in this direction is the increasing number of calls for *status confessionis* approaches to controversial issues by activist segments in the churches. In recent years these segments have branded participation in multinational corporations and support for nuclear deterrence as beyond the pale of Christian legitimacy.

These examples of left-leaning straight-line thinking can be matched by a like number of examples from the more fevered swamps of right-wing religious groups. Some religious ultraconservative organizations have even compiled checklists on legislative issues to determine whether senators

5. Ibid.

and representatives voted in a "Christian way." Both left and right have been tempted to stamp ambiguous policies with the seal of God's approval as it is perceived by them. As I have argued many times earlier, the paradoxical vision resists such identifications.

Finally, when the church does make public policy statements directly as an institution, it should remember the means-ends distinction. Most Christians agree on the general goals that we should be pursuing; for example, serious Christians abhor high unemployment and war. The debate centers on the means we use to avoid specific evils or to reach worthy goals. Here a good deal of latitude for discussion should be allowed.

It would be ideal for the church to encourage far more discourse on differing means. Such an approach would be helpful in both church and society. One way of stimulating such discourse might be the following. After a church statement projects its basic principles and goals clearly and develops relevant middle principles, it might put forth two or three ways that policy makers, using those middle principles, propose to reach those goals. Then after critical reflection it could raise pros and cons about each set of means. Except in moments of great clarity and consensus, the church would not agree on one prescriptive option. It would allow persons to make up their minds on ambiguous policies that offer no perfect solutions.

For example, it is increasingly clear that Christians can hold to a variety of strategies to counter international aggression. Such an instance of aggression occurred when Saddam Hussein invaded Kuwait. None of the proposed strategies were conclusively correct or effective, let alone "Christian"; each involved a mix of trade-offs and ambiguous effects. To claim moral legitimacy for only one strategy— the pacifist option was preferred by the mainstream churches—is foolish and dangerous. Unfortunately, many churches have painted themselves into corners by opting for one highly debatable option. Often the course of events brings an embarrassing verdict of judgment on their ill-chosen policy. (Such I believe is the case with the mainstream churches' tip toward "nuclear freeze" policies in the mid-1980s.)

3. INTELLIGIBILITY.

The first requirement under this rubric of intelligibility is that the church's statements be persuasive to its own members. I have already argued this above in the section on indirect and intentional influence (see pp. 194). But I am assuming that churches intend also to address society directly. This introduces other items into our discussion of the criterion of intelligibility.

In his book, *Love and Power: The Role of Religion and Morality in American Politics,* Michael J. Perry, a Catholic law professor, has an extended discussion of how religion ought to enter public debate. His concern for what he calls "ecumenical political dialogue" includes detailed attention to the way religious traditions ought to articulate public arguments. Several of his insights are important to us at this point.[6]

When the church addresses the public world, Perry believes, it should not shrink from drawing upon its specifically religious symbols and values. He disagrees with those in both the Catholic and Lutheran communities who argue that the church's approach to the public sphere ought to be exclusively on the basis of "universal" rational principles. Perry is enough of a historicist to doubt that such principles—ensconced in either natural law or the orders of creation—have the kind of unversality claimed for them. Indeed, such claims themselves are generally part of a particular tradition of reflection.

6. Michael J. Perry, *Love and Power: The Role of Religion and Morality in American Politics* (New York: Oxford, 1991), pp. 83-127. This book contains a thorough discussion of the possibilities and limitations of theological communication in public debate. It counters the arguments of secularists who believe that specifically religious rhetoric has no place in the public sphere, as well as those of religious particularists who tend to be impatient with and intolerant of the plurality of opinions in the public square.

Further, he believes that religious arguments flowing from core religious and moral convictions will be healthily challenged and enriched by "robust external deliberation."[7]

But there are more compelling reasons why the specific symbols of a religious tradition should be employed in public argument. First, they are not necessarily unintelligible. The religious community can communicate in ways that "clarify rather than obscure the scriptural and other theological warrants for its understanding/interpretation."[8] Perry cites the reflections of Bryan Hehir, who did so much to make the Catholic bishops' letters intelligible to the broader community:

> When a religious claim will affect the wider public, it should be proposed in a fashion which the public can evaluate, accept or reject on its own terms. The point is not to banish religious insight and argument from public life, but only to establish a test for the religious communites to meet: to probe our commitments deeply and broadly enough that we can translate their best insights to others.[9]

Second, a public argument shorn of its basic religious presuppositions is "finally and radically incomplete without such beliefs." Perry goes on to quote a Catholic colleague, David Hollenbach:

> If the church is intent on making a contribution to debates about social, political and economic life, it must state forthrightly and publicly its own most basic convictions about the nature and destiny of human beings. . . . The church must respond to the most basic questions about the meaning of human life in its social teachings as well as its doctrinal theology. . . . Such questions are religious questions, demanding religious and theological answers.[10]

7. Ibid., p. 103.
8. Ibid., p. 104.
9. Ibid., p. 108.
10. Ibid., p. 105.

Third, the society needs such substantive proposals. In a political world dominated by interest group liberalism, where the adjudication of claims is attempted purely on procedural grounds, substantive moral traditions are increasingly necessary for the health of public discourse itself. A public square denuded of substantive moral proposals will likely revert to struggles of private power rather than public persuasion, thus decreasing the chance for peaceful accommodation of competing claims.

I am not suggesting that religious communities with natural law traditions should not use them. Indeed, such traditions can call upon common rational and experiential grounds that will broaden their persuasive appeal. Moreover, they will elicit positive responses from reservoirs of Christian teaching that have deeply permeated all the cultures of the West. They may remind a secular world of rich roots it has neglected.

The criterion of intelligibility has certainly been met by the three public theologians discussed in chapter 5. Niebuhr, Tinder, and Neuhaus have all succeeded in translating core Christian religious and moral values into arguments thoroughly understandable to non-Christians. As Christian apologists, they have put forth specifically Christian arguments without being either sectarian or authoritarian. There are no compelling reasons why social statements constructed by formal religious bodies cannot also make the modulations necessary to render key Christian insights publicly intelligible.

However, it is important to conclude with several cautionary notes. Church statements first of all should be directed to their internal constituency. The church must first be able to convince its own communicants of its social teachings before it presumes to persuade the public, and it must devote far more attention to this internal task. Second, Neuhaus's rather extreme principle, discussed in chapter 5 (p. 174-175), should be heeded without necessarily being followed. "When it is not necessary for the church to speak, it is necessary for the church not to speak." Third, when the church does speak, it ought to make sure that it is speaking with the authentic voice of its own tradition, not with the cacophonous clamor of "politically correct" interest groups.

EXERCISING POWER: DIRECT AND INTENTIONAL ACTION

This final way that the church affects public life is highly controversial and risky for both church and society, but particularly for the church. Western societies have so many secular concentrations of power that it is unlikely that any religious group could exert enough power to threaten the freedom and order of society. Certainly no religious group in the West has anything like the power it would take for such a threat, contrary to the alarmist claims to that effect expressed by some secular groups. Compared to governmental, corporate, or military power, church power is puny.

Direct action, however, does involve great risks for the church, as I will contend later. For the moment, however, I will define and describe what I mean by "direct and intentional action." Direct and intentional action differs rather dramatically from all the earlier modes of church-public connections. In this approach the church uses power to realize its intentions, and it does so directly as the church. Moreover, it intends to change policy or move society in specific directions through its exercise of power. This approach entails a high degree of either authority or consensus, which enables the church to exercise the kind of decisiveness that wielding of power demands.

In this approach the church no longer relies on the persuasiveness of argument or example; it commits its funds, political weight, and people-power to pressure decision makers to move toward a well-defined policy objective. While influence and power are not absolutely distinguishable categories, they do point to clear tendencies. Power includes all those levels of pressure ranging from threat to force that get people to do what one wants them to do, whether or not they really want to do it.

Church involvement in direct action receives wide media coverage. In a world where people are accustomed to power being wielded by secular agencies, it becomes newsworthy when religious institutions try to wield power. Such behavior surprises and alarms secularists who believe that religion has been thoroughly relegated to the private sphere of life. Further, there is in such heightened attention an inchoate sense that religious institutions should not, for intrinsic reasons, be involved in such power moves. When they do become involved, there is something vaguely scandalous about it.

The West is still aghast at the resurgent political power of militant Islam. Religion was supposed to have waned in importance as modernization progressed throughout the world. But militant Islam possesses culture-transforming power. It is neither weak nor private. Some of its adherents aim at creating "Islamic republics" by direct use of power.

Other examples from around the world abound. The Catholic church in the Philippines exercised effective political power in deposing Ferdinand Marcos and electing Corazon Aquino. In Poland its direct support of Solidarity enabled that movement to play a crucial role in bringing down the Communist hegemony. Its "preferential option for the poor" in Central and Latin America has often meant direct support for organizations of the poor demanding their rights.

Protestants also have been and are involved in direct action. Presbyterians in South Korea directly support democratic movements. Lutherans in East Germany gave direct support to protestors on the eve of the Communist collapse in the fall of 1989. Methodists gave money to liberation groups in the Philippines. The World Council of Churches directly supported the Southwest African Peoples Organization (SWAPO) in the Namibian liberation struggle, as well as other liberation organizations in southern Africa.

Many more examples of direct action could be listed. These would not even include the many instances of direct action by the numerous voluntary associations indirectly connected with the church, such as the large array of pro- or anti-abortion groups. The question is not whether religious traditions engage in direct action, but rather whether they *ought* to, and under what conditions. There are, in addition, constitutional questions about how far churches can participate in direct forms of political action and yet maintain their tax-exempt status.

For several reasons the general presumption of the paradoxical vision moves against direct action. The first has to do with mission and integrity of the church. From the point of view of the paradoxical vision, the church's mission is not to wield power in the realm of the law, but to proclaim the gospel. True, as I argued earlier in this chapter, the church is also charged with addressing the law to the society. This gives it warrant to engage in direct and intentional influence, albeit carefully and sparingly.

But such a warrant does not include the exercise of coercive power. God gives the church the authority of the Word, not the power of the sword, to exercise in the world. The Reformation was mounted partly out of conviction on this principle. The Catholic church throughout the ages had flirted with the direct exercise of power, and this had led, according to Luther, not only to confusion about its proper mission, but also to a good deal of corruption. Lord Acton's famous remark about the corrupting tendencies of power could not apply better than to the church.

Such direct action threatens to instrumentalize and secularize the sacred symbols of the church in pursuit of very secular, partisan agendas. The church loses its needed distance from all political action; its claim to point to transcendence collapses if it draws too close to a political program of action. Consequently it has a more difficult time proclaiming a universal gospel to all repentant sinners regardless of what side of the political fence they are on. Certainly this has been a tendency of all churches too closely allied to political authority and too deeply involved in political power.

Other more practical problems arise. In an era of diminished authority among religious bodies and of pluralism in political opinions, who is represented when the church acts directly? This is not only a hazard for direct influence approaches, but is infinitely more problematic when coercive power is applied. Protestors arise within churches that exert direct power. They exclaim, "That certainly does not represent my opinion, and I object to my money being used for that cause in that manner!" Direct action is very prone to introducing serious conflict into church life at every level of organization.

The Case of Advocacy

The possibilities and limitations of direct action are particularly emphasized in church debates about "advocacy." Advocacy is "that activity by which the Lutheran church as an institution, in an intentional and organized way, seeks to influence public policy and civil legislation on the basis of its moral convictions."[11] Predecessor Lutheran churches were involved in advocacy, but ELCA involvement has been more extensive. The ELCA has Offices of Governmental Affairs in Washington, New York (United Nations), and a number of state capitals.

Advocacy is a "soft" form of direct action. It does not lean heavily toward the coercive side of the persuasion-power continuum. Advocates are charged to testify about issues and/or support legislation on the basis of the social practice statements of the church. No one assumes that the advocates are speaking for large numbers in the church nor that any real muscle lies behind the church's decision to support this or that legislation. Nevertheless, advocacy does intend to pressure legislators in a specific direction.

Many strong arguments can be made for advocacy activities. Since the government is now the instrument of so much

11. "The Evangelical Lutheran Church in America and Public Policy Advocacy" (Chicago: ELCA, 1990), p. 77.

social care in our society, it is right that the church as a corporate body add its voice to those who speak in the public realm. The church, so the argument goes, is more likely to support the causes of justice than are more powerful and self-interested parties. To limit its action to that of individual Christians is to refuse to support very worthy causes. Politics today is a main channel for serving one's neighbor in the modern world. The church must be involved.

Moreover, the choice of the term *advocacy* is itself instructive. "Advocacy means standing beside those in need in order to speak on their behalf to others."[12] Advocacy is to be distinguished from lobbying, in which lobbyists support their organizations' self-interest, not the interest of others, particularly not that of the poor and the vulnerable. Advocacy has a strong biblical warrant in the activities of the prophets who spoke to king and people on behalf of the poor.

Some of the arguments on the other side have already been mentioned. Advocacy gets the church involved with power, contrary to its nature and mission. The church often does "lobby" for its self-interest and therefore engages in hypocrisy when it claims to be advocating for others. Advocacy is partisan; it favors liberal thinking and policies. It extends far beyond what the church has actually said in its social statements; it has no warrant for much of what it does. In fact, according to these arguments, the advocacy activities of the church reflect the political views of church bureaucrats rather than of the church or its communicants. It divides the church unnecessarily and usurps the citizenship vocation of individual Christians.[13]

The argument about advocacy becomes even more intense when the coercive element is increased. This happens in many churches that get involved in "socially responsible investing." In the ELCA this activity is carried out by the Office for

12. Ibid., p. 9.
13. These objections are listed and explained by John Stumme in his helpful essay, "The ELCA and Public Policy Advocacy: A Preparatory Study," in *ELCA and Public Policy*, pp. 4–25.

Corporate Social Responsibility. This office vigorously challenges many banks, corporations, and financial organizations to abide by the policies the church has enunciated in its social practice statements.

In recent years this has, above all, meant pressuring private sector institutions to divest from involvements, direct or indirect, in South Africa. But it has also meant lodging stockholder resolutions concerning numerous other issues with many corporations and banks in which the church has a financial stake. The church often has no direct statement on many of these issues; the task force engages in much imaginative extension and application of the corporate conscience of the ELCA.

Thus the task force charged with this activity is very busy indeed. It engages in much discourse, makes threats to withdraw, and does withdraw the church's funds from economic organizations that maintain practices that are inimical, in the task force's estimation, to the values espoused by the church. It also invests church money in what it considers to be worthy enterprises, both private and public.

The church's pension funds are directed in a similar fashion. The Board of Pensions, upon orders from the church assembly or church council, invests some of its large amounts of money in "social purpose funds." These funds, among other things, are free of direct investment in firms doing business in South Africa. Moreover, the funds are "screened" on the basis of many other criteria, some of them politically charged. This profusion of criteria expands the area of sharp disagreement among those who either object in principle to such "screening" or who have different political criteria in mind.

The board continues to allow individuals choice in where they invest their pensions, but its strategy is gradually to withdraw from all enterprises involved in South Africa. As the South African situation changes, it will be interesting to see how long the South Africa-free funds are maintained.

As one might surmise, such "corporate social responsibility" activities in the private sector are even more controversial than advocacy with the government. They involve threats or punitive actions. They intervene frequently in organizational processes about which the task force can know relatively little. They put considerable amounts of money in the service of enterprises whose purposes may or may not be supported by church members whose money is being used.

The church's use of pension money for "social purposes" is a particularly volatile issue since that money technically belongs to the individual, not to the church. The church is only the administrator of these funds and is obligated to invest them solely for the interest of the owner. In fact, it seems that other purposes are guiding the use of money, purposes with which the owner of the funds may not agree. Further, ELCA members cannot withdraw their pension money and place it elsewhere.

Do the noble intentions and presumably significant good effects of advocacy overturn the presumption against direct action? Only partially, it seems. The furor surrounding advocacy is a signal of its borderline legitimacy. The church needs to think clearly about its involvement in direct action. I propose the following principles to guide and limit its involvement.

1. CALLING ATTENTION IS MORE IMPORTANT THAN TRYING TO CALL THE SHOTS.

If the church really is called to be an advocate, and I believe there is a good case for such a calling, then it is far more important to call attention to an injustice or social evil than to prescribe or even support legislative measures to address it. This is a variation on Neuhaus's negative principle that the church should speak proscriptively, not prescriptively. The church should use whatever moral weight it has to point powerfully to the presence of great challenges to our society.

Given the ambiguous effects of even the best legislation, however, it is prudent for the church to let policy makers shape legislation. The church can provide a further service if it is able to reflect critically on all legislation from its perspective, drawing out the pros and cons as it sees them. Only in rare cases of great clarity should the church actually support particular policy proposals.

2. FOCUS ON EXTREMES BUT LEAVE THE GREAT MIDDLE GROUND ALONE.

This principle applies to both public sector and private sector advocacy. Great evils and great goods should be the focus of public sector advocacy. The church should be able to bring its prophetic concerns to bear on behalf of those persons who are experiencing great suffering. The church will be most effective at this task if it can speak of that suffering firsthand from its ministry to suffering persons. Likewise, the church should provide a vision of the common good that is both hopeful and realistic, but it should not purport to identify the particular policies that will contribute to that vision.

Such a principle should also be applicable to the church's social responsibility in investing its money in the private sector. Efforts should be made to identify corporations that engage in activities the church clearly does not want to support—for example, distilleries, tobacco companies, and pornography publishers—and enterprises that successfully engage in activities the church clearly does want to support—for example, community renewal in poor neighborhoods and sound investments in developing countries. The same general principle would apply to the internal organizational practices of enterprises.

The great middle range of enterprise activity should be left alone. Such a posture would concentrate on the extremes and avoid busybody interventions in companies that are neither despicably sinful nor admirably saintly. Perhaps a strategy based on such a principle would take seriously ethical criteria in the use of the church's money without becoming unduly bold. Conversely, to fail to make any judgments whatever is to abdicate responsibility. Such reluctance would decide by failing to decide.

Like the church's efforts in articulating its corporate conscience, less may be more in the arena of direct action. The church should not squander its limited power on frequent attempts at exercising power. A few well-performed efforts will be far more effective than the current hyperactivity. While such restraint certainly will not dispel all controversy surrounding this high-risk activity, it may make the pain worthwhile by showing significant impact in the places it does intervene.

Restraint would certainly help to avoid snafus like the recent case of two different ELCA agencies testifying on opposite sides of the same legislation. In 1989 an amendment to day-care legislation was proposed to allow day-care certificates to be used in religiously oriented centers. The Lutheran staff in Washington opposed it while the ELCA Division for Education supported it.[14]

In conclusion, the presumption against direct action is still an important one. Evidence for overturning it should be very strong. As one commentator has put it, "Not to put too fine a point on the matter, religion's capital is frequently maximized when it is not a capital religion."[15] This is especially true in a free society where many organizations other than the church can provide vehicles for direct action by Christians. Such may not be the case in other societies where the church may be the sole vehicle for political protest, but in the West the church generally should locate itself at some distance from the political process.

Allen Hertzke, a lay proponent of the paradoxical vision, has said:

> To the extent that political activism divides the ELCA or diverts it from strengthening its spiritual nurture of members, it undermines its own efficacy. Even more, it jeopardizes its role in the moral socialization of future generations of American citizens. I know of no way to finesse this paradox. Politics

14. Hertzke, "Lutheran Political Witness," in ibid., p. 62.
15. Demerath, *Religious Capital*, p. 21.

needs the moral discernment and, yes, the prophetic witness of religious people. But a preoccupation with political activity can undermine the foundation upon which the church is built. What we need to ponder is this: maybe the church's cultural role is more vital than its modest political impact. If so, perhaps focusing on "being the church" in a secular age is the greatest, most long lasting, political contribution it can make.[16]

16. Hertzke, "Lutheran Political Witness," p. 62.

8

▼ ▼ ▼ ▼

CONCLUSION

I have nearly completed my sketch of the paradoxical vision's implications for public theology. In exploring the character of a particular religious tradition's engagement with the public world, my argument has been twofold. First, I have asserted that the paradoxical vision provides a crucially important framework for doing public theology now and in the future. Its four basic themes stipulate a structure within which Christian public theology can and must proceed if it is to avoid compromising fundamental elements of the Christian vision itself. Further, that framework leads toward the preference of some ways of engagement over others. It values indirect over direct ways of relating to the public world.

Second, I have contended that the paradoxical vision has been forcefully articulated by formal Lutheran bodies and by individual practitioners of its central themes. Formal Lutheran statements have been given less attention than they deserve, but individuals such as Reinhold Niebuhr, Glenn Tinder, Richard Neuhaus, and many others have represented the vision in the public world when that world has not been particularly attentive to church institutions. Together, church and individuals have given American public theology a definite Lutheran nudge.

Several questions remain. One has to do with my claim that the paradoxical vision provides a framework for public theology rather than a substantive social ethic itself. Is such a claim true? If it is, does the paradoxical vision then fall victim to Troeltsch's charge that it is chameleon-like, adapting to whatever social or political context it finds itself in? If such a claim is not, true, is then a particular social ethic being smuggled in under the guise of a neutral framework? In either case, this claim is seriously challenged.

My reply to this question is that the paradoxical vision is indeed *primarily* a framework, but one that provides a *general* direction for a social ethic. Its primary character as a framework supplies needed protection for the radicality and universality of the gospel and for the integrity of the church. The first and third themes of the vision—the qualitative distinction between God's redemption in Christ and all human actions, and the twofold reign of God through law and gospel—provide such protection. Without something at least very similar to the framework I have proposed, the gospel and the church are compromised in the serious ways I enumerated in chapter 3. Moreover, the third theme augurs for indirect methods in the church's engagement with society.

Admittedly, however, the framework is not merely a framework. It has important substantive implications for social ethics. Its second and fourth themes provide the substantive thrust. The paradoxes of human nature and history press Christian social ethics in certain general directions. Niebuhr, Tinder, and Neuhaus employ them in their arguments for democracy, pluralism, tolerance, community, and a reformist rather than a revolutionary approach to historical change. The paradoxical vision at its best leads toward vigorous but nonutopian efforts to improve our historical lot. At the same time, it emphasizes that our historical destiny is not all there is. We are ultimately not completely at home in history. The phrase "Christian realism" is in fact an accurate catchphrase for the direction toward which the paradoxical vision leads.

A second cluster of questions presents itself. Is such a vision fit for the world of the twenty-first century? Are the implications of a Pauline-Augustinian-Lutheran way of relating

Christ and culture relevant for a contemporary public theology? In grappling with these questions, I wish to spend a bit of time on a fascinating theory of religion's role in our modernizing and secularizing world.

Rodney Stark, a distinguished sociologist of religion, has proposed a provocative new theory of religion's role in the modernizing and secularizing societies of the West. It differs considerably from those theories that have repeatedly predicted the decline of religion as those processes advance. Stark believes, on the contrary, that the meaning-seeking aspirations in human nature itself guarantee the continuing vitality of religion. Religion does not disappear in modern secular societies; it merely takes a different form.[1]

Borrowing from H. Richard Niebuhr, Stark applies Niebuhr's famous Christ and culture typology to the trajectory of the dominant religious tradition within a whole society. With regard to Christianity in America, Stark suggests that it is constantly moving toward "ever-lower tension with its sociocultural environment." The combination of accommodation and secularization leads to two possible kinds of religious response. If, as seems to be the case in America, secularization has not reached advanced levels, the dominant religious tradition will spawn sect-like renewal movements that will revive that tradition. If, however, as seems the case in radically secularized countries such as the Scandinavian countries, secularization has reached a very advanced stage, the religious renewal will take the form of new religions— "cult movements which represent an unconventional religious tradition." According to Stark, the Mormons are such a new religion, and they show their greatest successes in precisely those parts of the West that are most highly secularized, such as Britain and Scandinavia.[2]

1. Rodney Stark, "Modernization, Secularization, and Mormon Success," in *In Gods We Trust: New Patterns of Religious Pluralism in America*, ed. Thomas Robbins and Dick Anthony (New Brunswick, N.J.: Transaction Press, 1991), pp. 201-18.

2. Ibid., pp. 202-7.

What does this have to do with the paradoxical vision? It seems arguable that the Lutheran tradition in America has precisely the combination of sect-like and church-like characteristics that will make it a fit participant in such a renewal of American religious life. This is true of both the vision's theological character and its churchly manifestation. Theologically, the paradoxical vision emphasizes the sharply "other" character of the gospel and of the way of being in the world that the gospel elicits. At the same time, it has theological warrants for vigorous worldly engagement without losing that "otherness." Christians are to be "in" but not "of" the world. Its posture, we have been arguing, is paradoxical.

In terms of churchly life, the Lutheran tradition has been able to maintain a measure of its confessional and evangelical-catholic identity amid the cultural challenges that have eviscerated much of mainstream Protestant Christianity. At the same time, that identity has not led to a sectarian withdrawal from the world. The "Lutheran difference" has meant neither identification with nor disengagement from culture.

This brings us to our final set of questions. Will that "Lutheran difference" survive among Lutherans? Does the paradoxical vision have a chance for survival and growth in the religious community that has brought it this far in American history? Can it continue to shape an ethos in the body of American Lutheranism?

It is clear that the paradoxical vision will continue to inspire individual Christians of all communities. It is so deeply embedded in the biblical and Christian traditions that it will repeatedly emerge as spiritual nourishment for the hungry soul. Solitary seekers will perpetually be grasped by its profundity. Public theology will always be shaped in part by those so grasped.

But what about the church? The Lutheran Church–Missouri Synod continues to be seriously distracted by deadly struggles characteristic of divisive fundamentalist churches. The ELCA, heavily acculturated to other segments of American culture, is buffeted by the strident feminism and multiculturalism of adversarial culture on the one hand, and by the religious individualism of mainstream culture on the other. True enough, there are strong confessional movements operating within the ELCA, but their constructive effect is diminished by serious disagreements among themselves.

Still there is hope. The residual strength of the paradoxical vision within Lutheranism is considerable. It can be regained and renewed. But like any religious tradition, it cannot flourish without the blessing of the Spirit. And we know not where the Spirit blows. Perhaps the mission of the gospel will be placed firmly in the hands of those we least expect. If it is, though, I expect that the paradoxical vision will be there.

BIBLIOGRAPHY
▼ ▼ ▼ ▼

Ahlstrom, Sydney. "American Religious Values and the Future of America." In *American Religious Values and the Future of America*, edited by Rodger Van Allen. Philadelphia: Fortress Press, 1978.

——. *A Religious History of the American People*. New York: Doubleday, 1975.

American Lutheran Church. *Social Statements*. Minneapolis: Augsburg Publishing House, 1970-84.

Aulen, Gustaf. *Church, Law and Society*. New York: Charles Scribner's Sons, 1948.

Becker, Carl. *The Heavenly City of the Eighteenth Century Philosophers*. New Haven: Yale University Press, 1921.

Becker, Gary. *The Economic Approach to Human Behavior*. Chicago: University of Chicago Press, 1976.

Bell, Jeffrey. *Populism and Elitism*. Washington, D.C.: Regnery Gateway, 1992.

Bellah, Robert, et al. *Habits of the Heart: Individualism and Commitment in American Life*. Berkeley: University of California Press, 1985.

Benne, Robert. "The Church and Politics: Four Possible Connections." *This World: A Journal of Religion and Public Life*, Spring 1989.

——. *The Ethic of Democratic Capitalism: A Moral Reassessment*. Philadelphia: Fortress Press, 1981.

——. *Ordinary Saints: An Introduction to the Christian Life*. Philadelphia: Fortress Press, 1988.

——. "Religion and Politics: Four Possible Connections." *In Discourse and the Two Cultures*, edited by Kenneth Thompson. Latham, MD: University Press of America, 1988.

——. *Wandering in the Wilderness: Christians and the New Culture*. Philadelphia: Fortress Press, 1971.

Benne, Robert, and Philip Hefner. *Defining America: A Christian Critique of the American Dream*. Philadelphia: Fortress Press, 1974.

Berger, Peter. *The Heretical Imperative*. New York: Doubleday, 1971.

Berger, Peter, and Richard John Neuhaus. *To Empower People: The Role of Mediating Structures in Public Policy*. Washington, D.C.: American Enterprise Institute for Public Policy Research, 1977.

Billing, Einar. *Our Calling*. Rock Island, Ill.: Augustana Book Concern, 1951.

Braaten, Carl. "The Doctrine of the Two Kingdoms Reexamined." *Currents in Theology and Mission*, summer 1981.

———. "God in Public Life: Rehabilitating the Orders of Creation." *First Things*, February 1990.

Brown, Charles. *Niebuhr and His Age: Reinhold Niebuhr's Prophetic Role in the Twentieth Century*. New York: Trinity Press International, 1992.

Burtchaell, James Tunstead. "The Decline and Fall of the Christian College, Parts I & II." *First Things*, April and May 1991.

Cady, Linell. "The Task of Public Theology." In *The Legacy of H. Richard Niebuhr*, ed. Ronald F. Thiemann. Minneapolis: Fortress Press, 1991.

Center for Concern. *The Road to Damascus: Kairos and Conversion*. Washington: Center for Concern, 1989.

Davis, Harry, and Robert Good, eds. *Reinhold Niebuhr on Politics*. New York: Charles Scribner's Sons, 1960.

Demerath, N. J. III. "Religious Capital and Capital Religions: Cross-cultural and Non-legal Factors in the Separation of Church and State." *Daedalus*, summer 1991.

Dietz, Reginald. "Eastern Lutheranism in American Society and American Christianity 1870–1914." Ph.D. diss., Yale University, 1943.

D'Souza, Christa. "Going Solo, By Choice." *The Sunday Times*, 20 September 1992.

Duchrow, Ulrich. *Two Kingdoms: The Use and Misuse of a Lutheran Theological Concept*. Geneva: Lutheran World Federation, 1977.

Elert, Werner. *The Christian Ethos*. Philadelphia: Muhlenberg Press, 1957.

Evangelical Lutheran Church in America. *Social Statements*. Chicago: Evangelical Lutheran Church in America, 1989–91.

Forell, George. *Faith Active in Love*. Minneapolis: Augsburg Publishing House, 1954.

———. "Luther and Politics." In *Luther and Culture*. Decorah, Iowa: Luther College Press, 1960.

Fox, Richard. *Reinhold Niebuhr: A Biography*. New York: Pantheon, 1985.

Gritsch, Eric, and Robert Jenson. *Lutheranism*. Philadelphia: Fortress Press, 1976.

Hauerwas, Stanley. *A Community of Character*. Notre Dame, Ind.: University of Notre Dame Press, 1981.

———. *The Peaceable Kingdom*. Notre Dame, Ind.: University of Notre Dame Press, 1983.

Hertz, Karl, ed. *Two Kingdoms and One World: A Sourcebook in Christian Social Ethics*. Minneapolis: Augsburg Publishing House, 1976.

Hertzke, Allen. "Lutheran Political Witness." In *The Evangelical Lutheran Church in America and Public Policy Advocacy*, edited by Roy Enquist. Chicago: Evangelical Lutheran Church in America, 1990.

Howard, Philip. "Defining the S-word Is Driving Some People Bananas." *The London Times*, 15 October 1992.

Hunter, James Davison. *Culture Wars: The Struggle to Define America*. New York: Basic Books, 1991.

Institute on Religion and Democracy. *Christianity and Democracy*. Washington, D.C.: Institute on Religion and Democracy, 1981.

Klein, Christa, and Christian von Dehsen. *Politics and Policy: The Genesis and Theology of Social Statements in the Lutheran Church in America*. Minneapolis: Fortress Press, 1989.
Kuenning, Paul. "American Lutheran Pietism: Activist and Abolitionist." Ph.D. diss., Marquette University, 1985.

Lazareth, William. *Luther on the Christian Home*. Philadelphia: Muhlenberg Press, 1960.
Lindbeck, George. "Tilting in the Ecumenical Wars." *Lutheran Forum*, November 1992.
Lindsay, Alfred. *The Essentials of Democracy*. London: Oxford University Press, 1948.
Lovin, Robin. *Christian Faith and Public Choices*. Philadelphia: Fortress Press, 1984.
Luther, Martin. *The Christian in Society*. Vol. 45 of *Luther's Works*. Philadelphia: Fortress Press, 1962.
———. *Christian Liberty*. Philadelphia: Fortress Press, 1985.
Lutheran Church in America. *By What Authority? The Making and Use of Social Statements*. Philadelphia: Division for Mission in North America, 1977.
———. *Social Statements*. Philadelphia: Lutheran Church in America, 1964–84.
Lutheran Church–Missouri Synod. *Reports of the Commission on Theology and Church Relations*. St. Louis: Lutheran Church–Missouri Synod, 1979–84.
Lutz, Charles. *Public Voice: Social Policy Developments in the American Lutheran Church, 1960–87*. Minneapolis: American Lutheran Church, 1987.

MacIntyre, Alasdair. *After Virtue*. Notre Dame, Ind.: Notre Dame University Press, 1984.
Marty, Martin E. *Righteous Empire: The Protestant Experience in America*. Fort Worth: Dial Press, 1970.

McCann, Dennis, and Max Stackhouse. "A Postcommunist Manifesto." *The Christian Century*, 16 January 1991.

McGovern, William. *From Luther to Hitler*. Boston: Beacon Press, 1941.

Neil, Andrew. "Laid Bare." *The London Sunday Times Magazine*, 18 October 1992.

Nelson, E. Clifford. *The Lutherans in North America*. Philadelphia: Fortress Press, 1975.

Neuhaus, Richard John. *The Naked Public Square*. Grand Rapids: Eerdmans, 1984.

———. "To Serve The Lord of All: Law, Gospel and Social Responsibility." *Dialog*, Fall 1990.

Neuhaus, Richard John, and Peter Berger. *To Empower People: The Role of Mediation Structures in Public Policy*. Washington, D.C.: American Enterprise Institute for Public Policy Research, 1977.

Niebuhr, H. Richard. *Christ and Culture*. New York: Harper and Brothers, 1956.

———. *The Kingdom of God in America*. New York: Harper and Brothers, 1959.

———. "The Responsibility of the Church for Society." In *The Gospel, the Church and the World*, edited by K. S. Latourette. New York: Harper and Brothers, 1946.

Niebuhr, Reinhold. *The Children of Light and the Children of Darkness*. New York: Charles Scribner's Sons, 1944.

———. *The Irony of American History*. New York: Charles Scribner's Sons, 1952.

———. *The Nature and Destiny of Man*, vols. 1 and 2. New York: Charles Scribner's Sons, 1949.

———. *Reinhold Niebuhr on Politics*. Edited by Harry Davis and Robert Good. New York: Charles Scribner's Sons, 1960.

Noll, Mark. "The Lutheran Difference." *First Things*, February 1992.

———. "The Public Church in Years of Conflict." *The Christian Century*, 15 May 1991.

Nygren, Anders. "Luther's Doctrine of the Two Kingdoms." *Ecumencial Review*, summer 1949.

Perry, Michael J. *Love and Power: The Role of Religion and Morality in American Politics*. New York: Oxford University Press, 1991.

Quanbeck, Warren, ed. *God and Caesar*. Minneapolis: Augsburg Publishing House, 1959.

Reichley, James. *Religion in American Public Life*. Washington, D.C.: The Brookings Institution, 1985.

Reuther, Rosemary Radford. *Gaia and God: An Ecofeminist Theology of Earth Healing*. San Francisco: Harper-Collins, 1992.

Rieff, Phillip. *The Feeling Intellect: Selected Writings*. Chicago: University of Chicago Press, 1990.

Schneider, Edward. "An Examination of the Social Statements of the American Lutheran Church from 1961 to 1972 from the Perspective of Luther and the Augsburg Confession." Ph.D. diss., University of Iowa, 1978.

Siegfied, Andre. *America Comes of Age: A French Analysis*. New York: Knopf, 1927.

Sittler, Joseph. *The Structure of Christian Ethics*. Baton Rouge, La.: Lousiana State University Press, 1958.

Stackhouse, Max. *Public Theology and Political Economy*. Grand Rapids: Eerdmans, 1987.

Stackhouse, Max, and Dennis McCann. "A Postcommunist Manifesto." *The Christian Century*, 16 January 1991.

Stark, Rodney. "Modernization, Secularization, and Mormon Success." In *In Gods We Trust: New Patterns of Religious Pluralism in America*, edited by T. Robbins and D. Anthony. New Brunswick, N.J.: Transaction Press, 1991.

Stone, Ronald. *Professor Reinhold Niebuhr: A Mentor of the Twentieth Century*. Louisville: Westminster/John Knox Press, 1992.

Stout, Harry. "The Historical Legacy of H. Richard Nie-
buhr." In *The Legacy of H. Richard Niebuhr*, edited by Ron-
ald Thiemann. Minneapolis: Fortress Press, 1991.
Stout, Jeffrey. *Ethics After Babel*. Boston: Beacon Press, 1988.
Stumme, John. "The ELCA and Public Policy Advocacy: A
Preparatory Study." In *The Evangelical Lutheran Church and
Public Policy Advocacy*, edited by Roy Enquist. Chicago:
Evangelical Lutheran Church, 1990.
Sullivan, Andrew. "Disappointed." *New Republic* 28
September 1992.
Svensbye, Lloyd. "The History of a Developing Social Re-
sponsibility among Lutherans in America from 1930 to
1960." Th.D. diss., Union Seminary, 1967.

Thiemann, Ronald. *Constructing a Public Theology: The Church
in a Pluralistic Culture*. Louisville: Westminster/John Knox
Press, 1991.
———, ed. *The Legacy of H. Richard Niebuhr*. Minneapolis:
Fortress Press, 1991.
Tinder, Glenn. *Against Fate: An Essay on Personal Dignity*.
Notre Dame, Ind.: University of Notre Dame Press, 1981.
———. "Can We Be Good without God?" *The Atantic Month-
ly*, December 1989.
———. *Community: Reflections on a Tragic Ideal*. Baton Rouge
and London: Louisiana State University Press, 1980.
———. *The Political Meaning of Christianity*. Baton Rouge:
Louisiana State University Press, 1989.
———. *Political Thinking: The Perennial Questions*. Glenview
and London: Scott, Foresman and Co., 1986.
Tracy, David. *The Analogical Imagination*. New York:
Crossroad, 1981.
———. "Defending the Public Character of Theology."
Christian Century, 1 April 1981.
———. *Plurality and Ambiguity*. San Francisco: Harper and
Row, 1987.
Troeltsch, Ernst. *The Social Teaching of the Christian Churches*.
London: George Allen & Unwin, Ltd., 1941.

Van Allen, Rodger, ed. *American Religious Values and the Future of America*. Philadelphia: Fortress Press, 1978.

Von Dehsen, Christian, and Christa Klein. *Politics and Policy: The Genesis and Theology of Social Statements in the Lutheran Church in America*. Minneapolis: Fortress Press, 1989.

Weber, Max. *The Protestant Ethic and the Spirit of Capitalism*. New York: Charles Scribner's Sons, 1958.

Wiener, Peter. *Martin Luther: Hitler's Spiritual Ancestor*. London: George Allen & Unwin, Ltd., 1945.

Wingren, Gustaf. *Creation and Law*. London: Oiver and Boyd, 1961.

———. *Luther on Vocation*. Philadelphia: Muhlenberg Press, 1957.

INDEX